HUMAN RIGHTS
PROBLEMS AND SOLUTIONS

HUMAN RIGHTS
PROBLEMS AND SOLUTIONS

D.R. KAARTHIKEYAN

GYAN PUBLISHING HOUSE
DELHI–110 002

Human Rights: Problems and Solutions

ISBN: 978-81-212-0824-6

Reprinted in 2013 in India by
Gyan Publishing House
5 , Ansari Road, Daryaganj,
New Delhi - 110002
Phones : 011-47034999, 9811692060

E-mail : books@gyanbooks.com
Website: gyanbooks.com

Printed at: G. Print Process, Delhi

Contents

Foreword

Today, more than ever before, there is increasing awareness of the need for realisation of Human Rights by the large masses of people living in different parts of the world and particularly in developing countries like India. There is a revolution of rising expectations amongst the people and they are clamouring for a new social order where the enjoyment of human rights will not remain confined to a fortunate few, but will encompass every human being irrespective of castge, creed, race, position or wealth. It is not merely enough to enunciate human rights or enact them in the Constitutions but what is necessary is to ensure implementation of human rights. But that is not possible unless awareness of human rights is spread amongst the people and for that a massive effort need to be made. I, therefore, welcome this book on "Human Rights: Problems and Solutions" produced by Mr. D.R. Kaarthikeyan, as it will go a long way towards promoting human rights awareness amongst the people. The book deals with the subject of human rights as they pertain to India but it also deals generally with human righrts applicable to the world at large. The coverage of issues is wide-ranging from the Right of Information, Right to Development and Gender Justice to the Rigour of Criminal Procedure and cryng issues of the functional autonomy of police and criminal law reform.

While the world saw two bloody world wars and countless other State conflicts in the 20th century, the 21st century holds promise for the future of human rights. While it may be said that much has been achieved so far in the realisation of human rights, there can be no doubt that much still remains to be done so that human rights become meaningful for the large masses of people, particularly in the developing countries. But there is no cause for despondency because the world over human rights movement is gaining ground as is evident from the establishment of the National Human Rights Institutions in several parts of the world, including India. The United Nations has also adopted several International Human Rights Instruments such as the International Covenant of Civil and Political Rights, the International Covenant of Economic,

Social and Cultural Rights, Convention on the Rights of the Child, Cnvention on the Elimination of Discrimination Against Women etc. These International Human Rights Instruments have been ratified by a large number of States and the implementation of human rights contained in these Human Rights Instruments is being monitored by the United Nations through Committees elected by the states which ratified these Instruments. This international mechanism for monitoring implementation of the human rights contained in the International Human Rights Instruments has succeeded to some extent in ensuring implementation of these human rights. These International Human Rights Instruments have led to vigorous human rights discourses and helped to discipline authoritarian regimes and, control State violation of human rights.

These International Human Rights Instruments embody the entire range of human rights which are necessary for ensuring freedom and liberty which are essential for human happiness. It is a common fallacy to believe that it is only Civil and Political Rights which constitute human rights and that Economic, Social and Cultural Rights cannot legitimately be called human rights. It is egregiously wrong misconception nurtured by the United States that Economic, Social and Cultural Rights are not human rights. But it is now universally accepted by all countries except the United States and its satellites that though Civil and Political Rights are priceless and invaluable because without them freedom and liberty cannot survive, they just do not exist for the vast masses of people in the developing countries who are suffering from poverty, want and destitution. It is only through realisation of Social, Economic and Cultural Rights that we can ensure that these large number of people that they can enjoy Civil and Political Rights. I am, therefore, glad that Mr. Kaarthikeyan has in this book laid as much emphasis on Economic, Social and Cultural Rights as on Civil & Political Rights and has dealt with the entire range of human rights which are essential for human happiness.

Mr. Kaarthikeyan has also dealt fairly extensively with the right to Development because the realisation of Civil and Political Rights as well as Economic, Social and Cultural Rights is not possible without proper alround development. The right to Development constitutes the culmination point of the evolution of the concept of human rights. Indeed it has been rightly called Human Right of the Third Generation. It has been recognised as an individual as well as the collective right in several Resolutions of U.N. General Assembly and the Human Rights Commission of ECOSOC. The realisation of the Right to Development is intended to secure integral development of the individual bringing about his multi-dimensional progress and development. It is necessary in order to ensure realisation of Right to Development that the people have effective access to—

- tangible resources to achieve their basic needs of productive and equitably paid work, sufficient nutrition, health care and hygiene, shelter, energy resources clean water and air;
- the necessary intangible resources, especially education and information, to enable them better to utilize resources better and to participate freely in the process of development.
- structures of production and government to assure the fair and equitable allocation of the above resources; and
- facilities and services to organise themselves to participate, monitor, evaluate and review development programmes and processes, and to hold accountable those responsible for their implementation.

These are the necessary conditions which must be fulfilled if everyone in the society is to be able to enjoy the entire catena of human rights which alone can ensure basic human dignity and complete self-fulfillment which is the objective and goal of human rights.

Mr. Kaarthikeyan has in this book dealt with the entire range of human rights, including Civil and Political Rights, Social, Economic and Cultural Rights and the Right to Development. The book emphasises the integrality of these three categories of human rights and presents them in a holistic manner and points out that both Civil and Political Rights as well as Social and Economic Rights need to be pursued with equal vigour since neither set of human rights can be realised without the other, so integrally connected they are. It is only through the realisation of both Civil and Political Rights and Social and Economic Rights that there can be true development of everyone in the society leading to realisation of human dignity and human happiness. This interdependence and integrality of all human rights is at the heart of human rights jurisprudence and this aspect has been rightly emphasised by the author.

The book is of special value since it is one of the very few, written by a lawyer turned Indian Police Service Officer and Human Rights activist. He has experience in policing of every kind—from investigation, maintenance of law and order, training, counter-terrorism and counter insurgency to successful investigation and prosecution of the most brutal and heinous assassination by a human bomb of the former Prime Minister Rajiv Gandhi. The fact that Mr. Justice Venkatachaliah heading the National Human Rights Commission invited him to join the Commission is a testimony to the reputation that he enjoys as an officer of integrity, deeply committed to the cause of human rights.

Mr. Kaarthikeyan's beginnings as a member of a rural agricultural family, has enabled him to approach the issue of development with a deep understanding of the suffering that rural and agricultural people are undergoing. He has always emphasised the importance and necessity of purity of investigation and independence of police machinery for maintenance of Rule of Law without which no real development encompassing the poor and deprived sections of the people is possible.

The author's concern over the near collapse of the Criminal Justice System in India deserves to be noted by every citizen who is concerned for the majesty and Preservation of the Rule of Law which lies at the basis of every provision of the Constitution of India. He is absolutely right that the Rule of Law cannot be maintained unless the nation undertakes immediate and comprehensive reform of the entire system of administration of criminal justice and unless the public administration, particularly the law enforcement machinery is freed from the virus of politicisation and corruption which have almost become the order of the day. It is a matter of deep regret that our investigating and prosecuting machinery is impotent to bring corrupt politicians to book and they remain secure and continue to dominate political life of the country since either they manage to stifle or delay investigation and prosecution and even when cases are filed, our justice system allows them to linger on for years. It is amazing that in the last 10 to 15 years not a single politician has faced conviction for corruption or abuse or misuse of power. This means that either there is no corruption or misuse or abuse of power in our political life and our politicians who wield power are paragons of virtue or there is something radically wrong with the independence, integrity and efficiency of our police machinery or the functioning of our judicial system. Some radical measures are necessary and they can be adopted only by a dynamic and alert citizenry which is aware of its human rights and is prepared to wage a struggle for their enforcement and realisation.

The narrative of the book is simple and never over-indulges in academic rhetoric, thus making it an ideal book for lay readers, as well as Civil Society activists.

P.N. Bhagwati
Former Chief Justice of India
Chairman, U.N. Human Rights Committee
Regional Adviser to the High Commissioner
for Human Rights in Asia Pacific Region

Chancellor, Hyderabad University

Preface

All humanity is one undivided and indivisible family, and each one of us is responsible for the misdeeds of all the others. I cannot detach myself from the wickedest soul.

– *Mahatma Gandhi*

This book does not claim to be a comprehensive treatise on all aspects of Human Rights, nor do I claim any expertise on the subject. I have always been a believer in human dignity, values and hence Human Rights.

I was born in a middle class agricultural family in a remote village. I grew up with certain values and attitudes, respect and care for human welfare and dignity. I had intolerance for any injustice or inhumane action on the part of anyone throughout my career as a lawyer and a police officer. My total conviction and dedication to Human Rights got reinforced by my providential association with eminent jurists and spiritual masters.

The day I superannuated and relinquished charge as Director CBI, I got a call from Justice Shri M.N. Venkatachaliah, then chairperson of the National Human Rights Commission, former Chief Justice of India, who later chaired the National Commission to Review the Working of the Constitution. He invited me for coffee the same evening at his official residence.

With unfailing grace and courtesy, as is his wont, he received me and invited me to join the National Human Rights Commission as Director General. He said he waited till the last day of my service, as he thought the Government might utilize my services by offering me suitable assignment in view of my distinguished service throughout and particularly as Chief of the Special Investigation Team that successfully investigated and prosecuted late Prime Minister Rajiv Gandhi's assassination case.

I told him that after I declined extension of service in principle, I had been offered a diplomatic assignment. I was advised by the all powerful Shri Brajesh Mishra, Principal Secretary to the then Prime Minister, not to commit myself to any other task. According to him, papers were already being processed in the Prime Minister's office. The new government of the National Democratic Alliance, headed by Shri Atal Behari Vajpayee, had just come into office a couple of weeks earlier.

Justice Shri Venkatachaliah once again impressed upon me that the NHRC is doing a noble task. By my joining the Commission I would have tremendous satisfaction, besides bringing in to the Commission enormous experience and prestige. He also added that many are willing to join the post but having watched my career throughout, he thought that I would be the best choice.

I responded by telling him that as long as I was holding office, I had refused to discuss and even think of my future plans as I did not want that consideration to even remotely affect my functioning in the CBI. I told him that I would take quite some time to make up my mind, though the government in the Home Ministry had written to me that even on retirement from service I should continue to live in Delhi and that the Government would provide me residential accommodation for security reasons for having undertaken the most dangerous assignment and having done it successfully.

Later I received several calls from the Secretary General and other senior officers of the NHRC from time to time asking for my consent to join the NHRC as the Chairperson was very particular to send the proposal to the government accordingly. Justice Shri J.S. Verma, the Supreme Court Judge whom I had the privilege of knowing since my appearing before the Justice J.S. Verma Commission of Inquiry related to Rajiv Gandhi assassination case, also advised me to join the National Human Rights Commission. With this background, when I was in Pune Symbiosis University, I received a call from Shri R.V. Pillai, the then Secretary General of the NHRC, persuading me to join the Commission as the Chairperson was very keen. At that moment I gave my consent to join the NHRC mainly because of the advice of eminent jurists.

A few days later, I got a call from Shri B.P. Singh, then Union Home Secretary. He asked me if I had given my consent to join the NHRC as the proposal has been received from the Commission for my appointment as Director General in the Commission. He told me that as already conveyed to me by Shri Brajesh Mishra, my posting as Head of a Mission was at the final stage of approval. Shri Singh said that personally he would prefer me to go as Head of the Mission abroad. I thanked him for his personal interest but told him that I would stand by my decision to join the NHRC for two reasons. One was of course because of my commitment to the eminent jurists that I would join the Commission. The other reason was that by my joining the NHRC, I would be in Delhi and would be able to assist prosecution as and when the appeal in Rajiv Gandhi assassination case would come up before the Supreme Court of India.

Within a few days I joined the Commission. As was expected, Rajiv Gandhi's assassination case appeal came up before the Supreme Court of India. I was asked by the Government at the highest levels to assist the Government side handling of the appeal in the Supreme Court. Though it meant my doing the NHRC work late in the evenings and holidays, I did attend the Supreme Court every day for more than three months, as that appeal turned up to be perhaps the longest ever heard criminal appeal in the apex court. In between, I had to brief the Additional Solicitor General and coordinate with the CBI to get all the material that he needed for his arguments.

My appearing in the Supreme Court and assisting the government side, was strongly objected to by pro-LTTE elements in Tamilnadu. They took out procession in the streets of Chennai carrying placards and shouting slogans. They also sent a memorandum to the Chairperson of the NHRC. In that they argued that while heading the Special Investigation Team of the CBI my taking enormous interest in the case was somewhat understandable, as a senior officer of the NHRC I should not be taking sides and supporting the government side. Hence they said that I should be removed from the NHRC.

Of course this was outright rejected by the Commission, as I was only doing my primary national duty and that too on the request of the Government of India and with the approval of the Commission. Ultimately, the three eminent judges of the Supreme Court pronounced judgement upholding my investigation. The court also praised my role as leader of the Special Investigation Team. Well before my tenure in the NHRC was coming to an end, I had informed the Commission and the Government that I would neither be seeking nor accepting extension, as I have always been against government officers accepting extension of service as that undermines their independence and dignity besides delaying promotion of officers expecting their long-awaited promotion and posting in service. Justice Shri J.S. Verma, who by then had become the Chairperson of the NHRC, and Shri Kamal Pande, the then Union Home Secretary representing the Government, persuaded me to accept extension in service and stay on as the rules permitted such extension. While I was moved by their confidence and goodwill, I had to very politely decline their offer due to my longstanding principle against extension in service.

In my farewell function at the Commission, Justice Shri J.S. Verma was gracious enough to mention that he was aware that even in the CBI, I had declined extension in service and in the NHRC again I was declining extension on principle. He expressed the hope that I would continue to be involved in Human Rights activities.

That proved to be prophetic as I found myself getting involved in Human Rights activities, particularly in the field of awareness, religious harmony, environment and rural issues, more than even before.

On my demitting office from the NHRC, Shri Brajesh Mishra, the then Principal Secretary to the then Prime Minister, once again was gracious enough to say that he would identify a foreign mission for my posting. I had no hesitation in thanking him profusely and saying that for the time being I had decided to be on my own, doing things which are dear to my heart. At that point of time I had some conscientious objection to accept such a position. Also, though retired from service, I was still quite physically energetic and mentally alert. Hence I wanted to devote myself to certain causes like religious harmony, spirituality, rural development and welfare of farmers. Having been born and brought up in a village, I was aware of the continuing neglect of farmers in rural areas by government after government. I took that decision without any hesitation as one was not sure how many years of life one is left with on this planet and one should devote one's energy and time in doing acts of service dear to one's heart.

This, in brief, is the story of my full-fledged involvement and commitment to Human Rights.

I have always been a firm believer and practitioner in recognizing, respecting and protecting Human Rights as a farmer, as a lawyer and as a police officer for more than four decades in dealing with investigation, law and order, insurgency and terrorism and in dealing with various sections of the society and various organizations.

When the Government of India requested me to take over as

Chief of the Special Investigation Team of the CBI to investigate the dastardly assassination of our former Prime Minister Rajiv Gandhi, I laid down two conditions, namely, I shall not allow any extraneous influence or political interference in the case, and I shall not permit any third degree or torture of suspects, whether the case is detected or not. By sticking to these values, I had to face enormous challenges and hardships.

I used to tell my officers in the SIT repeatedly that we shall strictly follow not only the law but also ethics and that if truth has the strength to stand by itself, let it stand, otherwise let the case collapse.

When the totally blind case was detected successfully, tributes were paid even by the defence lawyers for the fair investigation and proper treatment of accused in custody.

I had the opportunity to prove that even in the most difficult case involving the deadliest terrorist organization, it is possible for the investigators to function effectively, always respecting Human Rights and ignoring political interference.

Even now when I am involved in various activities and organizations, I have been preaching, promoting, observing and respecting "all the Human Rights of all".

Yet, I continue to remain a humble student of Human Rights. Somehow I have been invited by many academic and other institutions and organizations inside and outside India to talk on Human Rights, among other subjects.

This compendium is a collection of my talks on certain aspects of human rights on various occasions both in India and abroad. Such lectures were not always from prepared papers. On the persistent persuasion of Shri Amit Garg of Gyan Publishers, an effort was made and we could get recordings of some talks from some organizers. The keen publisher took the trouble to transcribe the CDs and cassettes obtained from the organizers of some such functions.

A lot that can be said on Human Rights has been said again and again by many scholars and Human Rights activists in various fora. I do not claim any originality in any of my talks on the subject. It is possible that I may have even quoted from speeches and writings of others, without specifically acknowledging the source, as during such talks it was not considered very essential. What was required for the impact was conveying a particular point of view that I believed in.

Of course, I have extensively quoted from many U.N. documents and NHRC guidelines and circulars, but every where I may not have specifically acknowledged the same.

The concept of Human Rights is wide-ranging and it varies from person to person, situation to situation and time to time. What I say on certain aspects of Human Rights may not fit into the views of some of the readers.

I thought it appropriate and relevant to add a chapter on Right to Information for the same being desideratum for realisation of Human Rights and the last three chapters on Human Rights and Custodial Justice issues, in view of the current global concern on some instances of grave violation of custodial rights by Armed Forces, who were entrusted with the task of establishing and guarding peace and freedom of all.

I will be more than satisfied if this book makes even a small contribution towards spreading the awareness and consciousness of certain aspects of Human Rights.

I am grateful to The Eminent ovrisy Hon'ble Justice Shri P.N. Bhagwati, former Chief Justice of India, Chairman UN Human Rights Committee, Regional Advisor to the High Commission for Human Rights in Asia Pacific Region and Chancellor Hyderabad University, for having contributed the valuable Foreword.

I thank Shri Shanmuga Patro, Advocate, Delhi and Shri Kailas Karthikeyan of the UNCTAD India programme, New Delhi, for their valuable assistance in bringing out this volume.

D.R. Kaarthikeyan

1

Human Rights in India*

"Om Sarvey bhavantu Sukhinaha
Sarvey Santu Niraamayaha
Sarvey Bhadraani Pashyantu
Ma kashchit dukhbhaak bhavet"

Vasudaiva Kutumbakam"[1]

Which means:
Om, May all be happy
May all be healthy
May all see auspiciousness
May none suffer.
Om, Peace be! Peace be!! Peace be!!!

The right to live is not restricted to mere animal existence, it means something more then just physical survival. The right to 'live' is not confined to the protection of any faculty or limb through which life is enjoyed or the soul communication with the outside world but it also includes the right to live with human dignity, and all those that goes with it. – Supreme Court of India in Francis Coralie vs. Union Territory of Delhi, 1981

The human rights movement in India is an offshoot of the social and cultural renaissance that began in nineteenth century British India. Establishment of British rule united the subcontinent. The pioneering work of orientalists such as Sir William Jones, James Prinsep, Charles Wilkin and Max Muller established and promoted intellectual unity. However, the ideals of modern-day human rights can be seen in various classic religious and secular sources, such as the Vedas, Puranas and epics. Although human rights in ancient Indian literature did not form a coherent unified structure, they could be seen spread all over. The Rig Veda talks about three civil liberties:

From the Introduction to a paper prepared by the Author for the United Nations University, Tokyo.

Tana (body), *Skridhi* (dwelling house) and *Jibazi* (life); *Mahabharata*, the great Indian epic, describes civil liberty of the individual in a political state. The Aitareya Brahmana states that the kings were required to act according to "whatever law there is and whatever is dictated by ethics and not opposed to politics." The Arthasastra, the greatest political treatise of ancient India, written by Kautilya, provides for detailed civil and legal rights. It states that, "the king shall provide the orphan, the aged, the infirm, the afflicted and helpless with maintenance. He shall also provide subsistence to the helpless expectant mothers and also to the children they give birth to." The *Manusmriti, Mahabharata* and *Arthashastra* also focus on the conduct of war—indicating that the major source of violation of human rights in ancient India was war. Besides, the underlying principle of *Vasudeva Kudumbakam* propounded the concept of universal equality.

In modern history, Raja Rammohun Roy can be considered as the father of India's human rights movement. He was the first to oppose all discriminations and evil practices against women. He raised his voice against polygamy and *sati* (widow burning) at two levels. First, he approached the British rulers directly to legally ban such practices, and second, he mobilized the masses in favour of such a ban. He published *Modern Encroachments on the Ancient Rights of Females according to the Hindu Law of Inheritance* in 1822 and established Brahmo Samaj in 1828. The Brahmo Samaj was against sacrifice and emphasized love of mankind, irrespective of colour, race or creed. As a result of his efforts, Lord William Bentinck, the then Governor-General of India, passed Regulation XVII in December 1829, which declared practice of '*sati*' illegal and punishable. Thus began the human rights movement in India in the 1820s. The formation of Brahmo Samaj led to the growth of an organised social movement, which gave importance to many modern-day human rights ideals.

Keshav Chandra Sen, following Rammohun Roy, took up issues such as women's education and intercaste marriage, and began campaign against child marriage. Sen started a fortnightly journal called the *Indian Mirror* (which later became the first Indian daily in India) to propagate these ideals. Jyotiba Phule took up the untouchable issue and began an organized crusade against untouchability. He formed Satya Shodak Samaj in 1873 to liberate the depressed castes and to create awareness among them. The

Theosophical Society was established in the 1870s and preached universal brotherhood of men irrespective of caste, creed and race.

The effects of these various nineteenth century movements were reflected in the Indian National Congress in the twentieth century. The Congress fought not only against the British but also the various social evils prevailing then in India. Long before Indian independence, Jawaharlal Nehru, Mahatma Gandhi and other Congress leaders created awareness on several human right issues. The Indian National Congress, to certain extent, can be considered as one of the largest human rights movements. The Nehru Committee, appointed in 1928, made recommendations that include the following: personal liberty and inviolability of dwelling place and property; freedom of conscience and of profession and practice of religion; right of free expression of opinion; right to free elementary education; and, equal treatment of all citizens by law of the land.

In the constitution of India some of these ideals were reflected especially in the chapters as Fundamental Rights and the Directive Principles of State Policy.

However, promulgation of a new constitution by incorporating several provisions to protect and promote human rights did not automatically do away with violations. The age-old traditions and evil practices, coupled with problems confronted a newly independent country and proved to be an effective stumbling block in achieving the human rights objectives. Even today, problems of nation building and society building haunt the country. Thus, human rights violations still persist despite the efforts taken in the last 53 years.

It is significant however to note that the deliberations vis-a-vis protection and promotion of human rights that took place during the formation of the UN and those discussions in the UN General Assembly, which ultimately led to the Universal Declaration of Human Rights, had a great impact on the Constituent Assembly of India and the founding fathers of Indian Constitution.

2

United Nations and Human Rights*

Human rights are inscribed in the hearts of people; they were there long before lawmakers drafted their first proclamation. –Mary Robinson, United Nations High Commissioner for Human Rights (1997-2002)

The theme of "All Human Rights for all" highlights the universality, indivisibility and the interrelationship of all human rights, above all it recognises the inalterable nature of human rights for human existence.

Mrs. Eleanor Roosevelt, who chaired the United Nations Human Rights Commission declared, "Where, after all do universal rights begin?" In small places, close to human—so close and so small that they cannot be seen from any of the impasses of the World, yet they are the world of individual persons, the neighbourhood he lives in; the school or college he attends; the factory, farm or place where he works. Such of other places where men, women and children seek equal justice, equal opportunity, equal dignity without discrimination.

Respecting human rights should be considered as our responsibility towards each fellow human being. At the same time, we cannot over-emphasise only the rights and ignore duties. The rights of the children imply corresponding duties of the parents; the rights of women implies corresponding duties of the men towards women folk; we should perceive them. If everybody does his duty, the question of rights will not arise at all. The education of human rights should be undertaken in this manner.

In Paris, on December 10, 1948, the UN adopted the Universal Declaration of Human Rights (UDHR). The UDHR was framed at the time when the world was recovering from a long period of bloody and horrific conflict. The conflict followed with a depression in the economic and social conditions of the people.

The declaration proclaims that human beings are born free

* Gist of Talk at a 'Human Rights Day' conference.

and are equal in dignity and rights. Its articles cover a wide range of nudimentary/basic rights including the, right to be presumed innocent until proven guilty, the right of freedom of speech and the principle that no one shall be subjected to slavery, torture or arbitrary arrest, detention or exile.

India, in recent years saw some remarkable decisions by Courts, the National Human Rights Commission (NHRC) and the Central Government itself. The people also got themselves organised, anywhere from a handful of individuals to more systematic organisations, which are continuing to address a range of human rights issues, special political and economic. A large number of network of various human rights groups have emerged in India, are fighting for the common causes in different parts of India.

Scrutiny by the NHRC and International Human Rights Organisations and the persistence of individuals including Judges, have resulted in a greater accountability of the security forces. The NHRC continues to play an important role in investigating and redressing human rights abuses all over the country.

The people living in the remotest parts of India, i.e., the rural, tribals and other marginalized sections of our society have always been deprived of their basic human rights. These people are not even aware of what their basic human rights are. Therefore, there is a need that these sections of our society are made aware of the same.

It is now one of the prime duties of the NHRC to not only take individual cases but also concentrate on cases where there are violation (s) of communal rights noted. The States of UP and Bihar alone account for about 54 per cent cases of human rights violations in India. It is unfortunate to note that the girl child from cradle to the grave is totally deprived of her basic human rights.

It is disturbing to note that micro projects which are sustainable and the need of the hour for poor people living in these remote areas, have been suspended in all those areas which have been declared as protected areas. According to the Indian Forest Act and the Wild Life Protection Act, the protected areas have to be free from any kind of interference, which again denies these people the right to live with security and dignity.

In a developing nation like India over 340 million people live below the poverty line and are trapped in a vicious cycle in which they remain because they are not able to acknowledge their basic human rights.

All Human Rights derive from the dignity and worth inherent

in the human person by virtue of his birth as a human being. Humans are the central subject of Human Rights and Fundamental Freedoms. Whatever required for a dignified and free existence of Human Beings should be regarded as Human Rights. Evolution and crystalization of this concept took a long time. Initially, there was confusion between the Natural Rights propounded by political philosophers in the bygone ages and the Human Rights. One must know that the latter is an all encompassing one.

In history and ancient scriptures, references to the basic Human Rights can easily be noticed though they were not referred to as rights. Modern Historians credit the origin of human rights to MAGNA CARTA A.D. 1521.

The term Human Rights was introduced in the United States' Declaration of Independence in 1776 and thereafter in the bill of rights in US constitution. The French Revolution gave birth to the Declaration of Rights of Man and Citizen in 1789. In 1929, the Institute of International Law, New York, USA, prepared a Declaration of Human Rights and Duties. In 1945, the Inter-American Conference passed a resolution seeking establishment of an International Forum for the furtherance of Human Rights of Mankind.

The unspeakable atrocities committed on political and ethnic minorities during the World War II, shocked the conscience of the world. The Charter of the United Nations Organisation in its Preamble declared "We the Peoples of the United Nations determined .... to reaffirm faith in the fundamental human rights, in the dignity and worth of human person, the equal rights of men and women and of the Nation large and small..........".

The United States in 1978 defined Human Rights in a Policy Document as follows :

"Freedom from arbitrary arrest and imprisonment; torture; unfair trial; cruel and unusual punishment; and invasion of privacy. Rights to food, shelter, health care, education and freedom of thought, speech, assembly, religion, press, movement and participation in Government."

In India, the protection of Human Rights Act 1993 defined Human Rights as 'the rights relating to liberty, equality and dignity of the Individual guaranteed by the Indian Constitution as embodied in the Fundamental Rights and the International Covenants".

The scope of the Human Rights concept is expanding day by

day. Broadly, they fall into categories of:

(a) Civil and Political Rights
(b) Economic, Social and Cultural Rights and
(c) Group Rights.

Entitlement and Human Rights

In the framework of Amartya Sen's thoughts, human rights have two main dimensions. One of them can be called negative freedom. 'No one will cramp my negative freedom. It is not negative in the sense that it is any less important, it is negative because such freedom is based on a bedrock of what cannot be done, rather than what can be.

The mainstream of the human rights movement has always clung to this notion of negative freedom. The opposition to tyranny of the State, social oppression and deprivation has inevitably been based on what cannot be done. This demand for negative freedom is very important, as is the organised struggle to extract it.

What is to be judged in this context is whether a person is being able to realize his physical and mental capabilities fully. Clearly, the importance of nutrition, education, health, good environment and opportunity for a reasonable job are paramount in this assessment of human value.

If one were to tell an unemployed, unfed, homeless, illiterate person, "You are given custom-made individual freedom, no one will torture you, but you will not ask for anything else either", it might fulfill the conditions of negative freedom, but would it alone be Just ? If that person says he wants freedom and food, shelter, clothing and health care, it certainly would not be an unreasonable demand. What he actually wants is 'entitlement'. Without this positive entitlement, negative freedom will always remain a limited concept.

At the core of Amartya Sen's model of economic development is the idea of entitlement. He has repeatedly said entitlement cannot be measured only in terms of national income or investment. That is why it is essential to directly determine social opportunities and the quality of life.

Understandably, we are up in arms against torture and oppression. But we do not build a movement around a child's right to education, a patient's rights to treatment, an unemployee's right to a meaningful occupation.

3

Human Rights Education

Liberty lies in the hearts of men and women; when it dies there, no constitution, no law, no court can even do much to help it. While it lies there it needs no constitution, no law, no court to save it. And what is this liberty which must lie in the hearts of men and women? It is not the ruthless, the unbridled will; it is not freedom to do as one likes. That is the denial of liberty, and leads straight to its overthrow. A society in which men recognize no check upon their freedom soon becomes a society where freedom is the possession of only a savage few; as we have learned to our sorrow.- Justice Learned Hand (1944), American jurist and Judge of Federal Court for 52 years

Education is a human right with immense power to transform. On its foundation rest the cornerstones of freedom, democracy and sustainable human development.- Kofi Annan, Secretary General of the United Nations.

Education on human rights and the dissemination of proper information, both theoretical and practical, play an important role in the promotion and respect of human rights with regard to all individuals without distinction of any kind such as race, sex, language or religion, and this should be integrated in the education policies at the national as well as international levels. - Vienna Declaration and Programme of Action adopted by the World Conference on Human Rights on 25 June 1993.

The Concept "Education for All" should be supported with necessary resources for its fulfilment. As the problem is to provide primary and secondary education to the children in the first instance which could be followed up with human rights literacy side-by-side. "Education for All' thus continues to be focal point. The Human

---

* Gist of speech delivered by the Author at Gandhi Gram Rural University inaugurating a seminar on "Curriculum Development on Human Rights Education and also at other educational institutions.

Rights Commission is of the view that human rights literacy could be introduced at different levels using different concepts through stories and anecdotes. At higher academic levels these values and concepts could be dealt with in greater detail.

Human rights education is essential to create an awareness of and respect for human rights. Acquaintance with such rights is but the beginning of awareness. The NHRC has observed existence of a clear linkage between the creation of society that is just in economic, social and cultural terms, and one in which a culture of human rights could take root, be sustained and flourish.

Section 12(h) of the Protection of Human Rights Act, 1993 requires the NHRC to spread human rights literacy among various sections of society and promote awareness of the safeguards available for the protection of these rights through publication, media, seminars and other available means. Nearly holding seminars in India would be to mock the circumstances of the unlettered and poor. For them, the way to best protect their rights is through good governance, responsive to their needs of food, clothing, shelter, education and health. A life of dignity and a capacity to better understand and assert their rights would flow out from good governance. Holding seminars for the comparatively privileged is also not enough. The Commission has accordingly sought to follow a multifolded strategy in its efforts to meet its responsibilities under the provision of Section 12(h) of the statute. The Commission has therefore tried to mobilise the educational system. It has worked intensively with the Department of Education (Ministry of Human Resource Development), the National Council for Educational Research and Training (NCERT), and the National Council for Teachers Education (NCTE) in respect of the manner in which human rights issues could be introduced into the schooling system.

Need for Long Term Strategy

The issue of human rights education is one which requires a long-term strategy and the involvement of all possible players, both governmental and non-governmental. The period 1995-2004 was designated by the United Nations as the UN Decade for Human Rights Education. While the ground work has been laid by the Commission and its partners for the observance of this Decade, far more needs to be done to bring its various elements and possibilities together. The Commission has therefore been in touch with the key ministries concerned, so that a cohesive program is devised for the country as a whole, drawing upon the talents and enthusiasm of all those who are interested in this subject.

The subject of human rights education should be viewed alongwith the ground reality in India. The main problem is that we have yet to realise 100 per cent literacy in our country. Out of a total of 5,75,926 villages in India, it is estimated that about 48,566 villages do not have any school at all. While we may be talking about human rights literacy, it is essential that children have access to literacy at the outset. Without the facility of education, it is felt that not much can be done about human rights literacy. The latest World Bank Report on Primary Education says that "India's primary education glass is 2/3 full and 1/3 empty." India has an ambitious plan of "Education for All" by 2004 A.D. And it has committed itself at the 1990 World Conference on interest in the subject being taught. One of the major objectives of teaching human dignity, and the recognition of student dignity in the class room context, is to allow and enhance the full development of the personality of students.

The dignity means, the "equal and moral worth of all human beings" irrespective of sex, ethnicity, caste, religion, social class, political belief or any other such distinction. In a plural society the understanding of human unity based on equality, transcending cultural diversity and/or inequality is of paramount importance in human rights teaching. The understanding and tolerance of human diversity based on gender, ethnicity or other distinction are equally important.

Teaching for human rights, to be effective, should start from primary and pre-school level. This was the method adopted by the Australian Human Rights Commission when it introduced human rights teaching into schools in 1985. This was also the method prescribed by the UN Centre for Human rights when it formulated guidelines for human rights teaching in 1989.

By the age of 12 years, it is argued, children may harbour well-formed attitudes towards attributes/issues such as gender, caste or race.

The objects of human rights teaching are five-folded :

1. What human rights are?
2. The need to learn human rights.
3. The importance of human rights in day to day life.
4. How human rights are to be safeguarded in one's own society.
5. How human rights can be maintained/promoted in one's own society.

Awareness of the following aspects of human right are also deemed as essential.

Duties and Rights
Diversity and Unity

Spread of Civilisation
Natural Resources

Basic Human Needs
Social Organisation and Social Living

Fundamental Rights

Social Systems

Social Living and Human Rights
Preservation of Human Rights.

It is logical to begin cognitive understanding of human rights by, first discussing basic human needs: the life itself, food, freedom, dignity, shelter, clean air, clean water, health care, employment etc. This can be enhanced by teaching human dignity separately in practical terms to students through brain storming, role play or any other such method which could create lively atmosphere.

The Principle of "digging deep into one's well" is necessary to be able to see how at the core of one's own culture one finds consonance with other people's cultures. This leads to an understanding of the inter-relatedness of cultures.

The call for the adoption of Universal Declaration of Human Responsibilities opens another aspect of the human rights debate that looks at the issue of responsibility. The call by Ms. Mary Robinson, UN High Commissioner on Human Rights, . . . "tracing the linkages between constitutional values on the one hand and the concepts, ideas and institutions which are central to Islam and the Hindu-Buddhist tradition or other traditions, the base for support for fundamental rights can be expanded and the claim to universality vindicated".

One of the major obstacles to human rights education in schools is the lack of opportunities for teachers to study and practice new ideas in teaching human rights. Past experiences show that the very atmosphere in schools create an attitude of disrespect for human rights. The authoritarian style of teachers, for example, is not a model for understanding the practice of human rights. The very idea is to inculcate respect for human rights in both knowledge input and practice.

Changing the mindset of bureaucrats regarding understanding of human rights and human rights education is another major concern of human rights educators. There seems to be a persistent perception that human rights is an anti-government concept and therefore useful only for those who oppose the government. Closely related is the sense of insecurity on the part of the teachers that make them think that human rights education would lead students to simply assert their rights in schools and undermine their authority. Resistance to human rights education in schools among the teachers because of fear that it adds more burden to their existing work load is also a major concern. The expected reaction is inclinations towards integrating the teaching of human rights into existing subjects rather than creating separate human rights subjects. A basic requirement is a better appreciation of the meaning of human rights and its relevance to various subjects in school from civics to mathematics.

The human rights education approach must be practical (rather merely academic exercises). It may also be secular in certain cases. Understanding of human rights can be made richer by relating the same to the positive and deeply-held values of the community such as respect for life, freedom from oppressive systems, importance of peaceful resolution of conflicts, protection for the weak, disabled and the old, and even respect for the environment and other (non-human) life forms.

There is however a clear understanding that there are negative aspects in every culture. One usual example is the caste system. Discrimination against women and girls is also cited as an example of negative aspect of culture.

Role of UNESCO

The report of UNESCO on Education for the Twenty-first century chaired by Jacques Delors, "Education is one of the principal means available to foster a deeper and more harmonious form of human development and thereby to reduce poverty, exclusion, ignorance, oppression and war. Education is the most powerful instrument for transforming our world and our image of each other, for liberating and harnessing those human energies that can assist in realising our collective aspirations." Statement made by Federico Mayor, Director-General of UNESCO: "Wars will not cease, either on the ground or people's minds unless each and every one of us resolutely embarks on the struggle against intolerance and violence by attacking the evil at its roots. Education offers us the means to do this. It also holds the key to development, to receptiveness to others, to population control and to the preservation of the environment."

Let us teach our children, from their earliest years to live without violence and to practice tolerance. Lasting peace is a prerequisite for the exercise of all human rights, not the peace of silence, but the peace of freedom, of happiness, equality and solidarity, in which all citizens count, live together and share. Everyone is concerned at the upsurge of intolerance and extremism, the increasing number of manifestations of racial hatred and the way in which discrimination and violence have become everyday occurrences. The reasons for this upsurge are not the same in every place, but everywhere it is the product of a complex association of economic, cultural, political and social factors.

In this world of violence and violation, we have to question ourselves on the role and function assigned to education and school. United Nations' action has been aimed at greater mutual understanding and growing cooperation between nations and individual on the basis of universal respect for justice, for the rule of law and for the human rights and fundamental freedoms which are affirmed for the peoples of the world, . . ." without distinction of race, sex, language or religion . . ."

Education demonstrates, its ability to promote the values and behaviour necessary for the training of citizens worthy of that name, its ability to encourage the readjustment, and the radical social transformation that is needed.

Values of peace, mutual respect and democracy must be constantly present in the minds and deeds of individuals and groups. This implies a sustained strength of will in order to develop in daily life, attitudes and behaviour founded on the recognition of the dignity and equality of all individuals. It presupposes that every human being has learned to behave as a responsible person, to control himself/herself and to be sufficiently open-minded towards others to understand them, respect them and accept that other people may manifest feelings or display ways of thinking and acting different from his/her own. It is thus essential that education opens up for all individuals in the world, and particularly children, the road to mutual understanding and respect.

Education for international understanding, peace and human rights must exert its influence from early childhood onward and through a broad range of disciplines, perception of other peoples and cultures. Better knowledge of others, thorough understanding of major problems, education is also called upon to inculcate attitudes of respect for every human being and every culture, together with the realisation that each one of us is responsible for the future of all.

Role of School

School has an important role to play in helping children who will become citizens of the future to develop awareness of world issues, in particular peace and human rights issues, and to develop appropriate attitudes from primary school onwards.

It has been well stated that "Constructing the defences of peace in the minds of men."

In order to prepare young people for their responsibilities in the world of tomorrow, it is important to start from the living realities in the family, in the school and at all levels of society; from their community on to national and international levels. They must be encouraged, through increasing awareness, knowledge and reflection, to acquaint themselves with major world problems; to analyse their nature and origins as well as evaluate their social, economic, political and cultural dimensions; to cultivate a critical understanding of questions concerning their possible manipulation; to form their own judgment, to develop their own positions; and, lastly, to cooperate with others in the search for solutions to these problems.

Education *per se* has been identified as the tool in creating a more skilled workforce, but unfortunately, it is more often than not to the detriment of the personal development of the individual. The long-term goals of maintaining the human values and moral principles of society are inclined to gradually lose their stronghold on humanity and become less important as they battle against the more dominant global forces of economic trends and market fluctuations. This has bred a growing concern that the constant deterioration of human rights and dignity is being overshadowed by an ever increasing upsurge of intolerance, discrimination and violence. Educational systems are indifferent with regard to human and ethical values. The schools shape the minds of those who can afford to have formal education. They have become the main medium for teaching ideas that relate to personal and societal relationships.

The impact of schools on the behaviour of people cannot be denied. But the contribution of schools to the development of society and the cultivation of peaceful relationship among people has always been the subject of debate. In recognising the significant role of the schools in shaping minds and behaviour, critiques would point to the failure of the schools to take on matters that are important to the welfare of the society. One such matter is human rights. Despite the international campaigns on human rights by both inter-governmental and non-governmental institutions, human rights have not become a popular subject of study in many schools. Appreciating human rights in the context of own culture makes the understanding of human rights more meaningful.

The development, the culture and civilisation of the countries should be assessed not by the economic growth, but by the respect and protection given to the human rights of the individuals, particularly by the well-being of the children. Each and every child in every nation is entitled to a whole series of rights called child rights.

We should look at the children's rights from the very beginning; with the right to be registered at birth. For millions of children, lack of birth registration means exclusion from the rights and privileges, a nation offers its citizens such as education and health care. We have seen dramatic progress in child immunization over the past two decades. But much more remains to be done. Over two million children still die because they lack access to this basic and inexpensive public health service.

Education–Upto-14 years as Fundamental Right

Education is empowerment–Hence, it should be made a fundamental right. All below the age of 14 must be educated. Now of course the parliament has introduced an article in the chapter of 'fundamental rights' to enable states to enact legislation to make free education to all between 6 to 14 yeas age group a fundamental right.

Child Labour. Any number of legal prohibitions would not work so long as the underlying problems of poverty were not addressed.

The Global Convention calls for immediate and effective measures to secure the prohibition and elimination of the worst forms of child labour, as a matter of urgency.

According to an ILO estimate in developing countries alone about 250 million children aged between 5-14 years are forced to work on paltry wages. Child labour is employed in hazardous industries like glass, chemical, fire works. Weaker sections become easy targets for recruitment of child labour.

The root causes like poverty and social backwardness need to be stressed. We should ensure that children have access to schools and their parents have jobs. The long term solution is in expanding primary education infrastructure so that poor children who are able to attend school instead of falling victim to exploitation by unscrupulous employers.

Every Society Claims that it Lives for its Children

Children's growth, protection and survival, makes qualitative regeneration of life possible. Yet,children around the world face death, deprivation and despair by being subjected to the worst forms of physical, emotional and sexual abuse at the very hands of those who are assigned to protect them. Different pressure situations persist in countries around the world which have made life increasingly difficult for children to live and grow into an adolescence and adulthood wholly beneficial to future societies. At a tender age they have become victims of war, violence, disease, poverty, perversions and greed of the adult world.

Children constitute 1/3 of Indian population. Over 50 per cent of them live in poverty, disease and exploitation. Neglected, abandoned, delinquent, HIV-injected and drug-addicted. Children become a menace not only to themselves but to the society at large.

The Constitution of India and Convention of the Declaration of the Rights of the Child the UN (20th November,1989) make it obligatory for parents, employers, community and governments to respect rights of the child under threat of punishments.

Rights Vis-a-Vis Corresponding Duties

Thus, the Human Rights should be considered as our responsibility towards our fellow human beings. Right of a child implies duty of parents; Right of woman implies duty of man towards her. Therefore, we should perceive them as duty of other persons to help him enjoy his rights. This enables us to understand each other's view point and helps create a cohesive atmosphere where Duties Come First. If everybody does his duties the question of rights will not arise. Hence while violation cases should be dealt by NGOs in strict legal sense, the education of Human Rights should be undertaken as explaining duties of others to allow their colleague enjoy his Human Rights.

The Challenges Today

The biggest challenge today is creating awareness about Human Rights and their education. The society in general is attracted towards the news of violation of Human Rights but the incidents are treated as passing phase by the people in general. The education of Human Rights to the masses should be given serious thoughts. Awareness of Human Rights must be created. To accomplish this India faces a peculiar situation where the country is having 70 per cent rural population - tribals and farmers and with high percentage of illiteracy. Therefore, it is imperative to search for such agencies which are involved with the masses so as to educate people about human rights.

All human beings great or small virtuous or vicious, should be respected and cared for simply by the virtue of the fact that they are human beings. The recognition of human rights under international law is relatively recent but the philosophy underlying the concept is ancient.

It has underlined the need for a fundamental transformation in the direction and approach to the curricula for teaching basic duties in schools and teacher education institutions in the country. Secondly, it has drawn attention to the work of non-governmental organisations in the related fields and how that work can be utilised to optimise benefits. Thirdly, it advocates the need to create an awareness of the fundamental 'duties among citizens through various programmes of sensitising the public mind. It has also been suggested that the Preamble to the Constitution and ten clauses of Article 51 A "Fundamental Duties" should be widely discussed in the assemblies of schools and through seminars, debates, competitions and through suitable display in the school text books, supplementary materials and general publications, which would be used by the students all over the country.

International Interaction Council for Drafting a Declaration of Human Responsibilities

On 1st September, 1997, the Interaction Council proposed a universal declaration of human responsibilities, just one year before the 50th anniversary of the Universal Declaration of Human Rights adopted by the United Nations. The basic point that has been made by the Universal Declaration of Human Responsibilities is that the concept of human obligations serves to balance the notions of freedom and responsibilities. Without a proper balance, unrestricted freedom is as dangerous as imposed social responsibilities. If we have the right to life then we have the obligation to respect life; and if we have right to liberty, then we have the obligation to respect other peoples' liberty too. The golden rule of responsibility is that we should not do to others what we do not wish to be done to us; or that we should do unto others as we would have them to do unto us.

This draft declaration which has been now submitted to the world community at large reaffirms that the time has come to talk about responsibilities, about obligations. The action taken by the Government of India to set up a Committee of Teaching Fundamental Duties is timely and that while we have talked for decades of value-education, we have now to take decisive action in implementing the programmes of value-education. Imparting of moral and spiritual values does not come within the purview of the prohibition that is laid down in the Constitution to impart religious education in educational institutions that are financially supported by the Government. Dr. S. Radhakrishnan had made a distinction between a religious education and education about religions and advocated that there is no constitutional disability in imparting education about religions in our educational system.

Fundamental Duties

The Fundamental Duties include, first and foremost the obligation on the part of the citizens to abide by the Constitution and to respect its ideals, and institutions. This would mean obligation to secure justice, liberty, equality, and fraternity as also the values that are embedded in the Fundamental Rights and the Directive Principles of the State Policy. In laying down the obligations to value and preservation of the rich heritage of our composite culture, the Constitution has stressed the wide range of values that have come to be cherished right from the times of the Vedas to the present day, which has played a role towards assimilation and synthesis. In laying down the duties to develop scientific temper, humanism, and the spirit of inquiry and reform, the emphasis has been laid on the value of truth, knowledge and freedom from dogmatism and obscurantism.

There is a dimension of values, which transcends the dimension of duties. Love for my own country as a duty is inferior to the love of a patriot that arises spontaneously in his heart and soul, as he looks upon his country as the very source of his breath and life. Search for truth and search for goodness is an end in itself and they have to be encouraged not as duties but as irresistible demands of our being.

Self-knowledge and self-control are the true foundations of value-education. As Socrates had pointed out, virtue is knowledge, and it is when knowledge is rightly pursued, that pursuit of virtue attains its right place as a spontaneous action and it has a lustre brighter than that obtains in performance of our duty.

Value-education does not merely remain a matter of do's and don'ts; it becomes a process of exploration, and it crosses the border of constraints that are felt in the performance of duties and leads us into a realm of freedom of which discipline for performance of duty is a happy product. Secondly, value-education opens before us the gates of the harmony between truth, beauty and goodness, which impart to us the sources of true humanism and even our true godliness. Value-education is absolutely imperative and that unless a good teacher is himself value-oriented, we cannot fulfil the objectives of value-education.

Just as swimming cannot be taught merely by lecturing, but by leading the learner to jump into the water and help him in the practical art of swimming in the midst of water, similarly, value-education requires of the teacher the ability to inspire the student to enter into the waters of life-situations and give him practical abilities and art of practising values in concrete situations of life. Value education is perhaps the most difficult domain among all domains of education.

Human Rights Education

(A) It has been my dream for many years to visit this great institution Gandhi Gram which was founded by a team of dedicated disciples of Gandhiji, when India attained independence in 1947.

(B) Gandhigram Rural Institute was started in the year 1956 on the pattern of Gandhiji's concept of basic education. The idea was to carry higher education to the door steps of the village community. The Institute fulfilled the expectations and its objectives so well that it was conferred the status of Deemed University in 1976 by the UGC.

(C) This unique institution has fulfilled the broad objectives of providing for instructions and learning and to promote a classless and casteless society. It has also provided for research and advancement and dissemination of knowledge and has functioned as a centre for extension work leading to integrated rural development.

(D) It has done commendable service in rural extension activity, scientific and social research on rural people and their environment, training of rural women, youth, local leaders and development functionaries for capacity building and promoted social welfare in close collaboration with NGOs, development organisations and the Government.

(E) Rajiv Gandhi Foundation has instituted a Chair for Panchayati Raj studies in the Department of Political Science and Development Administration to activate grass root democracy like conducting action research, creating awareness and training of Panchayat leaders.

(F) I am very happy to note that Gandhigram Rural Institute has been discharging its social responsibility by means of admitting students from rural areas in large numbers and has been successful in transforming rural India through rural higher education. This Deemed University with a distinction of having President of India as its Chancellor has been living up to Mahatma Gandhi's definition of education meaning "drawing the best from mind, body and soul".

(G) I consider it a privilege to be invited by this great institution to inaugurate the national workshop on Curriculum Development in Human Right Education.

The UGC Ninth Plan Approach Paper on promotion of human rights education in universities and colleges makes an interesting reading.

The Human Rights movement represents historical journey travelled by mankind ever since the beginning of an institutionalised political and social order.

Human rights concept is a dynamic one which will find expanded expression and constantly covering new areas as human society continues to evolve to higher levels of development.

The original content of philosophy of fundamental freedom was limited in the main to civil and political rights of the individual, often referred to as "first generation" rights, which to a large extent called for a negative obligation on the part of the governments to desist from interfering with the exercise of individual liberties.

The concept of human rights in its expanding comprehension has now travelled to encompass what are called "third generation" rights which include right to self-determination, right to sovereignty over natural wealth and resources of the country and, right to development as well as rights of disadvantaged groups to special protection. Thus, the growth of the human rights movement has been historic and impressive.

Till recently, the study and concern about human rights remained largely confined to international lawyers, diplomats and statesmen. In the recent years, these rights are increasingly becoming the concern of every one. Respect and realisation of human rights require evolving a culture that is more sensitive to the basic needs of every human being. The preamble of the Constitution assures every citizen, justice - social, economic and political and fair and equal opportunities for growth and development to every individual and group of people. Human rights protect every one from being subjected to the whims of State and its arbitrary exercise of power and use of force by its agencies.

Even five decades after the Constitution came into force, the goal of ushering in human rights culture has remained a distant reality.

Amongst other causes, lack of recognising the significance and importance of education as a key instrument in bringing changes in social and cultural attitudes is perhaps the most important reason responsible for the situation. It is only in the last few years the national policy makers, educationists and education planners have begun realising the importance of education in relation to human rights.

The right to education is a fundamental obligation of all governments in the civilised world. The Constitution of India says that the State shall make effective provisions for securing the right to education and also provide for free and compulsory education for all children till they complete the age of 14 years. This is fundamental to the governance in the country and the Supreme Court has conferred the status of enforceable fundamental rights on the right to education upto the age of 14 years.

Article 26(1) of the Universal Declaration of Human Rights 1948 declares that "every one has the right to education".

Article 26 (2) says "education shall be directed to the full development of the human personality and to strengthening of respect for human rights and fundamental freedoms. It shall promote understanding, tolerance and friendship amongst nations, racial or religious groups".

Article 13 of the International Covenant on Economic, Social and Cultural Rights says that "education shall be directed to the full development of the human personality and the sense of its dignity, and shall strengthen the respect for human rights and fundamental freedoms". This provides for a clear link between education and human rights.

The World Conference in Vienna in 1993 clearly recognized that "human rights education and training are essential for the promotion and achievement of stable and harmonious relations among communities and for fostering mutual understanding, tolerance and peace". The General Assembly of the United Nations proclaimed in 1954 a United Nations' Decade for Human Rights Education (1995-2004). We are now right in the middle of the decade. The General Assembly called upon governments, international organisations, non-governmental organisations, professional associations and all other sectors of civil society to establish a partnership and to concentrate their efforts on promoting a "Universal Culture of Human Rights".

The goal of evolving a universal culture of human rights requires operating at various levels such as:

(a) Spreading awareness among masses, about these rights and also their duty for respecting the rights of others;

(b) Not only creating awareness amongst masses particularly amongst weaker, poor and vulnerable groups, but also imparting capacities and confidence in them to stand for protection and preservation of their rights.

(c) Requiring the people to shed away some of their prejudices and reform some of the attitudes which are derogatory to others' dignity.

(d) Creating different kind of knowledge, innovating or reforming structures, methodologies and normative regimes, and imparting new skills and competencies so that policy making, its enforcement and realisation become more sensitive to the demands of human rights culture.

(e) Establishing new structures of accountability and making existing modes of accountability more effective so that the State, its agencies and its personnel can be easily, effectively and meaningfully made responsible for human rights violation on, one hand and can be made to internalise respect for these rights on the other.

Education is an exercise for assimilating, creating and disseminating knowledge. It is a powerful means of influencing and bringing attitudinal change in the citizens in general and among members of professional groups in particular. Education, as a tool, to spread awareness, information and knowledge can play a critical role at each of these levels for the promotion of human rights culture. Till recently, the education system in India particularly at higher levels, has hardly shown any reliable signs of being a partner in the efforts of evolving human rights culture in the country. People must be made to realise that human rights are not a gift conferred by the State's generosity but are derived from the inherent dignity and equality in all human beings.

There is a spiritual spark in every human being and hence the human personality is precious, invaluable and to be respected and not to be humiliated or trampled upon.

Human rights should be in the curricula of every great institution starting from the children whose minds are not yet polluted by the forces of materialism, consumerism and communalism. Lessons in human rights should begin at the primary level. Young mind will readily appreciate the value of human rights, and respond positively and with sensitivity to violation of human rights. History of the movements for human rights and story of defenders and champions of human rights, their efforts and sacrifices will instill greater respect for human rights than merely learning by heart the provisions of the Constitution and Articles of the International Covenants. Songs, plays or documentaries based on certain human rights themes such as freedom of expression, equality, freedom from torture and the cruel degrading punishment will convey the pangs and horrors of racial and social discrimination and inequality.

One of the causes of violation of human rights is the perpetuation of prejudices and stereotypes, with regard to certain racial and religious groups. Persons belonging to certain groups are portrayed as cruel, violent, lazy or criminal by nature. These prejudices over the ages somehow get entrenched in one's mind and are transmitted from one generation to another and prove a great obstacle to promotion of mutual understanding, friendship and tolerance. One of the major cases of violation of the rights of persons belonging to ethnic, linguistic and religious minorities is intolerance which stems from mutual distrust because of these inherent prejudices. National and international peace and stability are dependent amongst other things, on the treatment of minorities in a country.

Article 5 (3) of the U.N. Declaration on the elimination of all forms of intolerance and discrimination based on religion or belief (25 November 1981) declares that "a child shall be brought up in a spirit of understanding, tolerance, friendship among people, peace and universal brotherhood, respect for freedom of religion or belief of others".

The need of the hour is to spread tolerance, understanding and respect for the views of others. The realisation of this objective should be the primary aim of human rights education, particularly so in our country which has a Chapter on Fundamental Duties. According to Article 51-A of our Constitution, one of the fundamental duties of every citizen is "to promote harmony and the spirit of common brotherhood amongst all the peoples of India transcending religious, linguistic and regional or sectional diversities; to renounce practices derogatory of women." This Article gives the essence, core and content of human rights education.

Human rights education should begin with the children but should not end when the child grows up. It should be a continuous process. The curriculum will vary in content at different stages in human rights course in school or college. But the quintessential message of human rights, namely, the dignity and worth of every human being should be loud and clear and must be vividly brought out. The Articles of the Convention on the Rights of the Child is a must in both school, college and university curriculum.

Violation of the basic human rights of life and liberty occur most frequently on account of the acts and omissions of those who are supposed to uphold and enforce the law. Regular courses in human rights are most essential for them. It is only by the human rights education we sensitize every citizen, more so the law enforcement officials to the value of human personality and the fact that the human rights are the natural birth right of every human being whatever his or her status.

Development is not merely development of material resources but also of people, infrastructure and betterment of quality of life of every member of society. A society that lacks or fails in its commitment to the preservation of human rights can hardly boast of democracy or development. Respect of every member of society as a distinct human being and welfare of every human member, is the common core of both democracy as well as development. Most of the activities undertaken for the sake of development result in mass uprooting of indigenous people, degradation of environment, imbalancing ecology due to an imbalanced approach to development and result in gross violation of human rights of those affected.

Sustainable development has also to accommodate preservation of environment and ecological balance. A social order which ensures full and free development of the potentialities of every member of the society and which cares and respects each member's distinct identity can only be created on the basis of total commitment to fundamental human rights.

People should realise the positive social and cultural value of diversity rather than treating it as a source of conflict. The human rights education must imbibe the understanding, tolerance and respect for differences and diversities.

It should be the concern of human rights education to expose all kinds of exploitation not only at the hands of the State but also by the members of the civil society. It should expose abominable practices like bonded labour, untouchability, sati, legal, social and economic discrimination against women and her exploitation, child labour in hazardous industries, child abuse and child prostitution.

Human rights education (HRE) has to be catalyst to expose these practices and lacunae and weaknesses in law and its enforcement and bringing about attitudinal and social change. Thus, human rights education should cover not only the rights relating to physical well-being of an individual, but must also expand to comprehend all those conditions in a society that makes human existence possible with dignity, honour and spirituality.

Human rights education cannot remain an intellectual exercise by merely imparting knowledge in the class-rooms. It has to cover all modalities, formal, non-formal and informal - which could sensitise a person, awaken his/her conscience and develop an attitude of mind imbibing respect for human rights of others. It has to build strong linkages between what happens in the society and what is taught in the class rooms. It has to build strong linkages and networking between colleges/universities and various NGOs and other social service groups working in the field and community to give HRE a grass root orientation.

HRE must also be backed by a strong research component - by strong multi-disciplinary research on various aspects of human rights and their complexities.

An important responsibility of the NHRC is to "spread human rights, literacy and promote awareness of the safeguards". Hence, coordination with NHRC will be useful for a more purposeful use of extension programmes of the universities and colleges.

Human rights education should be inter- disciplinary. The content of the course should incorporate and reflect the concerns for democracy, development, peace, social justice, distributive justice, individual development, national development, environment protection and ecological balance.

Human rights is an extremely expanding field. Curriculum development in human rights has, therefore, to be a continuous exercise through workshops, seminars, training courses and academic discussions.

Media Role of Informer, Educator, Creator

The general public is unaware of human rights; it needs to be awakened. The press needs to be educated in human rights and human rights should form a part of the curriculum in mass education programmes at college and university levels. It is only when it is educated that the media can function as an informer, an enabler, a creater. Modalities are infinite. Human Rights issues must be mainstream issues of news content.

Secondly, media not only informs and educates but also empowers with requisite knowledge, improving skills; capacities and talents. Information is a one-time, one-track input, education is a ceaseless process that develops faculties and empowers for a calling. It gives a personality to society. In shaping society, media itself becomes a social institution in caring for its needs with sensitivity and eventually a leader - a responsible corporate citizen-who places national interest above commercial benefits.

The education of human rights must be relevant and meaningful to our cultural conditioning and to add value to our information and education those media must be used which will bring about the desired effect - the awareness of human rights and their achievement for bringing about a new social order.

4

Right to Information*

It is crucial, nay fundamental, to the survival of democracy that we must have absolute freedom of information except slicing out a small portion which is impinging on the security of the country. - Justice V.R.Krishna Iyer, Judge Supreme Court of India (1973 -1980)

Introduction

The right to information and the assurance of widespread citizen participation in public affairs and an active civil society are essential for the full realization of democracy - a system of government that is actively responsible for the needs of its citizens.The adage 'Knowledge is Power' when applied to human rights holds equally true for the phrase 'Information is Power'. The right to information is inherent in democratic governance because in a democracy 'state power' ultimately vests with the people - and effective power can not be exercised by the people unless information flows to the people from the state.

In India restrictions on the free flow of information not only erode the historic and constitutional principles of democracy but also come at the cost of the poor, as they are not able to exercise adequate checks on government policies and development programmes that are specifically meant for the poor. The denial of information by government is a major cause for political, social and economic exclusion of millions of people - these people could range from urban middle class citizens to the most backward of rural and tribal poor.

Human rights are essentially there to safeguard against the arbitrary or capricious exercises of governmental power. The right to information assumes both a preventive and curative role. The preventive role is assured insofar as when full information is available to the people there is less likelihood that governmental power will be abused in view of fear of censure. The curative role is that if there is any irregularity in governance the people would be able to

* Gist of Talk at an Anti-Corruption conference.

detect maladministration and take appropriate remedial action against the same either politically or legally.

The right to information is also one of the best tools to fight the cancer of corruption because corruption and transparency are incompatible. The right to information would encompass the right to know the assets and finances of elected representatives.

Another major source and cause of corruption is secrecy and delay in decision making. Right to information, if ensured to all the citizens, will be the most effective way of minimizing, if not altogether eliminating, the cancer of corruption, that has been undermining development, democracy and the people's faith in governance.

In essence therefore Right to Information is the key to Democracy and Development in :

1. Making participatory democracy meaningful
2. Cementing Trust in Government
3. Supporting People-Centred Development
4. Facilitating Equitable Economic Growth
5. Tackling Corruption

History of the Right to Information Movement in India

Several ancient accounts of history are replete with instances of active and informed participatory governance of people. There are also recounts of how people actively participated in open meetings at village and other levels. It can be therefore said that the concept of Right to Information is not alien to India.

The Right to Information was never recognized when India was under colonial rule. This was because information suppression was an integral part of exercise of colonial power and in some sense was a colonial attitude. This manifested itself in the form of laws such as the Official Secrets Act, 1923 and other forms of governmental legislation. It is indeed ironic that India did not abandon these colonial vestiges when it attained Independence as a Democratic State. While the founders of the Constitution and early rulers of India displayed immense personal integrity in ensuring participatory governance, it is unfortunate that they did not insert by way of constitutional provision - the right to information.

The struggle for an explicit Right to Information law has its roots in people's movements that were working to secure minimum wages, property rights and freedom from corruption for the rural poor in Rajasthan. In 1994, the Mazdoor Kisan Shakti Sangathan (MKSS) was able to clearly link corruption and the denial of rights to the poor, to the lack of right to information and this generated a fast growing movement around the same. In 1994-95 public hearings in rural Rajasthan were conducted and they began uncovering to the public gaze, scam after scam, neatly filed up in documents on development expenditure of local self-governments.

The new wave sought to impose democratic accountability on an arbitrary and corrupt governance system. The then Rajasthan Government was slow in implementing assurances made in the state assembly, of granting people the right to obtain photocopies of all documents pertaining to Panchayati Raj Institutions. It took two long sit-in strikes of 40 days and 53 days in 1996 and 1997 respectively, for the state government to finally relent and fulfill its promise by amending the rules of Rajasthan Panchayati Raj, to include the people's right to access information relating to Panchayati Raj institutions within their ambit, by inspecting and obtaining photocopies of documents. These efforts ultimately resulted in Rajasthan Legislature enacting a law on the Right to Information in 2000.

As the Rajasthan movement and these advocacy and networking exercises made right to information the buzzword in may parts of the Country, Tamil Nadu and Goa became the first two states to legislate on the subject in 1997. In Madhya Pradesh, more than 50 government departments passed orders for providing photocopies of government documents on demand and on payment of a nominal fee. Some of these orders also pertained to proactive or *suo moto* information sharing by the government in matters gravely affecting the public. Now there are Right to Information Acts in Karnataka, Maharashtra, Delhi and Assam too.

Initiatives to get a national legislation on the Right to Information also emerged. The two major sit-in strikes by the MKSS in 1996 and 1997 triggered advocacy efforts in different parts of the country and a small group called the National Campaign for People's Right to Information (NCPRI) was formed with senior journalists, lawyers, sympathetic bureaucrats, academics and NGO activists in it. The high point of these advocacy efforts was an attempt to draw up a model draft bill on the right to information that would be submitted for the consideration of the Central Government. The Press

Council of India, under Justice Mr. P. B. Sawant, took up the matter in right earnest in mid 1996. By the end of the year, the NCPRI and the Press Council of India did succeed in drafting a model Right to Information Bill, which was later revised at a workshop organised jointly by the Press Council and the National Institute of Rural Development (NIRD), Hyderabad.

Faced with a persistent public demand and a model bill submitted for its consideration by the NCPRI and the Press Council of India, in 1997 the then union government formed a committee under consumer movement activist H. D. Shourie. The H.D.Shourie Committee submitted report in May 1997 with a draft bill titled the Freedom of Information Bill 1997. This bill was modified by the government and placed before the cabinet. After being in a state of referral to a Group of Ministers for close to three years, the Freedom of Information Bill 2000 was introduced in the Lok Sabha. This 'Bill of 2000' was referred to the Parliamentary Standing Committee on Home Affairs in September 2000. The Parliamentary Committee invited suggestions of various Non-government and government bodies / individuals including the MKSS and NCPRI in the year 2001. After considering all the submissions, the Committee made its recommendations, very few of which have found their way in to the Freedom of Information Act, 2002 passed by the Parliament in December, 2002, five-and-a-half years after the central government began an exercise in this direction by appointing the Shourie Committee in May 1997.

Tested against the expectations derived from the civil society debate in the wake of the grassroots Right to Information movement in Rajasthan, the Constitution of India and the international experience, these legislative efforts both in the states and the centre disappoint in varying degrees. It would be useful to see judicial opinion on the matter before I proceed to suggest essential elements of the Right to Information legislation.

Judicial Intervention and Pronouncements

The Supreme Court has in at least two Constitution Bench decisions, held that citizens have the right to get information about all aspects of government functioning, *viz.*: Indira Gandhi's Election Case (Reported as State of U.P Vs. Raj Narain : (1975) 3 SCR 333), where the court had rejected the government's claim of privilege on the blue book containing security instructions for the Prime Minister;

and the Judges' Appointment Case (Reported as S.P.Gupta Vs. Union of India : AIR 1982 SC 149: 1981 Supp SCC 87), where the court rejected the claim of privilege of the Government on the correspondence between the Chief Justice of India and the Law Minister regarding the appointment of certain High Court Judges. This was held on the basis that the fundamental right to speech and expression could only be effectuated meaningfully only if the citizens had an effective right to access information available with the government.

It was also pointed out by the Supreme Court, that in a democracy, all public servants exercise power only on behalf of the people and it would be an anathema if information about what they did were hidden from the people. The Supreme Court has also held that the Right to Know is an integral part of the Right to Life and unless one has the Right to Information, the Right of Life cannot be exercised. After these judgments, there have been several other judgments of the Supreme Court where it has upheld the right to information as a fundamental right, including most recently, the Election Reforms Case (Reported as UOI Vs. Association for Democratic Reforms and another with PUCL and another Vs. UOI and another: 2002 (5) SCC 294) where the Bench had directed the Election Commission to compel disclosure by candidates of information regarding their criminal antecedents and their assets and liabilities.

What are the Essential Features of a Right to Information Legislation ?

For a Right to Information legislation to be effective the following elements are essential :

1. *Scope.* It should apply to all organs and instrumentalities of the state. 'State' should also apply to private bodies that perform public functions for the purposes of this legislation.
2. *Imposition of Explicit Duty to provide information.* There must be a clear and explicit imposition of a non-discretionary and mandatory duty on the state body to part with information once a request for information is made to it.
3. *Access to Information as a General Rule.* The Legislation must confer the right of access to all information as a general rule and explicitly give exceptions to this general rule.
4. *Exceptions to be narrow and limited.* The exceptions to the grant

of right to information should be narrow and confined to only reasons such as those where the information has a 'direct bearing' on the 'security, sovereignty and integrity of the Nation of India' or 'public order' or to protect 'privacy' of other citizens.

5. ***Application procedure to be simple and clearly defined.*** Procedural law should not defeat substantive law. The application process needs to be clearly defined and a specific official ought to be identified for accepting and responding to the application. The application should have a simple format. Where the applicant is illiterate assistance ought to be provided to reduce an oral request into one of writing.
6. ***Time Limit for Response.*** Information delayed is information denied. Very often, time is of the essence, and the failure to provide information in time can render the information useless. While most of the existing Right to Information laws in India provide for a 30 day ceiling limit, situations may occur where information is required on an urgent basis. The Goa Law provides for issuance of information within 48 hours in cases where it becomes urgent.
7. ***Reasonable fees.*** Only reasonable fees should be charged to applicants. Fees should only be charged towards physical copying and paper costs. An upward limit on the fee should be placed. Given the abject and widespread poverty that exists in India, fee waiver must be given to all indigent applicants, particularly those who are below the poverty line.
8. ***Need for remedy mechanism.*** The mere conferment of substantive and procedural rights to information may not result in applicants obtaining information at the first instance. A speedy review or appellate mechanism is therefore of the utmost essence, in case the applicant feels that his application for information is not being considered properly. It would be important to keep not too many levels of review process as this would only accentuate difficulties and cause avoidable delays. There must be stringent penalties for those officers who do not comply in providing information in accordance with law. An umbrella remedy should be provided to address non-compliance of disclosure or information requirements that may be prescribed in other statutes. (eg. receipt of copy of FIR as required under Cr.PC or the need to conduct public hearings while completing Environmental Impact Assessments under

the Environmental Protection Act).

9. ***Publicity and Training.*** Any law on the Right to Information is of little use unless the public is made aware of its contents. Many laws conferring rights are passed without educating people on how to invoke their rights. The people must be taught how to agitate their right to information in case they feel aggrieved. The law must also contain a strong aspect of training and orientation of public servants at all levels in order to bring out changes in the mindsets of government servants.
10. ***Whistle blowers.*** Any Right to Information legislation must necessarily protect whistle blowers who come out with critical information of public concern that would not have been otherwise produced on grounds purportedly falling within the exceptions of the general rule of disclosure.

Conclusion

The right to information is in essence a fundamental right. Accountability lies at the heart of the Indian Constitution and the culture of democratic governance - accountability cannot be ensured without Information. A constitutional or legal right to have access to State held information will ensure the transparency and accountability of all state bodies, and boost the quality of citizen participation in governance from mere casting of vote, to vigilant involvement in decision-making (national, state level and local) that affects his or her life. The single act of conferment of Right to Information will also go significantly towards erasing the cancer of corruption that has undermined development in India. The right to information is a basic right that underpins good governance, democracy, poverty eradication and the practical realisation of human rights.

5

Women and Human Rights*

Discrimination against women violates the principles of equality of rights and respect for human dignity, is an obstacle to the participation of women, on equal terms with men, in the political, social, economic and cultural life of their countries, hampers the growth of the prosperity of society and the family and makes more difficult the full development of the potentialities of women in the service of their countries and of humanity. - Convention on the Elimination of All Forms of Discrimination against Women 1979 adopted in 1979 by the UN General Assembly

I

I consider it a privilege and honour to be invited to deliver the Padma Bhushan Dr. T.S. Avinashilingam Seventh Memorial Lecture.*

The earlier six memorial lectures have been delivered by eminent personalities. I join the millions, particularly the womenfolk in paying our respectful homage and grateful tributes to Iyya Dr. Avinashilingam AVL, for the unique services rendered to humanity in general and our nation in particular. He was a unique personality, born in a wealthy family, graduated in politics, economics and law, but dedicated himself to the cause of spirituality, education and the nation.

Very early in life, he came under the spiritual influence of Sri Ramakrishna Paramahansa, Swami Vivekananda and Mahatma Gandhiji. He joined the freedom struggle and went to jail a number of times in Salt Satyagraha, Civil Disobedience Movement, Individual Satyagraha and Quit India Movement.

---

* From Dr T.S. Avinashilingam Memorial Lecture delivered by the author at Avinashilingam Women's Home Science University, Coimbatore and other seminars by Women's organisations.

He dedicated his entire life to the service of the nation, particularly in the cause of rural and women's education. He founded Sri Ramakrishna Mission Vidayalaya in 1930, consisting of twelve institutions, including institutions for Ph.D. Courses. He founded Sri Avinashilingam Rural Centre and Tamil Academy. He has several publications to his credit, including Tamil Encyclopaedia in ten volumes. As Minister of Education in Composite Madras State, he introduced Tamil as medium of instruction in high schools and colleges.

The flagship of the countless institutions that he founded is, Sri Avinashilingam Home Science College which blossomed into the Avinashilingam Deemed University for women in the year 1988.

If he could achieve all this in a lifetime, it was made possible by the total dedication, hard work, brilliance, efficiency and competence of Dr. Rajammal Devadas, a household name all over the world in the field of Home Science and Women's education. It is fruitful association of five decades which made it possible for this institution to grow into the first university of home science for women which is acknowledged all over the world for its excellence and innovative methods of teaching and research. Her life itself is a living example and model of women's emancipation, education and service to the cause of women, education and humanity. Her bio data is perhaps the most lengthy and impressive one I have ever seen. She has attended all possible national and international conferences concerning home science and women's education. She is a leading nutrition scientist and an acknowledged expert whose advice and views are sought after the world over. She has trained several thousands of students and teachers. She has 40 books and over 400 research papers to her credit. She has given lectures in almost all leading universities all over the world. She has been Chancellor of the university since last 5 years after serving the institution in various capacities.

I am grateful to her for inviting me and giving me the honour and pleasure of being with all of you today. This unique university for Home Science and higher education for women has many noble objectives like :

1. Inculcate ethical values and social and moral standards in all disciplines of study.
2. Give the much needed awareness to women about their rights and status through adults and non formal

education.

3. Serve as a centre for national integration to bring women from all parts of the country and develop an all India perspective.
4. Function as a centre for the development of women and children.
5. Provide knowledge in Home Science, Humanities and fine arts to the highest level.

This institution has been upholding a life of purity, discipline and service to the less privileged community, by integrating value orientation as its component at different levels of teaching and learning.

High ideals are being imparted to the students to prepare them to meet the challenges of life in the family and society. Here the teachers are aware that mere knowledge and skills is not education. The right values, attitudes and character make education wholesome and complete.

What impressed me most about this great institution is not only excellence in knowledge and skills but also cultivating ethical, social and spiritual values and spirit of national integration and patriotism. The Sunday sarvodaya prayer imparts spiritual values and respect for all religions.

I am delighted to note that apart from national days and other important events, 'Human Rights Day' is also being celebrated. Let us share some thoughts on 'Human Rights' which ensure human dignity. After the second world war, a tired world appalled by the savagery of human degradation that it saw and experienced, looked forward to an era of peace. It dreamed of a new world order of peace and international understanding. But the dream turned sour. There have been senseless ethnic, racial, religious and linguistic conflicts all over the world.

What relevance have human rights in the lives of these great masses of humanity living in poverty and deprivation? Economic and social developments are critical dimensions of human rights conditions. It is rightly said that "poverty by itself is a human right violation." The human rights regime now forms an indelible part of legal, political and moral landscape.

Progressive Development

The subject of human rights is itself a progressive development of the status of the individual in the international legal system. Human rights stem from a baseline of equal concern for the interest of everyone. This moral idea is a reflection of a deep rooted moral sentiment that "all human beings, great or small, virtuous or vicious, should be respected and cared for simply by virtue of the fact that they are human beings". To speak of human rights requires a conception of what rights one possesses by virtue of being human. It means, the rights that human being have, simply because they are born as human beings on this planet. It is independent of their varying social circumstances and degrees of merit.

The recognition of human rights under international law is relatively recent but the philosophy underlying the concept is ancient. What does it mean to be a human being? What is the purpose of life on this earth? What should be our intellectual and emotional attitude to one another? Human Rights are essentially a codification of mainly spiritual laws. The underlying unity is eloquently articulated in the ethical systems of different faiths as in the teaching that "we should treat others as we ourselves wish to be treated".

India endorsed the Declaration of Human Rights. As in many other ancient civilisations, the issues of human rights were debated in our land for many centuries - starting from the Vedas. The moral percepts we have known all along, when incorporated into our governance and public functionaries have become what the declaration of human rights is about.

The recognition that the human rights of women and girls are inalienable, integral and indivisible part of universal human rights is one of the significant milestones of the world conference on human rights in Vienna in 1993. It was forcefully restated at the fourth World Conference on Women in Beijing in 1995.

Why is that Women's rights are more important than any other human rights? Because it is women who bear most of their family and community. They already grow most of the developing world's food, market most of its produce, fetch most of its water, collect most of its fuel, feed most of its animals and weed out most of its fields.

And when their work outside the home is done, they light the third world's fire, cook its meals, clean its compounds, wash its clothes, shop for its needs and look after its old and its ill. And they bear and care for its children. These are the multiple burdens of womanhood almost everywhere in the world.

When we look at the rights of children and girls, they are part and parcel of women's rights. We look at the children's rights beginning with the right to be registered at birth. For millions of children, lack of birth registration means exclusion from the rights and privileges, a nation offers its citizens such as education and health care. Rest of the important aspects like public health service, nutrition, child immunization are very well known to those like you, who have had the privilege of getting meaningful education.

When it comes to girls' rights, we realize that in countries of every economic and social profile, gender, inequity is deeply ingrained in society.

In the declaration on the elimination of violence against women article 3 says "women are entitled to the equal enjoyment and protection of all human rights and fundamental freedoms in the political, economic, social, cultural and civil fields. These rights include :

1. The right to life.
2. Equality.
3. Liberty and security of the person.
4. To be free from all forms of discrimination.
5. To the highest standard attainable of physical and mental health.
6. To just and favourable conditions of work.
7. Not to be subjected to torture or other cruel inhuman or degrading treatment or punishment."

Gender Violence

Let us have a glimpse of the various types of Gender Violence throughout the lifecycle of women.

Parental — sex selective abortion, battering during pregnancy.

Foeticide—In certain areas in the country, including Tamil Nadu, where female infanticide is endemic, the increasing instances of foeticide employing modern tools of medical technology, raise vital questions.

Sex—specific abortions assisted in many instances by doctors and paramedical personnel continue to be performed, sometimes at great risk to the woman. The long term sociological consequences of those unlawful unethical acts are serious in the extreme.

Infancy—female infanticide, emotional and physical abuse, differential access to food and medical care.

Childhood—Child labour, child marriage, child abuse and

child prostitution.

Adolescence – Drug abuse, dating and courtship, violence, eve teasing, harassment and abuse at work place, trafficking, in women and forced prostitution.

Reproductive stage – dowry abuse, psychological abuse, wife battering, frequent pregnancies.

Old age – elder abuse, and abuse of widows.

Adolescence has long been viewed as a distinct stage of life in the industrialised world. Now it is also emerging as a key period between childhood and adulthood. Young people of age10 to 19 years account for the sixth of the population on earth and 85 per cent of them live in developing countries making them a force for profound change. Adolescence should be the time of greatest hope and promise in life. It can be a springboard, producing self confident young adults equipped, with the knowledge they need, to create a successful future for themselves and their societies. Or it can be a point, where everything goes wrong when all their promises and potential are lost. If it goes wrong for today's adolescents, it goes wrong for the world.

HIV Posing a Menace to India

In 1997 alone around 3 million young people aged 15-24 years became infected with HIV and in that about two thirds of them are girls. Girls of the age 15-19 years give birth to 15 million babies a year. Around the globe 73 million children consisting 59 per cent girls and 48 per cent boys are not enrolled in secondary schools.

Women's life experience across the world and statistics and writing on women are testimony to the fact that violence against women is the gravest and most pervasive form of violation of human rights. Now let us look at some of the most serious violations of women's rights.

Human Rights Abuse in the Family

Research has shown that for millions of women, their homes are dens of terror and that a huge chunk of violence that is perpetrated against women is committed by their own family members. Human rights abuse within the family takes different shapes such as domestic violence, dowry related violence. Such violence cuts across income, class and culture. Crimes that occur in the family are rarely reported or even if they are reported they are reported when it is too late to change the situation. Many victims do not speak out, in fear of retaliation and further violence, while for many others it is the question of using their pride and dishonouring the family.

In India dowry-related violence claims the lives of at least 5000 women every year. It is important to take note of the fact that the occurrence of violence against women in the family context is not limited to developing countries alone. Industrialised countries also suffer from this serious malady.

In 1996 the NCRB of the Government of India recorded a total of over one lakh cases of crimes against women.

Crimes against women show an increase year after year. Eveteasing cases alone have increased by 18 per cent. May be the increasing awareness on the part of the women on their rights, is a factor responsible for this. But we must recognize that a vast majority of crimes against women go unreported due to the social stigma attached to them.

War Crimes Against Women

War and insurgency situations have a severe and dramatic impact on the human rights of women. Violence against women often continues even after hostilities end or women flee them. About three quarters of the world's 20 million refugees are women and their dependents. Women and children account for more than 80 per cent of those living in refugee camps and they are vulnerable to violence and abuse . While statistics suggest the frequency of violent assaults against women in situations of upheaval, it is impossible to fully document the continuing terror and dread that invade the daily life of women struggling not only to survive under these conditions but also to protect children and elders.

Economic Discrimination and Exploitation

Both the world summit for social development 1995 and the Fourth World Conference on Women 1995 acknowledged that while globalisation is changing markets and economic opportunities worldwide, the feminisation of poverty is a persistent trend. Improving women's economic status requires that women have equal access to decision making about economic policies; they need to have access to and control of the economic resources.

Political and Social Rights

It has been seen throughout political history right from the time of Aristotle who described women as unintelligent and therefore not politically capable, to the present day where in America the symbol of liberal democracy, not a single woman has occupied the post of president in its history. Even in countries like India and Sri Lanka though women became the president and prime minister they did so more out of the virtue of being connected to political dynasty families rather than in the capacity as a citizen or as a woman. The Women Reservation Bill regarding getting 33 per cent reservation in Parliament and Legislative Assemblies is still to be passed as it has many opponents.

Challenges

Eradication of violation of human rights calls for a combination of strategies, enactment and enforcement of laws and availability of services for survivors and victims of violence. Research on the prevalence of the problem, sensitisation and training for law enforcement officials, legal and health professionals, appropriate counselling of those who are in trouble, raising public awareness and introduction of human rights as a subject in schools and colleges are the needs of the hour.

Look at the word responsibility, it is response and ability – the ability to choose your response. Responsible people do not blame circumstances and rationalise through concepts like 'fate'. Blaming others is really juvenile behaviour. The mature mind says 'Try me' instead of 'why me'. Perhaps the Japanese success in building their economy out of the ashes of World War II was their willingness to learn, to borrow, copy and assimilate ideas, having a clear focus on quality. There is nothing free in this world. One has to pay a price for everything. To become individually great and make the nation great, the people have to grow and growth will come only with the right kind of education, intelligence and inception of humanistic qualities. Human rights should be considered as our responsibility towards our fellow human beings. This enables us to understand each other's viewpoint and helps create a cohesive atmosphere where duties come first. If everybody does his duties, the question of rights will not arise. Sensitivity towards our fellow human beings is not something which is acquired through knowledge. It is something which is a part of all of us regardless of our culture, class and creed. Sensitivity is not assimilated, sensitivity arises when we give up our prejudices biases and social contexts to see the innate natural truth of the most basic human force compassion.

II

Gender – Suggestions

I appreciate the Gender Training Institute and the Police Training College, New Delhi, for organising the "Training of Trainers on Gender Sensitisation for the police personnel" to sensitise the police personnel on this very important segment, who constitute 50 per cent of the population.

Without a total, complete and proper understanding of the sensibilities and concerns of the women and their problems, no police force can be successful in the discharge of their duties.

Every human being is endowed with certain basic, fundamental, inalienable and universal rights, by the mere fact that they are born on this planet. All human rights are indivisible, inter-dependent and interrelated. They include civil, political, economic, social and cultural rights. It is the duty of the State Government and authorities, regardless of their political, economic and cultural systems, to promote and protect such human rights.

Human rights issues have real application and relevance for every citizen. The affirmation and implementation of human rights form the foundation of a just society. They are vital for a just order fairness and justice as also for the peace and prosperity of every society.

If men and women take due responsibility as parent, home-makers, good citizens and guardians of the life and well-being of every child, they will contribute as they should, to ensuring the survival and development of both boy and girl children and the building of a better society.

Women getting their just place in every society is vital to the well-being of the community because it is they who bear most of the burden of meeting the needs of their family. They already grow most of the developing world's food market, most of its crops, fetch most of its water, collect most ot its fuel, feed most of its animals and work most of its fields.

And when their work outside the home is done, they light the third world's fires, cook its meals, clean, its compounds, wash and look after its old and its ill. And they bear and care for its children. These are the multiple burdens of womanhood, almost everywhere in the world. Although most nations promise equality of opportunity for women few come close to delivering it and that failure has a huge impact on the ability of half of the world's population to contribute fully to the economic and social, civil and political spheres of the community's activities.

Women earn less for paid employment than men: they have less livelihood of inheriting and other assets than their brothers; they are more likely to be physically assaulted regularly by members of their own families; they are less likely to serve in Government in senior positions. Now, they are being injected with the HIV/AIDS virus at a faster rate than men simply because they lack the information with which to protect themselves or the right or ability to refuse intimate relationships be it with their own husbands or with the rapists.

In 1993, the World Conference on Human Rights concluded that the human rights of women and of the girl-child are inalienable, integral and indivisible part of universal human rights. The full and equal participation of women in political, civil, economic 'social and cultural life at the national, regional and international levels and the eradication of all forms of discrimination on grounds of sex are priority objectives of the international community. The World Conference urged Governments, institutions, inter-Governmental and non-Governmental organisations to intensify their efforts for the protection and promotion of human rights of women and the girl-child.

The barriers which women must overcome are to be found not only in the reform of the law, but also in the reform of attitudes, traditions and beliefs.

It is in the making of policy or in the working of Government agencies such as the police that women's human rights will be implemented or frustrated. We have to ensure that women are treated with dignity, that they have equal access to justice and that the outcome for them is one of true equality.

The Convention on the elimination of all forms of discrimination against women is unique in that it recognises the role of education of both men and women in changing attitudes, so that equality of rights and responsibilities become willingly and fully accepted and prejudices and practices based on tradition are overcome. In the Convention, the discrimination against women is defined as "Any distinction, exclusion or restriction made on the basis of sex which has the effect or purpose of impairing or making the recognition, enjoyment or exercise by women, irrespective of their marital status, on the basis of equality of men and women, of human right and fundamental freedom in political, economic, social, cultural, civil or any other field."

Political participation by women is a must for the progress of a nation. The low numbers of women occupying position of influence in public and political life has detrimental effect on the health of a political life of a country. The low level of literacy among women in our country is against the interests of their human rights. This has an impact on the environment, on the health of the population and on a nation's economic status.

Woman, who are educated, are better able to provide for their children. They can accede to public information concerning health and justice. The work done by National Commission for Women through its "intensive and extensive legal literacy campaign" is an invaluable contribution to the goal of ensuring that women have access to justice.

A woman, who cannot read, 'may not know that certain crimes perpetrated against her are forbidden by law; nor will she know that she may have the same rights as men to housing and jobs and nor will she have access to nutrition advice, or advice on how to avoid the terrible diseases like AIDS. In nations where women are educated to a reasonable standard, the birth-rate decreases, the health of families improves and environment and the economy benefits and their human rights are asserted and better protected.

Very often, due to ignorance, the expectant mothers do not have nutritious food resulting in the children being born with a half brain capacity to a normal child. Thus, a large number of children born without the capability of understanding suffer for no fault of theirs. A mother's education would enable the knowledge and awareness of proper nutritious food which is important for the growth of the child.

It is now widely acknowledged that violence against women prevents them from participating fully in the family, in the work-place and in their community. Due to low literacy level, poor health and inadequate income, there is reduced ability to participate in community. Life is a vast waste of the talents and education of one half of the world's population where women are not treated equally not only do their families suffer, but the community itself loses access to an extremely valuable human resource.

The human rights of women relate not just to their status in society, but have, a real and serious impact on the general health and well-being of the, whole community.

Without their contribution, society will continue to be poorer.

III

Reproductive and Child Health (RCH)

The curative approach to the advanced of women entails several facilities given to them. RCH is one major stride to achieve this goal.

The 1994 international conference on Population and Development in Cairo and its aftermath emphasized that a narrow focus on population control was likely to be counter-productive for economic and social development. The RCH approach with its forcus on individual reproductive choice, access to information and health services and the empowerment of women emerged as the solution. This can contribute directly to reduced infant, child and maternal mortality, and infuses in female literacy with measurable gains in human development.

To illustrate, a reduction in the infant mortality rate from the existing all India levels to levels already achieved in Kerala, would increase life expectancy at birth by nearly 3.8 years and move the country seven rungs up in the ranking of countries by the human development index.

If these were combined with a Kerala-type improvement in female literacy rates, India would be catapulted out of the ranks of countries with low human development achievements. High quality maternal and child health care is likely to yield significant monetary saving in India, currently nearly 50% of public and private health spending is on primary curative health services. These resources could be economists have indicated that increased schooling would have significant effect on the growth of real GDP per capita.

Secondly, improved health of mothers and infants contributes to the national output by its effect on the quality and size of the labour force.

World Development Report of 1993 clearly indicated that direct interventions aimed at childhood communicable diseases and reproductive health were much more cost effective than health interventions focusing on heart disease, accidents] diabetes, etc. Investments in female education are high yielding. Returns to female primary education become significantly higher once benefits in terms of reduced infant and child mortality, fertility and better nutrition are included in the calculations.

IV

*Bringing new life into the world is a wondrous event. Even though a woman is supposed to be at the threshold of death at the time of child birth, she forgets all the pain the moment she hears her baby cry. To realise that the same woman is ready to kill her baby - a baby of her own gender - is hard to believe, but true even today in certain areas. One can imagine the tremendous amount of societal pressure that is brought to bear on such a woman to commit such a heinous act.

This is only one aspect of the generalized sexual bias and discriminatory behaviour in a male dominated patriarchal society. Why this perpetuation of gender bias against females? Particularly if we bear in mind it is the women who bear most of the burden and responsibility of the family and the community. They grow most of the developing world's food, market most of its produce, fetch most of its water, collect most of its fuel, feed most of its animals and weed out most of its fields.

When their work outside the home is over, their responsibility to the family starts. They light the third world's fire, cook its meals, clean its compounds, wash its clothes, shop for its needs and they also look after the old and ill in the families. They bear and care for the children. These are the multiple burdens of womanhood almost everywhere in the world.

Let us have a glimpse of the various types of Gender Violence throughout the life cycle of women:

Parental	Sex selective abortions, battering during pregnancy.
Foeticide	In certain areas of the globe, where female infanticide is endemic, increasing instances of foeticide are seen employing modern tools of medical technology or age old time - tested crude methods.

---

* Gist of the speech made by Shri D.R. Kaarthikeyan, Director General, National Human Rights Commission, while launching the booklet and the video documentary on Global Campaign for the Elimination of Gender Based Violence - on 27th April, 1999 at the Conference Hall, UNDP.

Abortion	Sex specific abortions sometimes at grave risk to the women continue to be performed very often assisted by doctors and paramedical personnel.
Infancy	Female infanticide, emotional and physical abuse – differential access to food and medical care - when the male child is always being preferred and pampered.
Childhood	Child labour, child marriage, child abuse and child prostitution.
Adolescence	Drug abuse. Abuse and violence even during dating and courtship - eve teasing very often endangering the life of the victim.
At work place	Sexual harassment, abuse and eve teasing trafficking in women forced prostitution.
After Marriage	Psychological abuse and physical violence- due to dowry, wife battering - frequent pregnancies even against the will - neglect and abuse of widows, and abuse and neglect in old age.

Human Rights Abuse in the Family

For nearly half the women victims of violence, their homes are dens of terror and horror. Such violence cuts across income, class and culture. Crimes that occur in the family are rarely reported and even if they are reported, they are reported when it is too late to change the situation. Many victims do not speak out under fear of retaliation and further violence, while for many others it is a question of their pride and prestige of the family. Crimes against women shows a steep increase year after year.

Women are entitled to equal enjoyment and protection of all rights and fundamental freedoms in the political, economical, social and cultural and civil fields.

All human beings, great or small, men or women, should be respected and cared for, simply by virtue of the fact that they are human beings. The discrimination and violence against women based on ignorance, illiteracy and tradition have gone on too long. It is high time the silent suffering of the women is ended.

I must compliment the very effective, thoughtful and imaginative campaign launched by Ms. Chandni Joshi and UNIFEM during the last one year. Certainly, the campaign has met the challenge effectively. The silence is shattered. We have to go a long way to achieve the object of ensuring the women realise their right of leading a life free of violence and full of dignity from the very beginning to the last end.

Apart from continuing the campaign of creating awareness by education and increasing the effectiveness and speedy disposal of cases by the investigation agencies and the judicial courts, what is of utmost importance is changing the attitude of the entire society, particularly all the males who are very often seen as the perpetrators of violence against women.

I have attended most of the functions of the UNIFEM. UNIFEM adopted every means during the campaign - seminars, workshops, rallies, painting competitions, dance performances and debates. Everyone of these functions have been organised with great forethought, planning and perfection.

I once again compliment and thank Ms. Chandni Joshi and her colleagues in the UNIFEM for the successful campaign and successful serving the great cause.

V

The Rights of Women

Women constitute half the world's population, perform two thirds of the world's work, receive only one-tenth of its income, and own less than one-hundredth of its property. Significant numbers of the world's population are routinely subjected to torture, starvation, terrorism, humiliation, mutilation and even murder because they are female. Violation of women's human right is distinctly connected to their being female - that is, women are discriminated against and abused on the basis of gender.

Article 2 of the Universal Declaration of Human Rights, confers on all "...the rights and freedoms set forth in this Declaration without distinction of any kind, such as race, colour, sex, language, religion, political or other opinion, national or social origin, property, birth or other status." Eleanor Roosevelt and the Latin American women who fought for the inclusion of sex in the Declaration and for its passage, clearly intended that it would address the problems of women's subordination.

Women as Leaders

Virginia Woolf said that "Even when the path is normally open-when there is nothing to prevent a woman from being a doctor, a lawyer, a civil servant. There are many phantoms and obstacles, I believe, glooming in her way".

In 1960, Sirimayo Bandaranaike of Sri Lanka became the world's first woman Prime Minister. Since then, Indira Gandhi, Gold-Meir, Margret Thatcher and many other women rose to occupy the highest positions in their countries. Thus, started the process of emergence of many more women as leaders in fields normally associated with men. The principle that authority flows from one who knows started applying impartially to women as well as men.

Prejudice dies hard and not until 19th century the age of progress - did women begin to emerge in larger numbers as leaders often in the face of disapproval.

In a family, better decisions are usually made when both sexes are involved, the same logic applies in industry. Women seem to have better intuitive capabilities and their deeper, in-built sense of fundamental responsibility. They tend to stick with details longer than men and to ensure that things are actually done right. They also have a different perception of other people's reactions and by and large, are more sensitive to them. The best decisions and the best results will come where men and women work together as a team, respecting their differences of view and contributing equally from their own experience and approach to the formation of the policies which they will then try to carry out.

Even in centuries and in cultures where the female sex was under-valued in contrast to the male and kept out of public life women could still be leaders of tribes, cities, states or nations. Many of these women actually showed outstanding, natural qualities and acquired skills as leaders.

Not until recent times has the door for leadership been slowly opened - or forced open for 'Women in almost all the areas of human work. Women who have no paid employment can still give leadership as wives and mothers, as neighbours, and citizens. A principle stand in our hope for the future must be in the awakening of women to the needs and responsibilities of leadership.

To enable more women to attain positions of strategic leadership responsibility in industry, commerce and the public services, should be one of the aims of society.

Great leaders have to pay a price for leadership, unceasing self-discipline, the constant taking of risks and responsibility, calmness in crisis unfailing courage, instinct, intuition, authority, charisma, humility, compassion, spirituality, patience, tolerance, a strong sense of justice, and unswerving loyalty to the cause and the team, strength of mind, magnanimity, moral stature and above all on dignity and strength of character.

Meaning of Leadership

Leadership potential can be developed but it does have to be there in the first place. Most people have some degree of aptitude forgetting things done with people. In this respect learning to lead and learning to swim are analogous. Most people can be taught to swim, but few will reach Olympics Standard and become great swimmers.

Lord Slim said—"there is no body who cannot vastly improve his or her powers of leadership by a little forethought and practice. Many of us do have hidden potential for leadership, which very often emerge's only in times of crisis, such as wars, yet the problems and opportunities of our troubled peace call for leadership on an unprecedented scale. As it is said, leadership is probably more caught than taught. The example of a few good leaders ignites in us the spirit of leadership, we in turn have the responsibility of passing on the torch to those who are ready to receive it. But the leaders of tomorrow will need a personal greatness as leaders which does not characterise many leaders today.

A leader has been defined as a person who creates followers. Even Alexander the Great found that he could not lead his Greeks against their better judgement. Discriminating and determined colleagues are as important as good leaders. Educated, intelligent, highly technically competent people today are,not likely to see themselves simply as followers.

Good leaders today will tend to see people as colleagues, companions or partners, not followers. As one progresses through levels of leadership, of course, many of those colleagues will be leaders in their own right.

Jesus told his disciples "No longer do I call you servants, for the servant (or slave) does not know what his master is doing. I have called you friends, for have made all known to you."

Nelson saw his captains as a "band of brothers and treated

them as such." True leaders want equals, not subordinates. John Hunt defined leadership as the art of inspiring others to give of their best and the courage to use this art. The leader operates from inside his group, not from above, it; that in setting a good example, he does not steal the initiative of the others in other words, that he takes his full share but no more than his share - of the job in hand. This implies, a willingness not merely to decentralise, or apportion the burden. Persuade each other member of the group that his is an equal essential job, and that each has his own liberty as well as responsibility to develop that part as a whole. Good leadership derives from a right attitude to the job of leading; that this is only one of the jobs to be done. A leader has been well described as a first companion. Then, of course, it is the art of blending the efforts of every one concerned to produce a combined result.

Dag Hammarkjold, Secretary General of the United Nations, the world's leading civil servant of 1953 till his death in a plane crash in 1958, wrote:

"Your position never gives you the right to command. It only imposes on you the duty of so living your life that others can receive your orders without being humiliated."

Such is the only kind of leadership that will really work over a longer period of time and among free and equal people. Thus, greatness now is more a matter of quality than degree. Such greatness even in the ordinary roles of leadership is what helps to constitute a great nation in the spiritual and moral sense of that word. In peace, as in war, there are many situations that call for personal greatness."

The price of greatness is responsibility, wrote Sir Winston Churchill, the position is really secondary. However, it is true that people who occupy the major roles or positions of leadership ought to lead and be trained to lead, but it is possible also for those in much humbler positions to achieve a degree of excellence in leadership and team work.

True leadership is simply an expression of human greatness. In its true sense leadership should mean, giving a lead by example, even without a position of authority. Our greatness lies in our ability to transcend ourselves in the service of that which has greater value to us than ourselves. There is not a single man or woman who has not had great moments, who has not risen to rare occasions. It is true that we need situations which call out the best in us as leaders, but all leaders can prepare themselves for such a time. Nor will opportunities be lacking.

A leader should be able to place himself or herself on an equal footing with the others involved, relying upon their authority of knowledge and personality to gain respect. Such an instance does require considerable inner confidence, people will sense if it is there. They will soon sense, too, if a leader can, show them the way forwards and lead them on their journey.

Leadership exists on different levels—team, operational, strategic, national and global. The philosophy of leadership applies to all those levels and transcends colour, race, gender, time and space as the underlying human natur is more or less the same.

Leadership comes into its own when people are free and equal. Leaders create not followers but partners in the common enterprise. Real excellence goes hand in hand with humility, with unlikely leadership virtue. Humility includes both saying the truth about oneself and also being open to learning more about good leadership.

To put it in John Buchan's words, "the task of leadership is not to put greatness into humanity, but to elicit it, for the greatness is there already."

Five decades of democratic politics and planned interventions through legislation and public programmes has not made a serious dent in the status of women. Shocking in particular is the abysmally low presence of women in decision making bodies. Why is it that we do not hear of women quotas in education and employment? After all, even at the level of literacy, the gender gap remains significant. And the proportion of women in formal public sector employment is no better. The private sector scene, particularly at non-clerical levels, too is dismal.

'Men make laws, women make manners.' American columnist Will Henry put it, 'Nature gave women too much power, the law gives them too little'.

'Women are one half of the world, but . . . it remains a man's world. The laws are man's laws, the government a man's government the country a man's country . . . This man's world must become a man's and a woman's world'.

The birth of the Indian National Congress in 1885 provided a political platform to Indian women. In 1900 the first women delegates attended the Calcutta session of the Congress and spoke from a political platform. This was the dawn of a new era, which saw Indian women take an increasingly active part in political activities. They emerged in their thousands in response to the call of the Mahatma and Sarojini Naidu became the first India's woman President of the Indian National Congress in 1925. Our women had become visible and their politicization had begun.

The Quit India Movement of 1942 saw the leaders of the movement arrested and jailed and women assumed leadership roles. They came from all age groups and classes, castes and religions. Their sympathy and support to the nationalist movement, including its militant activities, epitomised by youngsters like Aruna Asaf Ali, unnerved even the British.

The participation of women in the nationalist movement was unique. For, at a time when women in the West were demanding suffrage, motivated by the interests of their own gender group, our women's primary concern was the freedom of their motherland. Motivated by a sense of nationalist commitment, the focus of their activity was not feminism, but nationalism. This is why equal rights for women were accepted without any hostility or resistance when freedom came. Adult franchise under a democratic Constitution brought women political equality. The major challenge to Indian democracy was how the world's largest electorate, most of whom were illiterate, would function. But our people, both men and women in rural and urban areas, have demonstrated a remarkably high level of maturity, fully justifying the faith which our Constitution makers had reposed in them.

India is far ahead of many developed economies in providing progressive legislation and positive intervention on behalf of women. The impact of these policies on the status of women has, however, been limited. The reasons for this are varied. Given the hierarchical structure of Indian society with its diverse and complex socio-economic institutions and cultural values, it is difficult to evolve a strategy which could be effective within different groups. The size of the country and the intervening state level administrative machinery has led to an uneven distribution of the gains of development.

Acknowledging the limitations in using law as an instrument of social change, policy-makers have been compelled to adopt positive discrimination in favour of women in certain areas. They have tried to identify the sources and factors for the economic dependence and social powerlessness of women and to remove, or at least reduce, them. In an effort to mitigate the enormous burden which women carry within and outside the family, they have sought to reduce their oppression through a series of welfare and economic policy pronouncements. Participatory planning and decentralization administration is also being attempted.

Electoral Role of Women

An analysis of women's participation in elections over the past four decades brings out the following facts:

(i) The extent, nature and level of Indian women's participation is much greater than in most other countries-developed or developing.

(ii) This participation has been steadily expanding over the years - by way of voting, as candidates, and participation in campaigning, and so on.

(iii) The gap in the turnout between men and women is narrowing.

(iv) The percentage of women elected to representative bodies is increasing.

The politicisation of women is increasingly combined with a degree of political awareness that is expressed not merely in terms of their mobilization at the time of voting but also in the way they cast their votes. It is now an accepted fact that women do not vote blindly, or as ordered by their men. Recent elections have shown that women have a mind of their own and exercise their vote independently, pointing to the decisive role of women in electoral outcomes.

Equally significant has been the delinking of female illiteracy from their voting behaviour. Literacy among women is, the lowest, particularly in the rural areas, and among the poorer classes and Harijans. Yet, most of the time they have demonstrated their political sensitivity and an awareness of the various issues confronting them.

The effective mobilization of women and their electoral behaviour, however, is diluted by other disquieting trends. These are:

(i) Despite an increase, women contesting elections still constitute less than five per cent of the total number of contestants. Of these women who get elected constitute a still smaller percentage

(ii) Political parties are, by and large, reluctant to field women as candidates.

(iii) Most of the women who contest gain their candidature by their birth/close relationship with established party leaders.

(iv) There is no correlation between female population, their voting percentage and their numbers in elected assemblies.

(v) For women, the cost of participation in formal politics is too high and therefore their participation is low - even lower than that of men from the weaker sections.

International Initiatives

The World Plan of Action adopted in Mexico City in 1975 put forward various suggestions for the recruitment, nomination and promotion of women in various branches of government, public bodies, trade unions and pressure groups. The Nairobi Declaration (1985) stressed: "Women by virtue of their gender, experience discrimination in terms of denial of equal access to the power structure that controls society and determines development issues and peace initiatives," and noted: "For the equality to become a reality for women, the sharing of power on equal terms with men must be a major strategy." The Beijing Platform of Action emphasized the importance of governmental and non-governmental organisations in educating women to exercise their civil, political and social rights, and stated that in this process of consciousness raising, efforts would have to be made to fix definite time bound targets and even resort to a quota system. In spite of all this, women everywhere continue to be marginally represented in decision-making processes which have a direct impact on them.

The significant result of international initiatives and UN meetings on women, in so far as Indian women are concerned, is a visible shift from viewing women as targets of welfare policies to their emergence as a critical factor in development. The scattered, piece-meal or curative approach to the advancement of women unrelated to policies and strategies for economic development, are now replaced by an integrated participatory approach, related to their needs, aspirations and choices, emphasizing the holistic approach for bringing women into the mainstream of national development programmes. Several states have formulated their own policies for the advancement of women while the central government is in the process of formulating a national policy for women.

The big task before us today is to ensure justice, to reduce the disparities in the opportunities and facilities available to women and to make them equal partners in development. It will be too much to expect that this can be achieved by governmental pronouncements alone. What is needed is the sincere cooperation and support of common people in this gigantic task.

V

Gender Bias

The Chairperson of the National Commission for Women states that "definite gender bias" still exists in text books. She wanted freedom from such "psychological partitioning". She quoted several examples, even from nursery rhymes, reinforcing the age-old prejudices. "Science is for boys while humanity is for girls; that the outdoors is for men while indoors is for women."

The early school years form the psychological bedrock on which a child's values and attitudes are based, which later show up in actions and behaviourial patterns. If patriarchal patterns are formed at an early stage in both boys and girls they continue life long.

Women's life experiences across the world and statistics and writings on women are testimony to the fact that violence against women is the gravest and most pervasive form of violation of Human Rights.

Beijing Platform for Action stated, "Violence against women violates and impairs or nullifies enjoyment by women of their human rights and fundamental freedoms. It is a blot on our collective conscience."

State inaction and society's tolerance are the major causes that allow such violence to continue. Prevalence of importance, custom, tradition and religion in some parts of the world perpetuates and even justifies violence against women.

New forms of violence, especially female foeticide and infanticide, reflected on the demographic profile in terms of sex ratio. According to Mehboob Haq, 74 million women are simply missing in South Asia.

In 1995, the UN General Assembly called for the creation of a trust fund in support of actions to eliminate violence against women. UNIFEM supports initiatives to combat violence against women in partnership with Human Right NGOs and Governments.

The declaration on the Elimination of Violence against women defines such violence as "any act of gender-based violence that results in, or is likely to result in, physical, sexual or psychological harm or suffering to women, including threats of such acts, coercion or arbitrary deprevation of liberty, whether occurring in public or private life.

As admitted by no less a person that Mrs. Hillary Rodham Clinton, the wife of the then President of US, that even in USA, women face poverty and discrimination and were not given equal pay or equal work.

Pt. Nehru was asked by Andre Malraux, "What has been your greatest difficulties since independence?" Nehruji answered, "Creating a just society by just means."

All the societies have gone through its very difficult period.

As it was said by an activist of the Women's Rights Movement, "Women are tightly wedged between laws, sometimes it is "in-laws" and sometimes the legal laws—and if she resists she is branded an outlaw."

It has been a constant struggle for the women to confront gender bias. In order to help her in struggle for equality, equity and gender justice, the International Human Rights Movement, the National Commission for Women, the National Human Rights Commission and the Judiciary, have spelt out and interpreted Fundamental Rights and Directive Principles enshrined in the Constitution.

All of us enjoy human rights not because they are conferred by the Constitution and laws. We are entitled to those rights simply because we are born as human beings and we have the rights and obligations which flow out of our human needs.

Human rights are human rights and they constitute 50 per cent of the population. The remaining 50 per cent also were given birth to by women. So they are entitled to not only the rights which are enjoyed by the men, but in fact because of their special role they should be entitled for more rights than men.

Status of Women in Society?

In all nations, women earn less from paid employment than men—they have less likelihood of inheriting land and other assets than their brothers—they are more likely to be physically assaulted regularly even by members of their own families—they are less likely to serve in governments in senior positions and they are the sole bread winners in more than 1/3rd of the families in the world.

Now they are being infected with HIV/AIDS virus at a faster rate than men simply because they lack the knowledge and information with which to protect themselves and also they lack the strength to refuse intimate relationships.

These barriers for gender justice and equality exist in all countries and more so in developing countries.

What is required is not only reform of the law, but also reform of the mindset, attitude, traditions and beliefs in the society.

The courts do play an important role but the process is too expensive and too time consuming to be thought of.

It is in the attitude and working of organizations like the Police that women's human rights can be recognized, preserved and protected.

In times of internal or international conflict, every one suffers but women will suffer more because of their gender. The CEDAW Convention process began in 1967 but finally adopted by the General Assembly in 1979. 150 out of the 185 member nations ratified the Convention.

The Convention emphasized that discrimination in any area of human life will hamper economic growth and prosperity and detrimental for the society as a whole.

The Convention recognized the role of Education or both men and women in changing attitudes, prejudices and practices.

The nations of the world recognized the need for a number of important steps to be taken to combat the evil of the prevalence of violence against women. It is acknowledged that violence against women prevents them from participating fully in the family, in the workplace and in their community.

As Prime Minister Jawaharlal Nehru said, "You can tell the condition of a nation by looking at the status of its women".

Amartya Sen pointed out that when he took up issues of women's welfare, he was accused in India of voicing "foreign concerns". "I was told Indian women don't think like that about equality. But I would like to argue that if they don't think like that they should be given a real opportunity to think like that."

The persistence of hunger, malnutrition and abject proverty in India and both parts of the world is due to a large extent to the subjugating, marginalisation and disempowerment of women. Women suffer from hunger and poverty in greater numbers and to a great degree than men. At the same time, it is women who bear the primary responsibility for actions needed to end hunger—education, nutrition, health and family income.

In India, which is the world's second most populous nation, at least 120 million women are living in poverty. Deaths of young girls in India exceed than of young boys. Every 6th infant death is specifically due to gender discrimination.

Higher female mortality between ages 1 and 5 and high maternal mortality rates result in a deficit of females in the population.

VI

Violence Against Women

The United Nations has developed a declaration on the elimination of violence against. women. In that declaration, the General Assembly proclaimed that: "Violence against women both violates and impairs or nullifies the enjoyment by women of human rights and fundamental freedom and is concerned about the long-standing failure to protect and promote those rights and freedoms in relation to violence against women.

Violence against women is defined in the Declaration as:

> Any act of gender based violence that results in, or is likely to result in, physical sexual or psychological harm to women, including threats of such acts, coercion or arbitrary deprivation of liberty, whether occurring in public or in private life.

Violence against women in Indian sub-continent mainly focuses on the following: dowry deaths, female infanticide and foeticide, *sati* (widow burning) and rape. Besides, there are other forms of violence, including sexual abuse, wife beating, eve teasting [Eve teasing is a form of harassment, especially the young girls in public places. While in most cases they were harmless, in certain cases, it has taken serious turns.] and no inheritance to women. The Indian National Crime Records Bureau (NCRB) provides statistics of crimes against women in the last decade.

Crime Against Women in India

Crime	*1990*	*1991*	*1999*
Rape	9,518	9,793	15,468
Kidnapping and abduction	11,699	12,300	15,962
Dowry deaths	4,836	5,157	6,699
Torture	13,450	15,949	43,823
Molestation	20,194	20,611	32,311
Sexual harassment	8,620	10,283	8,858

The increase in crimes figures is mainly due to increased reporting of them. Awareness over the rights of women, pressure on law enforcing agencies and the role of voluntary organisations has mainly resulted in increased reporting.

According to statistics, the states of Rajasthan, Madhya Pradesh and Delhi have the most crimes against women, whereas states like Nagaland, Meghalaya and Punjab have reported less. Crime against women are less in certain areas mainly due to high level of literacy, especially female literacy.

Among the various levels, women belonging to lower class suffer the most, as the following statistics reveal.

Composition of Crimes Against Women by Social Status (in Percentage

Level	*Rape*	*Kidnap/ Abduction*	*Dowry Death*	*Molestation*	*Sexual Harassment*	*Cruelty at Home*
Low	34.02	25.04	12.20	11.68	1.26	15.80
Lower-Middle	11.21	17.31	7.74	23.04	5.73	34.95
Upper-Middle	16.72	19.46	2.46	33.76	3.91	23.68
High	14.27	14.47	5.25	28.12	5.25	32.62

Dowry

Dowry is one of the major issues in crimes against women. Dowry is defined as any property or valuable security given or agreed to be given, directly or indirectly, by one party to marriage, or by parents of either party to marriage, or by any person to either party to the marriage or to any other person at or before or at any time after the marriage, in connection with the marriage of the said parties.

Being one of the most significant factors in violence against women it results in harassment, beating, and in many cases, murder. According to the NCRB, in 1999 alone there were 6699 dowry deaths. Dowry deaths per year have increased significantly since the beginning of the 1990s, mainly due to their increased reporting. Dowry-related violence against women, in which women were subjected to harassment by their husbands and his family, has also been increasing. In 1999, 43,823 cases have been registered. It should also be noted that the NCRB figures might not be accurate, as many dowry related violence goes unreported. Lack of awareness, fear of retaliation, distrust of legal instruments, or inability to take legal measures prevent families from reporting dowry-related violence to the police. It should also be kept in mind that the reasons for the increased figures could also be because of increased awareness, led by the various women movements in all parts of India. [Some of the women movements are Self Employed Women's Association (SEWA), Forum against Oppression of Women, Maitri, Sakshi, Women's Rights Initiative etc.]

Most of the victims of dowry belong to the middle class and are of the age group 21-24. Dowry deaths are found more among the middle and upper castes than the lower caste. They are prevalent more in urban semi-urban areas than rural areas. One of the main reasons for dowry deaths has been lack of economic self-sufficiency among victims.

The above mentioned statistics show that rape as a crime against women has been increasing. Most of the victims belong to the age group of 16-30, and are from all classes of society.

Female Infanticide and Foeticide

The female infanticide and foeticide is yet another form of crime against women. In most cases it takes place with the consent of the parents after the baby is born. The main reason for female infanticide in India is the cost of raising a girl child in a patriarchal society. Female foeticide involves aborting the female foetus, once its sex is determined. The reasons are the same as those for female infanticide. Female infanticide is more prevalent among the lower classes, whereas foeticide is prevalent among the middle and upper classes.

Sex Ratio in India 1901-2001

Census Year	*Sex Ratio*
1901	972
1951	946
1961	941
1971	930
1981	934
1991	927
2001	933

According to the 2001 Census in India, though the overall sex ratio has increased from 927 females per 1000 males in 1991 to 933 females per 1000 in 2001, there is a decline in sex ratio of the population in the age group of 0-6. An analysis of the last 40 years would reveal the steady decline in the sex ratio in India.

Though the sex ratio has increased in states like Bihar, Jharkhand, Rajasthan and Tamil Nadu, there has been a decline in Haryana, Himachal Pradesh, Punjab and Chandigarh.

The difference is mainly due to selective abortion of female foetus and female infanticide.

Sex Ratio and Child Population between 0-6 Age Group in Select States of India in 1991 and 2001

States and Union Territories	*Total Population*		*Child Population (0-6)*	
	1991	*2001*	*1991*	*2001*
Himachal Pradesh	976	970	951	897
Punjab	882	874	875	793
Chandigarh	790	773	899	845
Uttaranchal	936	964	948	906
Haryana	865	861	879	820
Delhi	827	821	915	865
Rajasthan	910	922	916	909
Uttar Pradesh	876	898	927	916
Bihar	907	921	953	938

Gujarat	934	921	928	878
Daman and Diu	969	709	958	925
Dadra and Nagar Haveli	952	811	1013	973
Maharashtra	934	922	946	917

The child sex ratio, especially in two states (Haryana and Punjab), shows the "rampant practice of female foeticide alongwith a certain amount of infanticide in these two states." [The child sex ratio is the number of girl children per 1000 births]

The IPC and Crimes Against Women

The Indian Penal Code (IPC) covers issues related to crimes against women—rape (Section 376); kidnapping and abduction (Sections 363-373); dowry killings (Sections 302 and 304B); molestation (Section 354); eve-teasing and sexual harassment (Section 509); and importation of girls (Section 366 B). The IPC is the basic criminal law, prescribing deterrent punishments. Cases under the IPC are investigated more seriously and tried in higher courts of law more effectively.

6

Gender Sensitization*

You are a human being. You have rights inherent in that reality. You have dignity and worth that exists prior to law. - Lyn Beth Neylon, Director of "Human Rights USA"

"When a woman is in need of justice, who does she turn to? The first post to be passed is always the police station where she has to make her basic complaint. But it is here that harassment begins. The gender sensitization course is designed to give a human face to the police force so that women get justice."

Gender sensitization is a challenge in the new millennium, we have to go through the learning process of gender sensitization in order to build up a new society. Woman alone cannot fight the battle on their own, they should have the support and partnership of the other half and this value should be imbibed right from the early stage of life.

In the ancient times, women enjoyed a very high status in the Indian society, but today they are exploited, discriminated and are the vulnerable section of the society. They are even denied their basic human rights.

Role of Police Force

The role and image of the Indian police force needs reinterpretation because women constitute 50 per cent of the population and whatever welfare measures are to be undertaken have to be done by keeping women as the focal point of those programmes.

A large number of police forces are recruited from rural areas where inequality among gender is an acceptable fact. This has to be changed through a learning process and make them more gender sensitized.

---

* Talk delivered to Delhi Police Officers at a workshop, organised by Gender Training Institute.

70 per cent of the police force come from a rural background and it is a massive effort to sensitize them on gender issue. If one police personnel is trained and sensitized, he is changing his family, his community and the society as well.

As a law-enforcing agency, the police has lot of responsibility to reform the civil society. Violence against women is the outcome of the fact that we think well about our daughters but we look at the daughters of others in a different perspective. Training is a learning opportunity and it is necessary to sensitize the police on gender issues in order to achieve an equitable society. There are two dichotomies of Indian Culture. Firstly, religious scriptures like Manu's slokas, Gurbani, Quran—in all these scriptures women have been placed on a high pedestal. Women are worshipped as Goddesses. How can one denigrate a woman who has given birth to a "Guru?" or "hands that rocks and cradle rules the universe". Secondly, women are discriminated and are kept backward deliberately. This mindset needs to be changed. Freedom of women is limited and she is over worked. Levels of subordination of women are a universal truth. If any change is perceptible, it is only the tip of the iceberg.

The core issues are attainment of "gender equity". Changes are coming in a slower way in institutions like family, education, marriage, workplace etc, in the urban sector and middle and higher middle class levels. The media plays a significant role in projecting the different roles of women.

Police as the "Transforming Agency" of special change needs to be gender sensitized, change of attitude is to be cultivated within one's own self. Change is difficult and changeable but it can be achieved if desired and can be done so through persuasion and introspection rather than exerting pressure or by punishing. Police is the most visible/powerful institution in the society and they should not be biased towards any kind of mindset.

Sex is a physical difference between men and women. It is a biological reality. It is universal and no change is possible.

'Gender' is a term through which society interprets the relationship between the two genders that is 'Male' and 'Female'. It is a social definition given to the expected roles of both men and women.

How they are expected to behave, and this leads to stereotyping of the roles. Gender also magnifies the only one biological dissimilarity to such proportions that it overshadows all similarities between men and women respectively. It is pervasive, through various institutions, it is relevant to time, place and culture and change is possible.

Family/kinship is about altruism and cooperation. The family or household is a caring, sharing unit. Somewhere, over the centuries the institution started favouring one gender and disfavouring the others—and all because of one discrimination that is child bearing. Each institution reinforces the same (wrong/biased) values and by the time it reaches the 'STATE' the gaps are widened. The irony is that many a time the wrong values keep on getting strengthened without realisation even as the policy, planners and implementers level, because all of them are the product of the basic unit that is the 'Home'.

All the institutions differ and are culturally variable. However, they do have some commonalities. All the institutions have five distinct but interrelated dimensions of social relations that are significant to the analysis of social inequality in general and gender inequality in particular. The five distinct but interrelated dimensions are rules, resources, people, activities and power. So to understand how social difference and inequalities in the institutions exist, each institution is to be analyzed under these five dimensions.

Rules: How things get done. Institutional behaviour is governed by rules.

Activities: What is done. Institutions do things, institutions are about achieving goals by following their own rules. These activities can be productive, distributive and regulative.

Resources: What is used, what is produced? At whose command these resources are? Institutions are also about mobilising the distribution of resources. Such resources may be human (labour, education and skills); material (food, assets, land, money) or intangible (information, political, clout, goodwill, contracts).

People: Who is in, who is out, who does what; Institutions are about people and are selective about—

Who they include and whom they exclude?

Who is assigned different resources, tasks and responsibilities?

Power: who decides, whose interests are served? Institutions are relations of power, which means that they embody relations of authority and control.

Trafficking in Women and Children

Trafficking in women and children is one of the worst, and most brazen, abuses of human rights. It is a blot on our collective consciousness as we prepare to enter the new millennium. It is a matter of shame that even after half a century since the adoption of the Declaration of Human Rights by the global community, trafficking continues to thrive.

One of the most visible and widespread is the trafficking of women and children for commercial sexual exploitation. The issue of the sexual exploitation of women and children itself is not new, as it goes back into the history, cultures and traditions of many societies. What is new, is the unscrupulous and massive scale of the problem, exacerbated by globalisation, modern technology, and its links to the tourists and sex industry. Trafficking is increasing dramatically in the Asia region, but the phenomenon spans the globe.

Consensus is lacking on precise definition of trafficking. The following is widely used: "The illicit and clandestine movements of persons across national borders, largely from developing countries and some countries with economies in transition, with the end goal of forcing women and girl children into sexually and economically". Oppressive and exploitative situations for profit of recruiters, traffickers and crime syndicates, as well as other illegal activities related to trafficking, such as forced domestic labour, false marriage, clandestine employment and false adoption." (United Nations General Assembly 1994)

Bangladesh, China, India, Myanmar, Nepal, Pakistan, Sri Lanka, Thailand have large number of women and children who are trafficked everyday. In India at least 25,000 children are engaged in prostitution in the metropolitan cities whereas other sources quote that 500,000 girl children below 18 years are victims of trafficking in India.

Gender and Human Rights

Human Rights is universally accepted as rights relating to life, liberty, equality and dignity of the individual and that it is the right of all human beings, be it men or women, old or young, working or non-working. India has the distinction of being a signatory to most of the international covenants and conventions on human rights. It has also translated into action its commitments to protect human rights of all its citizens by adopting a progressive constitution and constitution of Commissions like the National Human Rights Commission and the National Commission for Women.

Statistics shows that in terms of numbers women are still far behind men. The 1991 census shows that female work participation rate is only 22.27 against male work participation rate of 51.61. Percentage of women in organised sector further comes down to 15.36 (1995) with share of public sector at 13.36 per cent. Central Govt. had 2.88 lakhs female employees in 1991, but in terms of percentage it dwindles down to 7.58 per cent of the total workforce of Government of India. According to the Human Development Report, 1996, only 2.3 per cent of administrators and managers are women in India against the world average of 14 per cent. In USA, their percentage is 42.

The above statistics indicates the wide gap existing between the professed philosophy of equality and the present reality. It also indicates the long and rough journey that women may have to traverse to achieve equality of status and opportunity in the real sense.

The representation of women is very poor in the police forces throughout the country. It would range from 2 per cent to 10 per cent only. The police officers who mostly handle the cases under investigation are men by themselves or men forming formidable groups in the team of investigators who handle the case. In such a male dominated milieu, there is every reason why the police officers should be adequately sensitized so that they could handle women and child with care so that:

- There is no secondary victimization.
- Basic human rights are not violated by anybody.
- No atrocities are committed on them and no modesty is outraged by taking advantage of the situation.
- Basic decency and courtesy is extended to women/ children.
- Minimum comforts and perquisites required for a human being especially a women is extended.
- A congenial atmosphere is created in which victim/ suspect/accused is free to speak out without fear or favour or any reservation.

- An atmosphere of camaraderie is built up so that person (especially the victim) helped to get out of the trauma, both physical and mental.

While dealing with children and women, it is most essential that the above mentioned code of conduct is clearly manifest and transparent. Sensitization of police officers is essential, as they need to realise that the victim has come for help only when she has reached the extreme state of helplessness.

There is no universally accepted definition of the rights of women. It is a fact that seems to be unknown to men that the dominant emotion in the lives of most women is fear.

Gender is the social interpretation of attitude, behaviour, relationships, moral values and social values of an individual on the basis of sex.

How can we create gender sensitivity in the system?

Through the socialisation tree, it was explained that if the roots are strong then the tree is healthy. It is important to inculcate strong values so that there is no gender bias and insensitivity towards women. Violence against women is one of the most outrageous forms of violence against women. It is threat that looms large over the heads of millions of women in India. The right to walk on the street with no threat of physical assault is a human right. This threat is a result of negative values. This is an issue not for women alone but the society at large.

There is a wide range of violations that women face in everyday life right from the day she is born to her last day. In a number of cases, it is the question of human rights that are being violated but the violation is based on her womanhood.

The fact that a woman does not enjoy many human rights because of being a woman is a serious social problem. There are rights, which are specifically women's right. One of the important roles that a woman plays is that of child bearing, a service that is indispensable for procreation of human kind. Any definition of human rights needs to take cognizance of the requirement that society needs to provide all those necessary conditions for women to perform this service in the most healthy and civilized manner.

Gender Violence

Since the birth of humanity women have been socially harassed in some way or the other. India has a patriarchal society and women are often said to be the man's shoes. Women are denied their basic rights they do not have a right over property, nor finance. Men have never wanted women to work shoulder to shoulder with them, her voice has always been silenced. She has always been identified as the mother, or daughter or wife of man.

Forms of Gender Violence

- Foeticide
- Deprivation of food
- Deprivation of medical care
- Emotional abuse
- Forced marriage
- Sati
- Rape
- Sexual assault
- Harassment
- Trafficking
- Forced prostitution
- Forced sterlization
- Torture
- Dowry death

Keeping the different forms of violence in view, it is the duty of the police to be sensitive to the victims. If one is helpful to others then it will give satisfaction to self.

Make gender sensitization a part of life.

Legal Provisions

The participants of this gender sensitization programme will know more about the legal provisions regarding violence.

1. Section 354 IPC penalty of imprisonment up to 2 years or both for assault or use of criminal force with intent to outrage her modesty.
2. Section 509 IPC simple imprisonment up to 1 year or fine or both for word gesture or act to insult to modesty.
3. Section 376 IPC Rape imprisonment up to 10 years.
4. Section 406 IPC Misappropriation of Streedhan.
5. Section 498 IPC physical and mental torture.
6. Section 304 B dowry death.
7. Section 228 IPC protects honour of victims of rape by

prohibition of disclosure of their name.

8. Section 327(2) CRPC 1972 in camera trial of rape cases.
9. Section 114 Evidence Act in case of alleged rape her evidence before the court that she did not consent the court will presume the same.

Mode of Violation

- *Physical Violation*
  1. Deprivation of food
  2. Deprivation of medical care
- *Sexual Abuse*
  1. Rape
  2. Harassment
  3. Intimidation
- *Emotional Abuse*
  1. Confinement
  2. Forced marriage

Steps to Combat Violation

- Promote women's economic rights and employment
- Facilitate women's equal access to resources market and trade
- Eliminate occupational segregation and forms of employment discrimination
- Promote harmonization of work and family place
- Full participation in power structure and decision making
- Increase women's participation in decision making and leadership
- Promote protection of human rights of women through full implementation of all human rights instruments, i.e., convention
- Ensure equality and non-discrimination under the law and in practice

Human Rights of Women

Sudan Moller Okin defines human rights as a 'claim to something (whether a freedom, a good or a benefit) of crucial importance for human life'. Milne defines human rights as implying a duty to act with respect for persons. Thus, if rights are viewed as respect for human beings, such rights include rights to life, to freedom from arbitrary coercion and to be respected as a human beings. The basic idea of human rights is thus embedded in the notion of respect for person.

The first is that human rights violations often takes different forms for men and women. For example, both males and females may suffer slavery and involuntary servitude, but females are more likely to suffer from sexual forms of slavery and, thereby, experience further violations of their human rights.

A second dimension focuses on the gender related circumstances which make it more likely that women will suffer disproportionately from a human rights violation than men, based on established patterns of discrimination and "traditional" gender roles. For example, women represent a greater proportion of the informal labour force than do men and as a result are less likely to enjoy the protections of legislation and policing guaranteeing their rights to safe working conditions and adequate standard of living, and socal security.

A third gender related aspect of human rights is that the consequences of violations can be gender specific. For example, although both men and women may be subject to rape as a weapon of war, unmarried women who are raped may become pregnant, and this fact alone may make them "unfit" for marriage, which can have devastating economic consequences.

A final gender dimension is the one which has received the most attention in recent years within project and programmes aimed as promoting women's "legal rights" namely that access to remedies is influenced by the gender related factors. This includes a lack of literacy and capacity to initiate legal action to redress a violation, community norms that discourage women from reporting violations; and the pervasive lack of sensitivity towards the needs of women by officials who are responsible for responding to violations.

Ignoring the Rights of the Child

The November 1989 Convention on Child Rights expressed the commitment of the international community to provide the child with a secure future. It emphasized that the enchancement of the child's health and nutrition was the first duty of the nation. It is felt that improving the status of women and ensuring them equal rights with men will be an advantage for the world's children.

Child labour, child abuse and child prostitution are some of the forms of torture that a child has to bear. The UNDP report shows that the number of child labourers in India ranges from 14 million to 140 million.

Child prostitution is the worst form of child labour and now there is a perceptible increase. Girl children are being exported and imported from our neighbouring countries for the flesh trade. It is estimated that there are about 2.5 million sex workers out of this slightly less than half are children. Trafficking in women and children are a violation of their human rights. These women and children who are trafficked are often criminalized in the receiving countries where there is no legal protection for them. Child abuse is another horrible torture that a child has to bear. Violence, physical, mental and sexual against the child is a fact in many houses. Child labour is the result of abject poverty. Many of these children who are left to fend for themselves do not even have a family to go back to. These children are often victims of police harassment. Our system of juvenile justice lacks sensitivity on the part of those who operate them. Destitute children are very often kept with those accused of various crimes.

Gender Justice

When you talk about gender awareness
You talk about absolute fairness
Its all about peace and equality
Divine justice in reality

Exploring yourself and expanding
your vision
Listening to your conscience and
making decision
You learn to conquer as well as
to surrender
To celebrate success as well as
to accept failure

Its all about humanity
Living together in tranquility
Where no one is powerless and powerful
Its land of beauties .... Beautiful!

It is women who bear most of the burden of meeting the need of their family and community. They already grow most of the developing world's food, market most of its crops, fetch most of its water, collect most of its fuel, feed most of its animals, weed most of its fields. And when their work outside the home is done, they light the third world's fires, cook its meals, clean its compounds, wash its clothes, shop for its needs, and look after its old and its ill. And they bear and care for its children. These are the multiple burdens of womanhood, almost everywhere in the world. If men and women take due responsibility as parents, home-makers, good citizens, producers and guardians of the life and well-being of every child, they will contribute as they should, to ensuring the survival and development of both boy and girl children, and the building of a better society.

Women have not achieved equality with men in any country. Of the world's 1.3 billion poor people, it is estimated that nearly 70 per cent are women. Between 75 and 80 per cent of the world's 27 million refugees are women and children. The first country to grant women the rights to vote was New Zealand in 1893. Only 24 women have been elected heads of State or Government in this century. Women hold 10.5 per cent of the seats in the world's parliaments. Of the 185 highest-ranking diplomats to the United Nations, seven are women. Of the world's nearly one billion illiterate adults, two-thirds are women. Two-thirds of the 130 million children world wide who are not in school are girls.

It was Pt. Jawaharlal Nehru who said, "You can tell the condition of the nation by looking at the status of its women". By this norm, India does not present a favourable picture.

No doubt, this country has always worshipped; Shakti, the Goddess. As the most powerful diety. But the living women have always been treated with prejudice.

India has the world's largest number of professionally qualified women. India has more female doctors, surgeons, scientists and professors than even the United States of America. India has more working women than any other country in the world. This includes female workers at all levels of skill—from the surgeon and the airline pilot to bus conductors and menial workers.

But at the same time, on an average, women in India are socially, politically and economically weaker than men. Women work roughly twice as many hours as men. Women suffer from hunger and poverty in greater numbers and to a greater degree than men. It is women who bear the primary responsibility for actions needed to end hunger, education, nutrition, health and family income.

India has exceptionally high rates of child malnutrition, because tradition in India requires that women eat less and least throughout their lives, even when pregnant. Malnourished women give birth to malnourished children, perpetuating the cycle. Females receive less health- care than males. Many women die in childbirth of easily preventable complications.

Women and girls receive far less education than men. India has the largest population of non-school going working girls. Overall, the literacy rate for women is 39 per cent as against 64 per cent for men. A large proportion of roughly 40 million "non-working" girls who are not in school are kept at home because of responsibilities in house work. Even the women's creative and intellectual potentials are either ignored or under-played in education in India.

India has a population of ne billion of whom 120 million women live in poverty. India's maternal mortality rates in rural areas are among the world's highest. India accounts for 19 per cent of all births and 27 per cent of all maternal deaths. Pregnancy related deaths account for one quarter of all fatalities among women aged 15 to 29, two-third of them considered preventable. Of the 15 million baby girls born in India each year, nearly 25 per cent do not live to see their 15th birthday. Surviving through a normal life cycle is a resource – poor women's greatest challenge.

Working women are invisible to most of the population. If all activities – including maintenance of kitchen gardens and poultry, grinding foodgrains, collecting water and firewood, etc. – are taken into account, then 88 per cent of rural housewives and 66 per cent of urban housewives can be considered as economically productive. Women's employment in family farms or businesses is rarely recognized as economically productive, either by men or women.

Women have unequal access to resources. If training women for economic activities requires them to leave their village, this is usually an insurmountable problem for them. In terms of skill development, women are impeded by the lack of mobility, low literacy and prejudicial attitude of the society towards women.

Even in the "Year of Women's Empowerment", the women continue to be ill-treated. The most cruel atrocities are by way of female infanticide, sex selective abortion and child prostitution.

Every 26 minutes, a woman is molested. Every 34 minutes, a rape takes place. Every 42 minutes, a sexual harassment incident occurs. Every 43 minutes, a woman is kidnapped and almost every hour, a woman is burnt to death over dowry. 25 per cent of the rapes involve girls in the age of 16, but the vast majority are never reported. Although the penalty is severe, convictions are rare. Legal protection of women's rights have not been effective in view of prevailing patriarchal traditions and the enormous delays in investigations and trials. Even after 33 years of existence of Dowry Prohibition Act, 6000 dowry deaths/murders are reported every year.

The spiral of violence against women is rising at an alarming rate and one of the least noticed aspects of this is that of domestic violence. Yet, there is no specific legislation in India that deals with domestic violence. Domestic violence is recognized by existing civil law only in the context of dissolution of a marriage and as being conduct amounting to cruelty and, therefore, ground for divorce. Domestic violence requires a separate law altogether since the nature of the relationship between the offender and the victim is intensely personal. Very often, in the Indian social million the victim is unable to escape from the offender. A new law should indentify the social and domestic relationships in which today violence is perpetrated with impunity.

A range of orders could be brought into force to protect victims of domestic violence. These could be restraining the respondent from indulging in abusive conduct, restraining entry into the matrimonial home, restraining the dispossession of the wife and children, providing maintenance and so on. Domestic violence laws in many countries provide for precisely such prohibitory orders.

Women's rights to inheritance are still not just and fair. Recently Prof. Amartya Sen observed, " The ramifications of gender inequality are much broader than believed." Prof. Sen said gender inequality is a social problem and a terrible affliction, which appears in different forms. In 1991, there were 95 girls per 100 boys. In the new census, however, the number of girls per 100 boys had declined to 93.7. Behind this moderate decline, there is an alarming picture which shows that northern and the western areas of India have a lower population of girls. The effects of gender inequality could even spill over to on men and children. A study had shown that the children of malnourished mothers at later stages in life suffer from various cardio-vascular diseases.

Even though one million women have actively entered political life after the introduction of Panchayat Raj, still women are far from getting their due share in governance.

We have to go a long way in ensuring the women's rights of justice and dignity. We have to transform the still prevailing social prejudice and discrimination against women. At the same time, we have to increase direct action in a time-bound manner to rapidly improve the social and economic status of women. Of equal importance is to create an alternative redressal structure and procedure, different from the existing criminal justice system, which is time consuming and costly. Women constitute nearly 50 per cent of the world's population. Unless gender justice in done and also seen to be done, there can be no peace and progress in the society.

7

Vital Areas of Human Rights : Poverty, Environment and Child Labour*

Peace can only last where human rights are respected. - Dalai Lama

The Right to live is a fundamental right under Article 21 of the Constitution and it includes the right of enjoyment of pollution-free water and air for full enjoyment of life. - Supreme Court of India in Subhash Kumar v. State of Bihar, 1991

Poverty is the mother of crime. —Marcus Aurelius

The poverty of our century is unlike that of any other. It is not, as poverty was before, the result of natural scarcity, but of a set of priorities imposed upon the rest of the world by the rich. Consequently, the modern poor are not pitied...but written off as trash. The twentieth-century consumer economy has produced the first culture for which a beggar is a reminder of nothing. - John Berger, British Actor, Critic.

Everyone has the right to a standard of living adequate for the health and well-being of himself and of his family, including food, clothing, housing and medical care and necessary social services, and the right to security in the event of unemployment, sickness, disability, widowhood, old age or other lack of livelihood in circumstances beyond his control.- Article 25 (1) of the Universal Declaration of Human Rights, 1948

Whenever there is a conflict between human rights and property rights, human rights must prevail. - Abraham Lincoln

On being sworn in as the first Prime Minister of independent India, Pandit Jawaharlal Nehru called for the ending of poverty, ignorance, disease and inequality of opportunity. Mahatma Gandhi

* Gist of inaugural speech at a seminar at Vishwa Yuvak Kendra, New Delhi.

had always insisted that India would become truly independent only when the poorest of its people would be free from human suffering.

The objective of the Nine Five-Year Plans was to raise the standard of living of the people with poverty eradication, economic equality, social justice and human development as key objectives.

In 57 years, the country has recorded impressive gains in many areas. There is significant reduction in the intensity of poverty. But human deprivations continue.

Per capita income has more than doubled. Food grain production increased four fold. Index of Industrial Production went up 15 times.

Still 35 per cent of country's population lives below the poverty line-defined as access to minimum calories needed for healthy living.

The county has achieved self-sufficiency in food grain production. It has built up a good safety stock of food gains. Famines have been virtually eliminated. But, yet 50 per cent of children under four year (some 60 million) remain malnourished.

Life expectancy doubled to 61 years. Infant mortality reduced by half. Still over 20 lakh young children (infants) die each year due to preventable and curable diseases.

Tamil Nadu is the second most urbanized State after Maharashtra. Even in Tamil Nadu, 70 per cent of its population lives in 12,619 Village Panchayats. 28 lakh families live below the poverty line—earning Rs. 310 per capita per month.

Incidence of poverty increases alongwith lack of access to health care, nutrition of the standard of 2,300 calories a day, sanitation and community infrastructure.

One-sixth of the world's population does not have access to clean drinking water. Nations will be ready to shed blood for fresh water. Already there are 300 confrontations, conflicts and quarrels over sharing rivers and lakes.

India and Pakistan could flare up over Indus. Within our own country, we have seen periodic disputes and eruptions of violence and agitations over the sharing of the sacred water of the Cauvery and other rivers.

There is large population growth. More people need more water. More people also pollute the Water Resources.

Rain Water Harvesting—careful use of water, saving forests and growing trees will help in bringing water from clouds. Urgent need of the hour is Economic use of water like Drip Irrigation and stopping pollution of water sources.

Green Revolution helped agricultural growth, but the benefits have not been distributed equitably. Conditions of farmers also have not improved proportionately.

Health and Educational facilities did not cover rural and remote areas adequately. Highter Education got disproportionately large allocation of the Budget at the cost of Basic Education in rural areas.

Certain other vital areas remain neglected. They are -

Child Labour, illiteracy, environmental degradation and pollution, caste discrimination, gender bias, women's health, domestic violence, maternal and child mal-nutrition, basic health, child abuse, child prostitution, urban and rural slums, manual scavenging, non-availability of safe drinking water, exploitation, discrimination.

Our country is vast, great and rich. Its history, geography, languages, culture, religion, traditions are all great. But our basic problems remain Poverty, Illiteracy, Disease, Discrimination, Exploitation and Corruption.

So, the result is : We have every thing, yet we have nothing.

People often value other things in life much more than income. Even to the very poor, self respect and good reputation mean a lot.

They often articulate their immediate needs as a good education for their children, access to good health care facilities and a safe environment.

They detest exploitation and discrimination. To most people to be treated with dignity and respect and a life free from fear of crime and terrorism matter much more than incomes.

Fundamentals of Development

The spirit of service

The priorities should be universal education, universal access to safe drinking water, shelter for living, a Job to do, fair living wages, access to credit, access to affordable basic health care.

We have seen that Governments alone cannot do everything. In fact they have been able to do much less than they promise. The solution is possible when well-meaning voluntary agencies, benevolent private companies, corporations and charitable individuals also discharge their social obligations towards the less fortunate and the less privileged in the society.

We should not think that we are doing a favour or kindness for those whom we are serving. It is actually the other way! They are giving us an opportunity to be of service to them and thereby allowing us to repay the debt that we all owe to the society and the nation.

We believe that in every Jiva, there is Shiva. The Lord dwells within the heart of everyone. When we serve with the spirit of humility, we should not expect any thing in return for the services, not even a single word of thanks. We should not believe or declare that by means of service-seva- we can reform, change or reshape the world-others. We may or may not, that does not matter. The real value of service is, that its most visible result is, that it reforms us, ennobles us.

If we do service as a spiritual discipline, then we will become humble and happy.

We need not claim we are improving others by service to others, we improve ourselves.

Make service-seva-an extension of Pooja, Japam and Dhyanam.

Service or Seva is for our own spiritual progress, to discharge our fundamental social responsibilities, to make this a better and more humane world, to live and let other live. More than anything else seva is to save our great, ancient and unique culture.

Service is the very first step in the growth of spirit. Seva is the manifestation of our willingness to work for others, for work is dedicated as worship. That attitude instills in the mind, the Divinity inherent in all creation.

Poverty Eradication

Poverty has become a major obstacle in achieving sustainable development—one that meets the needs of the present generation without affecting the abilities of future generations to meet their own needs. It is due to this fact poverty is said to be the "Cause and Effect" of environmental degradation. Poverty anywhere is a threat to prosperity every where. So the World Bank recently committed itself to the creation of "A World Free from Poverty".

Development Assistance Committee of the Organisation for Economic Cooperation and Development (OECD) published a policy paper in May 1996 calling for global participation to a new development strategy focusing on reducing by half the proportion of people in extreme poverty by 2015.

The face of poverty varies across time, space and societies. The conventional method of measuring poverty in terms of per capita income or consumption gives only a partial picture. In fact, poverty has many non-income dimensions which include powerlessness, vulnerability, humiliation, isolation, frustration, gender discrimination and inequality, lack of autonomy, self-respect and self-esteem, lack of productive assets, deprivation of bare minimum needs such as shelter, food, safe drinking water, education and health care system.

Prof. Amartya sen says, "the concept of poverty should be changed from 'commodities' to 'capabilities' to overcome these non-income deprivations. Hence, the institutional capacity of the poor should be built up in such a way that they are able to reap the benefits from economic growth. From the poor's perspective, poverty has multiple, interlocking dimensions, which combine to create and sustain powerlessness, a lack of freedom, choice and action. Each dimension of poverty causes or reinforces the others to keep the poor in a vicious circle. The psychological experience of multiple deprivations is more intense and painful.

The poor are often powerless to influence the policies which affect their lives and unable to reap the benefits of the economic growth resulting from the market-driven economy.

Poverty is not just about income but encompasses various disadvantages, deprivations and wants of human life.

U.N. H.D.P. report declares, "Human Poverty is more than any poverty – it is the denial of choices and opportunities for living honourable life".

Real wealth of a nation is its people and the purpose of its development is to create an environment for people to enjoy longer, healthy and creative lives.

Shrinking space, shrinking time and disappearing borders are shrinking people's life more intensely and more immediately than ever before. Four out of the six billion people of the world, living mostly in developing countries still do not have some of the most basic choices.

More than one billion people do not have access to clean drinking water. Living below poverty line.

What the best and wisest parent wants for his (or her) own child that must the community want for all its children.

Environmental Issues and Human Rights

Major environmental problems in India include air and water pollution, besides deforestation, discharge of hazardous wastes by industries and land degradation. These problems result in respiratory diseases, lung cancer, etc.

According to a data compiled by Greenpeace, until September 2000, more than 100,800 tons of hazardous wastes have entered the country illegally. According to Greenpeace :

"Wastes such as zinc ash, residues and skimmings; lead waste and scrap; used batteries; and waste and scrap of metals such as cadmium, chromium, cobalt, antimony, jhafnium and thallium have been exported to India from countries including OECD nations such as Germany, USA, Australia, Denmark, the Netherlands, UK, Belgium and Norway. These imports have occurred without any authorization or the knowledge of the Indian Ministry of Environment. Lack of Effective laws and loopholes in them and inadequate and outdated state administration are some of the factors that contribute to this failure. Some of these waste items are also illegal under the laws of European Union nations and Australia, both of which have banned the exports of hazardous wastes to non-OECD countries."

Protection of environment, access to pure water, air, etc., have been viewed in India as a part of human rights, especially since the 1990s. Though the government and the people in general are yet to become aware of this issue, the Judiciary and NGOs have been championing the issue.

The rights of people towards pollution-free air and water has been seen as a part of Article 21 of the Indian Constitution, which states that "No person shall be deprived of his life or personal liberty except according to the procedure established by law."

In one of its verdicts, the High Court of Andhra Pradesh argued that,

"The enjoyment of life and its attainment and fulfillment guaranteed by Article 21 of Constitution embraces the protection and preservation of nature's gifts... The slow poisoning by polluted atmosphere caused by environmental pollution and spoilation should be regarded as amounting to violation of Article 21 of the Constitution."

Violence Against Children: Child Labour and Abuse

According to the 1991 census estimates, some 11.3 million children out of 200 million between ages 5 and 14 are engaged in child labour. Census in India takes place every ten years. The latest census was taken in 2001, but till now there has been no official report on the issue. These children work in various spheres, from agriculture to mining. The practice continues despite a ban and a series of court verdicts. But encouragingly, child labour is in decline. According to the National Sample Survey in 1981 there were 16.3 million child labourers in India which had come down to 11.3 million in 1991.

There are at least three types of child labour. First, there is domestic labour, which is non-monetary; girl children, in this case, do most of the domestic work. Second, there is monetary labour, which is non-domestic. Here, children are employed as wage labourers in organised and unorganised sectors, both in rural and urban areas. Third, there is bonded labour, where children are pledged by their parents. Most of the child labourers are employed primarily in agricultural sector as workers. Besides, they also work in industries including leather factories, hosiery units, carpet factories, glass factories, textile units and plastics industries. Some work as servants in private homes. Worse, some work as bonded labourers and sex workers. According to *UNDP Position Paper on Child Labour,* India accounts for the largest number of child workers in the world.

Field of Work of Child Labour

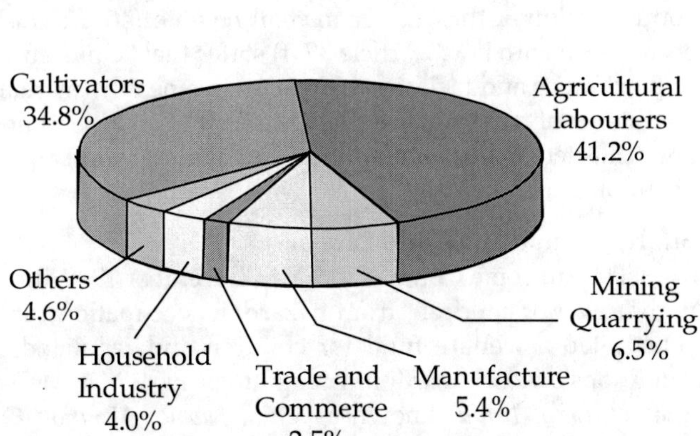

According to UNICEF study, there are more than 100,000 child labourers in Mirzapur carpet industries, 50,000 in Firozabad glass industries, 30,000 in Moradabad brass industries, and 10,000 in

Aligarh lock industries. (Mirzapur, Firozabad and Moradabad are leading industrial towns in Uttar Pradesh State of India)

Government and Child Labour

The Indian government has passed several laws prohibiting child labour, the most important being the Child Labour (Prohibition and Regulation) Act of 1986. The Act prohibits employment of children below 14 years of age in specified hazardous occupations and processes. The Juvenile Justice Act (1986) superseded all existing legislation related to children in different States and Union Territories. The Act provides for the creation of Advisory Boards and the establishment of State Children Funds, whose objective is to protect the children and to provide educational, training and rehabilitation facilities for neglected children. In 1993, the Union Government set up a National Authority to eliminate child labour and provided rupees 850 crore (US$185 million), which aimed to benefit two million child labourers, by undertaking measures on education, poverty reduction and awareness creation.

Constitution and Child Labour

The following articles of the Indian Constitution prohibit child labour: Article 23 says, "traffic in human beings and beggar and other similar forms of forced labour are prohibited and any contravention of this provision shall be an offence punishable in accordance with law." Article 39 (f) states that "children are given opportunities and facilities to develop in a healthy manner and in conditions of freedom and dignity and that childhood and youth are protected against exploitation and against moral and material abandonment."

Supreme Court and Child Labour

The Supreme Court of India, in December 1999, directed the withdrawal of children from hazardous occupations. It has also constituted a welfare fund for children and regulated working conditions in non-hazardous occupations. Earlier, in *M.C. Mehta v. State of Tamil Nadu* (known as *Child Labour Abolition Case*), the Supreme Court ruled that children below 14 years cannot be employed in any hazardous industrial, mining or other employment. Besides, the Court also directed the government to set up a Children Labour Rehabilitation Welfare Fund, and asked the offending employers to pay each child Rs. 20,000 (US$ 435) as compensation.

In case of non-hazardous jobs, children's working hours should not be more than 4 to 6 hours and the employer should provide education for them.

The implementation of these judicial decisions varies from place to place depending upon the level of awareness and political commitment of the states. But, increasing role of the NGOs, media and a proactive judiciary, to a great extent has made it sure that these regulations are adhered to and carried out.

Conclusion

The State is no doubt repressive, but it could also be responsive at least occasionally. The repressive nature of the State is certainly much more in evidence, for after all, the State represents the dominant interests of the ruling classes.

At the same time, to an extent, the State is often trying to appropriate the human rights agenda and to co-opt some of the peoples movements.

However, one need not feel apprehensive of these efforts if they tend to make State less inhuman, if not more human. If the State and the bureaucracy adopt, accept and act upon the agenda of Human Rights, it should indeed be a welcome development.

In the ultimate analysis, there is no substitute for genuine peoples movements. The struggle for Human Rights is a part of a larger struggle for democratizing the society, and Human Rights can really flourish only in democratic society.

It is sarcastically said, "The solidarity of the people signifies the spirit of our age and the recalcitrant power of the State constitutes the realities of our times".

8

Human Rights of the Disabled*

Self-pity is our worst enemy and if we yield to it, we can never do anything good in the world.

The best and most beautiful things in the world cannot be seen or even touched. They must be felt within the heart.

Although the world is full of suffering, it is full also of the overcoming of it.

Keep your face to the sunshine and you cannot see the shadow.
—Helen Keller (1880 - 1968), Deaf and Blind US Educator

Hearing Impaired

Hearing may well be the most important of our five senses. Through our ears we keep in touch with the sound of our environment.

The human ear is divided into three basic parts: the outer ear—which carries the sound inward; the middle ear—a small cavity containing three tiny bones which make up a chain; and the inner ear—containing fluid which carries vibrations throughout the length of the inner ear.

There are four kinds of hearing losses. These are classified as: conductive losses, sensor neural losses, central losses, and mixed losses.

A conductive hearing loss is a problem of the outer or middle ear. A blockage, malformation, or damage of the middle ear structure may be the cause of a conductive hearing loss. Such a loss may be corrected by medication or surgery.

A sensory-neural hearing loss involves the inner ear. This usually occurs when there is damage or malformation in the internal ear structure or of the auditory nerve. Such losses in children cannot normally be medically treated; however, the use of a hearing aid

---

* Gist of talk on All India Radio, New Delhi.

may be recommended.

Central hearing losses may occur when there is damage or malformation of the nerve structures in the brain. This malady is difficult to determine and is still a mystery to many.

A mixed hearing loss occurs when there is a combination of conductive and sensor neural hearing impairments.

The hard of hearing child means a child who, with a hearing aid, can develop a language system adequate to successful achievement and social growth.

"Hearing impairment means an impairment in hearing, whether permanent or fluctuating, that adversely affects a child's educational performance but that is not included under the definition of deafness in this section."

Visual impairment and hearing impairment are very common hidden disabilities.

People with learning difficulties are prone to both sight and hearing problems.

Unfortunately many people with learning difficulties frequently go through their lives unnecessarily handicapped because staff and careers have not recognised hearing loss or visual problems or have not tried to get help. Many people have quite inaccurate ideas about what it means to be deaf or hard of hearing.

There are well over 123 million persons with hearing loss of the approximately 64100 billion world population and this category ranks second among persons with severe activity limitation (WHO, 1998). There are 32,42,000 persons with hearing impairment in India.

Population suffering from hearing impairment in India is 0.3 million in 0-4 year age group as per the Report of Human Development, 1999. 1 per cent of children are born with hearing impairments.

Prevalence of disability is highly correlated with poverty and social disadvantage. Impairment not corrected leads to limitation of activities (disability) using the impaired organ and which if left uncorrected leads to limited participation in social life (handicap) irrespective of the age of onset. A child with mild hearing loss if left uncorrected, behaves like a severely hearing impaired person. There are only 5288 professionals (RCI, 1999) in the field of hearing impairment.

Empowering Panchayat Raj Institutions, not only to keep count but also to keep track of promoting the quality of life of persons with hearing impairment, is a felt need.

A World Health Organisation (WHO) (1990) report summarizes the main causes of hearing impairment in India as: Infectious, Neglect and Ignorance. Among the major causes of hearing impairment, the primary preventive measures can be taken with respect to Infectious diseases. Our country has a huge population of hearing impaired children. According to the latest survey, four children per every 1000 children born in India, suffer from severe to profound hearing loss.

The improvement in neonatal care is saving many pre-mature and low birth weight babies who would not have survived a few years back. However, many of these children are later found to have hearing loss. Many babies with hydrocephalus are saved today by shunt surgery. Again, some of these children are later diagnosed as hearing impaired. Even though we talk about education for all children, it is not going to be possible unless we give 'hearing-for all children'.

Even though the number of hearing impaired children is high, they are scattered. There may be a few hearing impaired children in a group of some 20 adjoining villages and it is not feasible to open a special school for them. Unless efforts are made to identify the hearing impaired children and provide them education according to their need it is impossible to achieve 'Universal Elementary Education (UEE)' in which India believes in the nation of 'Education for all' irrespective of gender, caste, creed, religion and disability of the children.

Keeping the aim of our country's motto Vikram Hospital established in 1999 a Specialised Project 'Hearing for all'. A few research doctoral and post-doctoral research projects are going to be undertaken.

Outreach Extension Service Unit (OESU) is going to be set up in order to conduct the sporadic Camp services throughout Tamil Nadu and Kerala. Initiated outreach services and training while creating a nationwide awareness campaign. Methods of preventing hearing impairment hearing loss going to be explored by the unit.

Hearing Impairment is any deviation from "normal" for the worse-whether in structure or in function. Therefore, any degree of hearing loss is a hearing impairment. Hearing Handicap is the disadvantage imposed on hard of hearing people by society such that it affects our efficiency in our daily lives. Even though we may have hearing losses (hearing impairment), we do not have to be handicapped if we live in a society that is sensitive to our needs. If all television programs were captioned, then whether we hear well or not doesn't make any difference—we can all understand the programs. As a result, we would not be handicapped in this situation. When society fails to meet our unique needs as hard of hearing people, we end up handicapped. This handicapping is not the fault of our hearing losses as such, but from society not "leveling the playing field" so we can live in society as equals.

Hearing disability is "an actual or presumed inability to remain employed at full wages." Hearing disability only comes about when society fails to meet our needs and thus handicaps us so it is difficult for us to compete fairly in a hearing society. In a nutshell, hearing.

No matter what hardships life throws at you, there is always tomorrow. No matter how cruel the world seems to you, it is no crueler than you let it be. Life is not always the way we want it to be but we have the power to make the best of what is given to us.

The National Handicapped Finance and Development Corporation set up by the Welfare Ministry with a view to facilitate education, training, developing the potential of the handicapped and thus gearing them for the betters professional tomorrow. We should also develop the concept of toy banks and reading rooms for the handicapped and disabled children as is being done in many advanced countries. There is also a need to educate, advise, and counsel normal children in schools on how to relate to their friends who are handicapped. Above all, it is important to portray them as equal participants in the social system, in mainstream electronic and print media.

Handicapped and Disadvantaged People Statistics and Their Rights

It is estimated that in India the population with disability is slightly above 90 million; nearly 10 per cent of the population. Of these 12 million are blind, 28.5 million are with low vision, 12 million are with speech, and hearing defects, 6 million orthopaedically handicapped, 24 million mentally retarded, 7.5 million mentally ill, 1.1 million leprosy cued.

There are nearly 24 million individuals in India with mental retardation, out of which approximately six million are moderately, severely or profoundly handicapped. In all countries of the world, people with disabilities are the largest minority group.

The disable have at last realized that all people with impairments, in all countries and cultures of the world have one experience in common, an experience that stares at them constantly, hurt them relentlessly. This single common experience, cutting across geographical, political and cultural boundaries, is Discrimination.

How They Suffer?

They are subjected to a long history of neglect, isolation segregation, poverty, deprivation, charity and even pity. They suffer multiple deprivations. The educational, social health, transport and residential arrangements made by local, State, Central governments or voluntary organizations frequently fall short of the demand for them.

The prejudices against the disabled and ignorance about their potential get institutionalised and are inevitably reflected in policy making, resource allocating, service provision and the status accorded to them.

Barriers

Disability, however, is a human right issue and it must be clearly realized by all that the disabled are an integral part of society and every effort must be made to involve them with the whole society. People with impairment feel disabled not because of their physical and/or mental handicaps but because of the barriers society chooses to put up to establish difference between the disabled and non-disabled. These barriers fall in three broad categories.

A. Environmental Barriers

These are inaccessible public and private buildings, schools, colleges, offices, factories. Shops, transport, information, communication system. These shut the disabled out or keep reminding them of their alleged shortcomings and shouting at them that you are not welcome.

B. Institutional Barriers

These include expulsion, exclusion and segregation from key social institutions including education, employment, health, law, recreation etc. Direct and indirect discrimination against the disabled prevents them from taking full advantage of these provisions.

C. Attitudinal Barriers

The non-diable, all over the world, view and treat the disabled with prejudice and in varying degrees, regard them as incapable, inadequate, resentful, bitter, pathetic, tragic, pitiable, abusive, aggressive, immoral, criminal, unhealthy, dependent or charity, costly for society to support, drain on family resources, inferior unemployable, etc.

Recommendations

Priority should be given to the prevention of disabilities, early diagnosis and treatment of those identified as disabled.

Priority should be given to provide financial assistance for the whole family in case of the primary bread winner becoming disabled. Barrier-free designs of public places, buildings, roads, footpaths, transport facilities should be promoted.

Priority must be given to poor person with disabilities in all poverty alleviation programmes.

Specific arrangements must be made so that people with visual handicap, hearing defects and intellectual impairment have direct access to information and they too learn about the world around them; make use of educational, employment, travel and entertainment facilities open to the non-disabled.

Distorted, negative and inaccurate images of persons with disabilities in films, TV serials, radio and television programmes, books, newspapers, should be prohibited and positive and appropriate image should be portrayed.

News coverage in both the print and electronic media must be made sensitive to the real struggles of disabled people—lack of education/employment and inaccessibility to opportunities/ information. They should be portrayed as real people and not as the objects of pity.

Discriminatory attitudes towards education-disabled people, with their roots in traditions and unfounded myths, must be replaced with progressive ideas and practices supported by relevant research findings.

New employment opportunities should be identified and created in formal and non-formal sectors, including the cooperations and self-employment schemes.

Disability and Education

Education, methodology has to be improved and special educators should be developed. Aids and special equipment should be acquired and officers adequately trained and motivated. The disabled should be enabled to use those facilities by removing the physical barriers and taking easy access to transport and buildings.

Today for an unattended disabled individual, traveling in a public transport bus can prove to be a suicidal exercise. Most school buildings, public buildings and private buildings are so ill-designed and dilapidated, particularly in rural areas, that a disabled student with crutches or on a wheel chair will found it impossible to attend classes or go to the toilet or even visit the school library.

The psychological pressure is extreme. Only a disabled person knows what it feels like to depend physically on classmates time and again. Others can only just pretend to understand how inadequate one up disabled student and construct accommodation, toilets and ramps.

The Rehabilitation Council of India is the statutory body for the disabled under the Medical Council of India. The Council plans to expand the definition of disability. The official estimate of all those who come under the expanded definition of disability—it included geriatric problems too—is no less than a tenth of our population. This is around 100 million, far more than the entire population of most of the countries in the world. The Council has planned a huge set of programmes for adults, who, for years, have been carrying for the disabled peoples in their family or their community, without any formal training.

All that the disabled people need is a little care and a little understanding. They are in no way less than us. They only need to be treated with affection and patience.

As estimated 118 persons with different types of disabilities have entered the portals of Delhi University. This was not so, in past records when people with disability hardly attended college.

Our educations systems is not geared towards including the physically/mentally handicapped child in mainstream schools. This is because is either clueless about the necessity of grooming each individual to achieve his/her full potential, or it is just too lethargic to bother. A progressive, open-minded individual leads to a progressive, open-minded society. After the family, the school is the second most important influence in shaping a child's mind and personality. Hence, it is important for every child to grow in the nurturing environment of peers and teachers.

The Disability Rights Act, 1995 which was enacted for the benefit of the disability sector, stipulates in clear terms that all persons with disability, up to age of 18 years, are to receive free and unconditional education in government and/or private schools. However, the directive is being openly flouted and these children are often denied admission on some pretext or the other. As a result, they are forced to receive their education wither at home or in school set up especially for them.

Now special education may be useful but it is not the ideals solution. Why? Since a special school admits only those who are handicapped, students there are not exposed to interacting with normal children on a one-on-one basis in their formative years. They impairs their confidence to interact with wider society later. Besides, they are treated with kid gloves here and are provided a sheltered, made-to-orders environment. Later, when they grow up and are faced with the outside world, life can become extremely difficult:

In a way, segregation never goes away. And this is detrimental not just to the child with disability but to a normal child as well. Normal children just do not get to see a disabled person often and so for them the disabled kid, and the term "disability" always remain outside the purview of their understanding. A child with disability will always remain "different". Someone to be helped and sympathized with, perhaps, but the understanding that disability is just a "condition" and could have occurred to anyone is not understood sufficiently.

To confront and change this scenario, it is vital that more interaction between a normal child and a child with disability is encouraged. The government should wake up to the fact that, by ignoring the educational needs of the differently-abled, they are not harnessing the vast potential of huge segment of society.

Action Plan

Government alone cannot provide equality and welfare to the disabled. Voluntary section also needs to play active part in this sector.

Empowerment of the disabled has to be approached first through economical empowerment in each case, the private sector also play an important role.

The principle of equality is not a luxury but a matter of right to the handicapped.

Over10 per cent of the population are disabled and out of them nearly 80 per cent live in the villages.

9

Terrorism and Human Rights*

"Freedom from fear" could be said to sum up the whole philosophy of human rights – Dag Hammarskjold, Former Secretary General of the United Nations.

"Injustice anywhere is threat to justice everywhere. We are caught in an inescapable network of mutuality, tied in a single garment of density. Whatever affects one directly affects all indirectly."- Martin Luther King Jr.

To a large extent, political violence in India affects human rights. It is manifested mainly in terrorist violence against the state and affects the common population. Terrorism results in the destruction of all human rights of large segments of the population. India, at present, is facing terrorist violence in two areas – Jammu and Kashmir and Northeast.

In Jammu and Kashmir, there has been an armed and organised violence against the state and the people since 1989. There are three major terrorist groups that are operating in Jammu and Kashmir – *Hizbul Mujahideen, Lashkar-e-Toiba* and *Jaish-e-Mohammad,* along with a number of minor groups. A look into human and material casualties shows the human rights violations by these terrorist groups.

Loss of Lives in Jammu and Kashmir since 1988

Year	*Incidents*	*Terrorists*	*Civilians*	*Security Force Personnel*	*Total*
1988	390	1	29	1	31
1989	2,154	0	79	13	92
1990	3,905	183	862	132	1,177
1991	3,122	614	594	185	1,393

* From the presentation at a seminar organised by the Army at Jammu

1992	4,971	873	859	177	1,909
1993	4,457	1,328	1,023	216	2,567
1994	4,484	1,651	1,012	236	2,899
1995	4,479	1,338	1,161	297	2,796
1996	4,224	1,194	1,333	376	2,903
1997	3,004	1,177	840	355	2,372
1998	2,993	1,045	877	339	2,261
1999	2,938	1,184	799	555	2,538
2000	2,835	1,808	842	638	3,288
2001-till June	1,628	760	503	278	1,541
Total	45,584	13,156	10,813	3,798	27,767

A cursory look into the captured weapons in Jammu and Kashmir would reveal the alarming human rights situation.

Of the seven states in India's Northeast, four states are most affected in terms of militancy—Assam, Manipur, Nagaland and Tripura. Assam has been witnessing militancy for the last two decades, ever since large-scale migration from Bangladesh (previously East Pakistan) started. There are more than 30 militant groups in Assam today, which include the following—United Liberation Front of Assam (ULFA); National Democratic Front of Bodoland (NDFB); Kamatapur Liberation Organisation (KLO); Bodo Liberation Tiger Force (BLTF); Dima Halim Daogah (DHD) and Karbi National Volunteers (KNV).

These militant groups in various parts of India have been fighting in various parts of India against the security forces of India and also among themselves. For example in India's northeastern states, most of the militant organisations are organised in tribal basis, where there exist many tribes. These intra tribal and tribe-state conflicts results in a number of human rights violations. Besides death and destruction, the common man is subject to a number of hazards in these conflict prone areas.

Manipur is yet another northeastern state facing both inter- and intra-ethnic tribal conflict, with more than 30 tribes in the

Weapons Recovered in Jammu and Kashmir since 1990

Year	AK-47/ 56/74 Rifle(s)	Pistols/ Revolver(s)	UMG(s)	Carbine(s)	RPG(s)	GPMG(s)	LMG/ SLR(s)	.303 Rif-les	Sniper Rifles	Rocket Laun-chers(s)	Rocket Booster(s)	Total
1990	1,240	751	77	0	65	0	0	0	0	108	74	2,315
1991	2,320	849	130	0	83	18	3	4	0	29	163	3,599
1992	3,504	756	164	0	97	0	1	7	9	62	135	4,735
1993	2,209	921	142	1	42	7	5	10	54	36	61	3,488
1994	2,196	940	127	34	84	11	14	22	41	31	66	3,566
1995	2,055	965	67	1	44	9	10	22	38	36	24	3,271
1996	2,150	1,052	84	6	48	9	9	36	49	43	119	3,605
1997	1,725	1,024	64	3	38	5	12	3	60	81	208	3,223
1998	1,520	584	71	7	104	3	7	7	34	140	293	2,770
1999	1,244	385	28	5	144	1	7	16	13	42	475	2,360
2000	1,405	482	21	0	53	0	2	7	16	59	273	2,318
2001	641	154	6	0	76	0	2	2	5	23	87	996
Total	22,209	8,863	981	57	878	63	72	136	319	690	1,978	36,067

states. Among the most prominent are the Meiteis, Nagas and Kukis. There are more than 30 militant groups operating in this small state, which include the United National Liberation Front (UNLF), People's Liberation Army (PLA), People's Revolutionary Party of Kangleipak (PREPAK), Kangleipak Communist Party (KCP), National Socialist Council of Nagaland – Isak-Muivah (NSCN-IM), Kuki National Front (KNF) and Kuki National Army (KNA).

Civilians Killed by Various Terrorist Groups in Assam

	1992	*1993*	*1994*	*1995*	*1996*	*1997*	*1998*	*1999*	*2000**
ULFA	35	48	49	16	59	68	97	55	35
NDFB	37	25	108	132	176	137	305	107	52
BLT & BTF	0	0	0	8	53	52	126	22	1
NSCN/ DHD	8	1	16	14	14	28	3	30	5
UPDS	0	0	0	0	0	0	0	0	33

*Data up to 28 June 2000.

Security Force Personnel Killed by Various Militant Groups in Assam

	1992	*1993*	*1994*	*1995*	*1996*	*1997*	*1998*	*1999*	*2000**
ULFA	10	15	7	14	48	50	42	29	28
NBFD	10	6	22	16	25	25	22	14	6
BLT & BTF	0	0	0	1	6	1	5	8	0
NSCN/ DHD	14	3	6	42	8	9	3	26	6
UPDS	–	–	–	–	–	–	0	2	0
Total	34	24	35	73	87	85	72	79	40

Security Force Personnel Killed by Various Militant Groups in Manipur

	1992	*1993*	*1994*	*1995*	*1996*	*1997*	*1998*	*1999*	*2000**
NSCN	27	80	104	30	21	27	20	6	0
MEITEI	43	119	79	139	90	62	57	75	26
KUKI	14	67	6	14	6	144	10	8	1

* Data up to 28 June 2000.

Security Force Personnel Killed by Various Militant Groups in Nagaland

	1992	*1993*	*1994*	*1995*	*1996*	*1997*	*1998*	*1999*	*2000**
NSCN	8	46	67	20	8	5	2	1	2
MEITEI	22	41	21	38	52	67	57	63	24
KUKI	0	4	10	6	5	39	3	0	0

NSCN is the major militant group operating in Nagaland. It is divided into two factions—Muviah and Khaplang. Besides their fight against the Indian security forces, the conflict between two factions is very intense.

Insurgency Related Killings in Nagaland

	1992	*1993*	*1994*	*1995*	*1996*	*1997*	*1998*	*1999*	*2000**
Civilians	34	62	110	80	144	104	26	26	5
Security Force	33	43	26	25	48	38	14	4	4
Militants	29	68	56	108	112	218	72	118	52

* Data up to 28 June 2000.

Caste Violence

Caste conflict is yet another source of human rights violation in India. Caste violence is predominant in states like Bihar, Uttar Pradesh, Tamil Nadu and Andhra Pradesh. The main reason for increased caste violence in these states have been due to the feudal nature of society, concentration of land in the hands of a select few, suppression of the lower castes by the land owned upper castes and the reluctance of the upper castes to provide equal social status to the lower castes.

The following section will focus especially on caste violence in Bihar as a case study, as caste violence there is more organised. In states such as Bihar and Uttar Pradesh, the caste violence is organised in the sense, many of the upper castes have come together and formed "sena" meaning caste militia, which are well funded and organised.

Bihar is a highly feudal society, where the caste lines are clearly drawn between the upper and lower castes. These caste groups have armed militias, known as *Senas*. Every caste group has a *Sena* for itself, as seen from the following table.

Senas (Caste Militias) of Bihar

Name of Sena	*Caste Affiliation*	*Year of Formation*	*Operational Districts*
Kuer Sena	Rajput	1979	Bhojpur, Rohtas
Kisan Suraksha Samiti	Kurmi	1979	Patna, Jehanabad, Gaya
Bhoomi Sena	Kurmi	1983	Patna, Nawada, Nalanda, Jehanabad
Lorik Sena	Yadav	1983	Patna, Jehanabad, Nalanda
Brahmarshi Sena	Bhumihar	1984	Bhojpur, Patna, Jehanabad, Aurangabad
Kisan Sangh	Rajput Brahmin	1984	Palamu
Kisan Sewak Samaj	Rajput	1985	Palamu, Aurangabad
Sunlight Sena	Pathans Rajput	1989	Palamu, Gaya, Garwah, Aurangabad
Swarna Liberation Front	Bhumihar	1990	Gaya, Jehanabad
Kisan Sangh	Bhumihar	1990	Patna, Bhojpur
Kisan Morcha	Rajputs	1989-90	Bhojpur

Ganga Sena	Bhumihar	1990	Bhojpur
Ranvir Sena	Rajput and Bhumihars	1994	Bhojpur, Patna, Jehanabad, Rohtas, Gaya, Aurangabad

Of these caste militias, *Ranvir Sena* is the most powerful militia. It has been involved in the most massacres, when compared with the other militias. Since its formation, it has been involved in more than 25 massacres, in which more than 250 persons have been killed.

Communal Violence

India is a multi-religious society composed of Hindus (82 per cent), Muslims (12 per cent), Christians (2 per cent), Sikhs (2 per cent) and other small communities (under 1 per cent each). Especially in the last few years, India has witnessed increased attacks on minority communities, especially Muslims and Christians. More than 600 incidents took place in 1998. In December 1998, churches and other Christian establishments were attacked in Gujarat in Dangs district. On 22-23 January 1999, an Australian missionary, Graham Staines, and his two sons were burnt alive. On 13 January, 1999, a church in Dangs district was burnt. A Muslim Dargah was razed to the ground in Surendranagar district of Gujarat. In April 1999, sectarian violence between Shias and Sunnis resulted in the killing of two persons. In the same month, two more persons were killed in Rai Bareli district in Uttar Pradesh in a communal clash. A priest of the Roman Catholic Church was killed in Koenjar district. Seven people were killed in Surat, Gujarat, in September 1999, over a communal clash during a Lord Ganesh procession.

Communal violence has been the result of religious conversions from one faith to another or rival claims over property or land. These situation and emotional issues are being handled carefully by various authorities. For example, processions taken out by Hindu community through a street where a mosque is located is handled with extreme care and caution by senior officers of the state. While the right of a community to take a procession need to be maintained, at the same time, keeping in mind the religious sentiments of another community. This is managed successfully by tactful and diplomatic handling of the situation, by ensuring that the procession does not involve in any loud music and drum beats while crossing select streets or places.

Terrorism vis-a-vis Human Rights

The observations of Senator, Mr. Jackson, when the safety of the American citizens was itself under terrorist's threat were : "The idea of that one person's terrorist is another's freedom fighter cannot be sanctioned. Freedom-fighters or revolutionaries do not blow up buses containing non-combatants, terrorist, murderers do. Freedom Fighters do not assassinate innocent men, women and children; terrorist murderers do. It is a matter of disgrace that democracies should allow the treasured word 'freedom' to be associated with acts of terrorist."

The best answer to those who believe human rights to be incompatibile with quelling of terrorism lies in the legislation in Northern Ireland. The region has been in the grips of terrorism for over two decades, but the law there does not provide even for preventive detention. It was tried briefly from August 1971 to December,1975 and given up as futile. A host of inquiries have been held on how to preserve human rights under the threat of terrorism, most notably by the Gardiner Committee to consider, in the context of civil liberties and human rights, measures to deal with terrorism.

In the Northern Ireland there is an independent Director of Public Prosecutions (DPP). Complaints against police are investigated by Chief Constable and he is required under law to submit investigation reports to the DPP is for possible prosecution. The DPP independent of government. The Court's approach to a case involving a soldier is that he is subject to ordinary law. Like any other citizen of the country.

There is in Northern Ireland institutional machinery for investigating complaints against the police. The citizen has a statutory right to lodge a formal complaint against a police officer whereupon the investigative machinery is set in motion.

Eradication of Terrorism

To eradicate terrorism is not easy task. Its relationship with human rights is complex. Those engaged in acts of terror are quick to seek the protection of precisely those rights that they violate without compunction and hold in contempt. Human rights are most readily invoked, without those engaged in acts of violations or themselves under seige. The invocation for such rights is an intrinsic part of the psychological and political inter-co-relation of what euphemistically, is called "low-intensity conflict" but which is, in reality often worked by proxy.

The Commission is of the view that all elements of such society must combine to fight the menace of terrorism, it is not a fight to be continued by the armed forces and police alone. Instead, it must be fought at the political level, at the economic and social level, at the level of ideas. But, above all it must be fought in a manner that respects human rights, whatever the difficulties this may entail for the State and to those who are engaged in this task.

The Commission believes that there must be full and uncompromising adherence to the provisions of the constitution, the laws of our land and the treaty commitments to which our nation is a party. The Commission has always made it clear that it will not countenance departures from these exacting standards.The security of the State can never be assured at the expense of the human dignity all those for whom the State exists. Respect for human rights must be an essential component in formulating any worthwhile policy of national security.

HUMAN RIGHTS/FUNDAMENTAL RIGHTS *versus* TERRORISM

Sovereign Immunity

By now it is well-established that the doctrine of sovereign immunity cannot be invoked by the state, where the fundamental right of a citizen has been violated.

The frontiers of public law are expanding far and wide and new concepts and doctrines which will change the complexion of the law are emerging fast all over the world.

The purpose of public law is to civilise public power and to assure the citizens that they live under a legal order which aims to protect their interest and preserve their rights. It is inherent in the concept of the rule of law that the state, no less than it's citizens and others, is bound by the laws.

Status of Individual

* Presentation at the Oxford Conference on International Cooperation in Criminal Matters. Balancing the Priduction of Human Rights with the needs of law enforcement.

According to Oppenhiem's classic; (1955) Edition

"Since the law of nations is primarily a law between states, states are, to that extent, the only subjects of the law of nations. But what is the normal position of individuals in international law, if they are not regularly subjects thereof? The answer can only be that, generally speaking, they are subjects of the law of nations.

The World Conference held in Vienna in 1993 proclaimed

"All human beings are universal, indivisible and inter related and inter dependent. The international community must treat human rights globally in a fair and equal manner, on the same footing and with the same emphasis".

"The subjects of human rights itself had it's origin in international law with the progressive development of the status of the individual in the international legal system. The effect of incorporation of individual rights in the Bill of Rights in a written constitution was to incorporate Human Rights into the municipal law of a State. Human Rights stem from a "base line of equal concern for the interest of everyone."

"All human beings have a natural right to an equality of concern and respect, a right they possess not by virtue of birth or characteristic or merit or excellence, but simply as human beings with the capacity to make plans and give justice." "All human beings, great or small, virtuous or vicious, should be respected and cared for simply by virtue of the fact that they are bom human beings."

Humanitarian base of the human rights regime assumed prominence fifty years ago when, chastened by the capacity of human species to destroy it's own kind through acts of war and barbarous inhumanity, the peoples of the world gave themselves two instruments designed to prevent forever the recurrence of self-destructive behaviour. They are the Charter of United Nations and the Universal Declaration of Human Rights. The rest of the rapid revolutionary developments in the field of Human Rights are too well-known to be recounted here. The declaration be 1948 and the two covenants of 1966 sought to put those great rights of man about the law of the land.

The Indian Experience

In India, article 5 1 (e) of the constitution mercy enjoins that the "state shall endeavour to foster respect for international law and treaty obligations". But the supreme court always endeavoured to interpret the existing statutes in consonance with the international covenants ratified by India.

In the Indian judicial experience, values of Human Rights have always influenced and inspired constitutional interpretation. The supreme court of India declared in Maneka Gandhi case :"The procedure established by law must be Right and Just and Fair and not arbitrary or oppressive".

Fundamental Rights and Human Rights

The supreme court of India held that fundamental rights are merely the modem name for what have been traditionally known as 'natural-rights'.

The fundamental rights are above ordinary laws. Ordinary laws cannot change them. They are not conferred rights. They need not be built into the law. They are placed above the law.

Respect for Human Rights is the greatest inspiration for integration of mankind, both internally and internationally.

The great change under the Indian constitution came about with the supreme court of India interpreting the directive principles and the fundamental rights in a harmonious way. The positive content to the fundamental rights arose from the infusion of the Directive Principles in such a way as to give meaning and content to the Fundamental Rights, though the Directive Pfinciples of state policy adumbrated in part IV of the constitution were 'proprio-vigore' unenforceable. They nevertheless became Fundamental to the governance of the country and became the sources or law in a welfare state.

The supreme court of India declared as early as in 1981 - "The fundamental right to life ... is the most precious right and ... forms the arc of all other rights" .... "Deprive a person of his right to livelihood and you shall have to deprive him of his life".

The supreme court added :

"An equally important facet of that right is the right to livelihood because, no person can live without the means of living, that is, the means of livelihood. If the right to livelihood is not treated as a part of the constitutional right to life, the easiest way of depriving a persons of his right to life would be to deprive him of his means of livelihood to the point of abrogation". Such deprivation would not only denude the life of it's effective content and meaningfulness but it should make life impossible to live. And yet, such deprivation would not have to be in accordance with the procedure established by law, if the right to livelihood is not regarded as a part of the right to live, leave aside what makes life liveable, must be deemed to be an integral component of the right to life."

India is a welfare state. It means, according to Oxford Dictionary, "a country so organised that every member of the community is assured of his/her due maintenance with the most advantage conditions possible for all".

Almost all natural rights or human rights as they have come to be celebrated all over the world, have been enshrined in the Indian Constitution in chapter III - under the caption 'Fundamental Rights'. The founding fathers of the Indian Constitution were deeply influenced by the Universal Declaration of Human Rights. In fact both these great events took place around the same period of human history. Hence the great similarities in the constitution of India and the Universal Declaration of Human Rights.

The Indian Judiciary with it's total independence and progressive attitude, guarding jealously the dignity of the individual, gave liberal interpretations in the exercise of it's power of judicial review.

Terrorism – The Biggest Threat to Civilised Existence of Humanity

Terrorism in some form and intensity or the other has become a global phenomenon.

The primary objective or the strategies to combat and control terrorist activity is the protection and maintenance of liberal democracy and the rule of law.

Any tyrant can solve the problem of political violence, if he is prepared to sacrifice all considerations of humanity and to trample down on all constitutional and human rights.

The common complaint is that a terrorist uses all unfair and illegal means and has, therefore, an advantage over the law-abiding policeman. It is an unequal fight when at stake is the very survival of the orderly society and all that go with it. Force, they say, has to be met with higher force and violence with counter-violence. The logic is tempting. In the short run it might even produce spectacular results. But quite apart altogether ftom the ethical side to it, even as strategy, the argument is stultifying.

Wardlaw on 'political terrorism' says :- "However serious the threat of terrorism, we must not be tempted to use repressive methods to combat it".

While we must avoid the easy move to repression as a counter to terrorism, it is equally vital that we do not allow ourselves to be so overcome by our democratic sensibilities that our response is weak and vacillating, and characterised by inaction . we must uphold constitutional authority and law and order, and we must do so with firmness and determination. To do so requires political will; but most importantly it requires citizen support. To gain such support the political will must be translated into effective action".

Any anti-terrorist measures must be, and be seen to be, directed only at terrorists. "The response must be hmited, well defined, and controlled. It must be both policy and practice for the government and its security forces to act within the law. Not only does failure to do so place the government in a morally difficult position (If the government does not obey the law, why should any one else do so?) but also such action is likely to undermine their support and provide valuable ammunition for a terrorist cause. Propaganda capital can very easily be made out of violations of law by government servants, and such propaganda can be used as additional justification for a terrorist campaign while the law can be a refuge for the law-breaker and a hindrance to the law enforcement official, the law is the basis of our system of government and must *be* upheld. Otherwise are we any better than the terrorist who argues also on the grounds of expediency?"

The biggest threat to the enjoyment of human rights is terrorism. Terrorists do not respect the rights of innocent citizens. The terrorists are no respecters of law. Intrumentalities of government dealing with terrorism have to strictly adhere to national and international norms. The tragedy and irony of such situations are exacerbated by the fact that terrorists, who themselves are the implacable enemies of civil society, and who hold the rights and values of such society including the right to life—in contempt, are quick to invoke the protection of rights when under seize.

Another paradoxical situation of the contemporary world is that while there is increasingly wide-spread concern for universal respect for and observance of human rights, gross violations of internationally recognised norms continue unabated. The obligations set out in scores of international conventions and accepted by most governments, are flouted with immunity.

It is not the severity of the punishment but the certainty of it that deters crime. It is not how strict and firm that criminals and law-breakers are dealt with that alienate the law-enforcer; it is the harshness and rudeness with which a law enforcer dealt with the honest law-abiding citizen that generate hostility and alienation.

Right to Peace — Most Basic Human Right

Human rights are value judgements which constitute the sounding board of domestic laws. But a balance has to be struck between the security of the state on the one hand and the individual freedom on the other.

The great violators of the most basic human right — the right to peace — are sovereign governments obsessed with national security. Whenever a sovereign government chooses to be a law unto itself, there is simply no effective power to stop it, particularly if it has, and is known to have a sufficient arsenal of weapons.

The sovereignty of the state, as opposed to the concept of the comity of nations, continues to be the single greatest threat to the human right to world peace, and so far there has not been seen any sustained and dedicated effort to make the peoples of the world aware of this important threat.

Dr Robert Oppenhiem, who invented the atom bomb and who lived to regret it, was asked to testify before the US Senate committee. He was asked if there is any defence against a nuclear weapon. He promptly replied, "yes - PEACE".

The following poignant sentence appears in the preamble to the constitution of UNESCO: -C4since wars begin in the minds of men, it is in the minds of men (and women) that the defences of peace must be "constructed".

Extradition and Mutual Assistance in Criminal Matters

Justice is the right to the maximum of individual independence compatible with the same liberty for others. Justice is the end purpose of the government. Because justice is not executed speedily, men (and women) persuade themselves that there is no such thing as justice.

Margaret Thatcher declared - "The acquittal of a guilty person constitutes as much a miscarriage of justice as the conviction of the innocent.

Increasing acts of transnational crimes and terrorism are posing the biggest challenges to civilised existence of societies and comity of nations.

Organised criminals and terrorists operate with impunity in any part of the world making a mockery of international co-operation and human rights.

Paris Minimum Standards Prescribe the sixteen non-derogable rights. Of these the most essential are:

(1) the right of life

(2) freedom from torture or cruel, inhuman or degrading treatment

(3) recognition as a person before me law

(4) freedom of thought, conscience and religion.

What is lacking is the will on the part of the world community: It is high time the member states agree on the terms, conditions, definitions and modalities to be adopted in matters of extradition and Yeordering mutual assistance in criminal matters.

'Injustice anywhere is a threat to justice everywhere, as Martin Luther King said.

It is high time the world community realises, "an act of terrorism anywhere in the world is a victory to the terrorists everywhere in the world".

The Commonwealth office deserves all the credit for organising this conference, which is timely. I am sure the Conference will prove to be a path-breaker in this vital area.

The Conference must urge the member states to act with a sense of urgency and speed up action on all matters of extradition and mutual assistance in criminal matters.

The world has shrunk into a global village. If you want peace, order and stability in your country, co-operate fully and speedily to ensure peace, order and stability everywhere Prof Ernest Baker says :

"The supreme sovereign which stands in the background of any politically organised community is Justice; justice in the sense of that right order of human relations which gives to the greatest possible number of persons the greatest possible opportunity for the highest development of all the capacities of their personality".

Holy rigveda, the ancient Indian scripture says "Ajyestaso Akanishtasa ete, sam. bhrataro va vridhutu sowbhagya"

(Rig veda-manda 5, sukta-60 mantra-5)

No one is superior or inferior. All are brothers who should strive collectively for the common welfare.

There is no dichotomy between rights of states and human rights. The dichotomy in fact, is between human rights of individuals and rights of state on the one hand and acts of terrorists and transnational criminals on the other.

10

Human Rights Violations and Police*

Undoubtedly, national security is of paramount importance. Without protecting the safety and security of the nation, individual rights cannot be protected. However, the worth of a nation is the worth of the individuals constituting it. Article 21 which guarantees a life with dignity is non-derogable. Both national integrity as well as individual dignity are core values in the Constitution, and are compatible and not inconsistent. The need is to balance the two.

—National Human Rights Commission, 2001

Police atrocities are considered a major area of human rights violations falling under the category of state violence. This includes torture and deaths in police custody, encounter deaths and atrocities against women including rape and illegal detentions. The government has also been accused of systematically violating international law "by using lethal force against peaceful demonstrators, and engaging in widespread and arbitrary arrests of persons suspected of sympathizing with the militants, and detaining them for extended periods without charge or trial." The state is determined to put down mindless violence by terrorists, while taking care to ensure protection of human rights of the people.

State Violence

Not only are non-state entities involved in violence, but the state, at times, is also involved in violence against its citizens. State violence takes place at four levels. First, it occurs in an insurgency situation where the armed forces are involved in tackling terrorist groups. There are a number of complaints against Indian armed forces deployed in Jammu and Kashmir and in the various North eastern states. Second, the police have used force to control organised political uprisings of armed groups, especially that of the naxalites [Naxalites are those armed groups who follow the teaching of Karl

* Gist of several talks by the author at Police Seminars and Training Institutions.

Marx and other Communist thinkers and leaders and believe in an armed conflict with the state and the select sections of the society to achieve their goals and caste militias. At present there are a number of naxalite groups in the states of Bihar, Jharkhand, Andhra Pradesh and Madhya Pradesh. Third, during political crises, especially in situations such as *bandhs* and processions, the state in the past has used force to bring disorderly situations under control.

Fourth, there are police atrocities in normal times. Police in India was constituted by the British to subserve their colonial interests. Even after independence, the police have not been able to transform their mindset to serve in a free and democratic society. Even after the independence, the laws of procedure and evidence continue to be as before – weighed against the police. Thousands of laws enacted place the entire burden on the police force that is inadequate and ill equipped to effectively discharge all their responsibilities. Police being the visible arm of the government, increasingly confront the public who are dis-enchanted with the failure of government to fulfill their election promises. The birth of organised crime, terrorism, insurgency and extremism also puts enormous pressure on the police. Unable to bear all such pressure of rising expectations of both the government and the public, the police force do lose their equilibrium and balance. To prove themselves to be effective, at times they resort to short hand methods and excesses. However, with the public increasingly becoming aware of their rights and with Human Rights organisations becoming active, efforts are being made to bring about law reforms. The situation seems to be changing for the better.

***Human Rights and CRPF (Para Military Forces)**

What are Human Rights? Human Rights are certain basic and fundamental rights which are inalienable and indivisible. Every human being, by the mere fact of being born on this planet, is endowed with such natural rights. These rights are not a gift or grant of some authority or the Government. Human Rights are essentially a codification of mainly spiritual laws which are themselves the cumulative achievement of the world's religious traditions. We must respect the Human Rights of others. In simple terms, what is meant is 'treat others with dignity'. We must treat others, as we would like to be treated by them.

---

* Talk delivered at CRPF Internal Security Academy.

Any public functionary and more so, any member of the law enforcement agency can effectively render any service to the society, only when one has full awareness of and utmost respect for human rights. In fact, protection and respect of human dignity, human decency and human rights are the very essence of the rule of law and social order in civilized society. How civilized a society is or a people are, is judged by the level of awareness, protection, preservation and observation of human rights.

Rights of Individuals vs. Rights of Society. Very often, the question is raised "which is more important - Safeguarding human rights of individuals or the collective rights of the entire society to live in peace?" Very often, it is also stated that the security forces have to strike a balance between safeguarding the human rights of individuals and defending the interests of the State as a whole against disorder. It is again argued that in order to be effective, some compromise has to be made while respecting and protecting human rights. It is stated that because of various factors like delays in investigation and trial, reluctance of witnesses to depose against notorious criminals out of fear, witnesses turning hostile on being won over and several loopholes in the criminal justice delivery system, organized crime is on the increase, threatening the very existence of civilized society.

Either due to such public pressure, campaign in the media or pressure from the Government itself, very often, the law enforcement agencies get "tempted" and "pressurized" to break or bend the law and resort to methods which are not permitted by the law of the land. The efforts to prove oneself "effective" by resorting to such illegalities only go to erode the credibility of the force, despite some short-term gains. Security forces which have sworn to abide by the Constitution and the law of the land should not under any circumstances, be tempted or pressurized to take the law into their own hands. They must strictly follow the procedure and the law prescribed however arduous it might appear to be in certain situations. If the enforcers of law themselves break the law, what will happen to the rule of law? Who can exercise any check or restraint? How can officers who have taken the oath not to usurp the authority of other institutions assume the role of law enforcer, investigator, judge and executioner? Then, who is safe? Where do we draw the line? Granting that in certain situations, even sections of the public applaud such 'effective' actions for immediate gains, it is dangerous to the entire society to accept, permit or tolerate such methods.

Respect for Law. It is the paramount duty of the leaders of the police forces to motivate, train and imbibe into every member of the force, that while discharging the onerous duty of maintaining law and order, investigating the crime and fighting insurgency, terrorism and extremism, they shall strictly abide by the procedure and law of the land clearly laid down by the Legislature and judgement of the Apex Court. While it is true that certain provisions of the law of procedure, evidence and substantive laws require drastic revision and amendments to effectively deal with the worsening situation, the right course will be for the leaders of the forces to convince the authorities concerned to bring in immediately necessary changes in the law and procedure. Unless and until such changes are effected in the law and procedure by the competent authority, the existing provisions should be strictly and scrupulously followed by every member of the force.

Earning the Trust. It is only by the police forces respecting the human rights of every individual, in all circumstances, that they will be able to regain the credibility and trust of the people. No security force can succeed in its mission, without total cooperation and trust of the people living in the area in which they are deployed and operate.

Supreme Sacrifice by Police Forces. On an average, every year, over a thousand officers, men and women of the police and paramilitary force make the 'supreme sacrifice' in fighting insurgency, terrorism, extremism, communal and anti-social forces to preserve order, unity, integrity and security of the nation. Without such a sacrifice, the country could not have made any progress and perhaps, could not have even survived as one nation. Also, several thousands of police officers, men and women work hard in most difficult situations, night and day to ensure peace and order even when the rest of the society is celebrating their holidays and festivals. Several thousands of police personnel of paramilitary forces spend months together away from their families, performing their duties in hostile climate and hazardous and remote areas of the country. No other force or a wing of the Government can claim to make so much of sacrifice and do so much of hard work for the peace and happiness of the rest of the nation. What should be the respect and trust enjoyed by such security forces in this country? Obviously, they must be the most trusted and respected organisations. But what is really the situation? The answer is obvious to all of us.

Treat People with Dignity. Why are the security forces not enjoying the respect and trust, which they fully deserve? It is certain aberrations, omissions and commissions on the part of some misguided and over-zealous officers, who by their high-handed behaviour totally disregard human rights, that is responsible for the lack of public trust in the police forces. Because a few police personnel indulge in rude behaviour, highhanded action, illegal detentions and false encounters, the sacrifice and hard work of the entire force gets diminished and goes unacknowledged and unsung. Unless the forces get the total cooperation and respect of the public whom they serve and amidst whom they perform their duties, they can never be effective and successful. To gain the trust and respect of the public, there is only one formula, i.e., treat the people with dignity, and treat others as you would like to be treated yourself. Respect the human rights of every individual. Any other attitude or behaviour will diminish ones own stature and personality.

Operational Achievements. The Central Reserve Police Force is the most important internal security force of the nation. The 1,80,000 strong force has rendered yeoman service throughout its glorious existence of sixty years. Its history is a saga of glory, achievement, service and sacrifice. The force has served in all theatres of operations. They fought shoulder-to-shoulder with the Indian Army in the Indo-Pak Wars, the Indo-Chinese conflict and also as part of the IPKF in the Sri Lanka operations. Wherever they were called upon to serve, they performed with admirable efficiency. CRPF is the most dependable, impartial, secular and effective force in any terrain, be it the North East, North West, high altitudes or jungles. It has proved its versatility in many operations, in fighting insurgency, terrorism, extremism and communalism.

A Unique Force. CRPF has also proved itself as a force full of compassion, by rendering appreciable service to the afflicted during natural calamities like floods, cyclones, earthquakes and railway accidents. It has endeared itself to the local population, wherever deployed. While being firm with hostile elements, the force has always functioned with a sense of service for the law abiding citizens. CRPF is also the most adaptable paramilitary force. It is comfortable working alongwith armed forces and the various State Police Forces. Its popularity with the people and the State Police Forces can be gauged by the fact that it is always in demand from various States and Union Territories, irrespective of the political colour of the Government and the type of problems. It is very difficult to imagine any General Election being conducted without the large-scale deployment of the CRPF. The force has earned laurels abroad by rendering admirable service in its various peace-keeping operations.

C.R.P.F.'s Service to Society. Apart from taking several welfare measures for its own personnel and dependants like providing education and rehabilitation, the CRPF has been serving humanity in various ways. At a macro level, afforestation has been undertaken by it on a large scale. Planting a tree is a way of not only repaying our debt to Mother Earth, but also enriching the environment of the campus, the city, the country and the planet as a whole. Every CRPF campus is full of greenery, making it a model campus. At a micro level, blood donation has been undertaken by the CRPF on a regular basis in every campus on a large scale.

An Enviable Record. Despite grave provocations, human rights violations by the CRPF are very few. The force leadership has never tolerated such human rights violations on the false and mistaken pretext of 'morale'. The leadership of the CRPF is fully aware, any condonation of such willful violation of human rights will only bring discredit to the Force adversely affecting the morale. On the contrary, when such violations are dealt with firmly, the credibility of the Force increases which in turn raises the morale of the Force. Such violations have been effectively dealt with by taking deterrent and strong action against the violators of human rights. Its neutrality, impartiality, secularism, the readiness to serve with distinction at any time anywhere, in any situation and the spirit of selfless sacrifice have endeared the force to the entire nation. CRPF marches on serving the nation with 'service and loyalty."

The record of the CRPF in recognizing, respecting, preserving, protecting and furthering human rights in unparalleled for a paramilitary force of its size and magnitude of its operations.

Is Police Brutality Avoidable?

Perspective of the Author

Every year, on an average, over a thousand officers, men and women belonging to the various police forces in the country sacrifice their lives in the line of duty, while fighting insurgency, terrorism, extremism and communalism to preserve the unity, integrity and security of the nation. Also, several thousands of police officers, men and women work hard for long hours, in the most difficult situations to ensure peace and order. They work day and night when the rest of society is safe in their homes celebrating holidays and festivals.

Police personnel spend months together away from their families, performing duties in a hostile climate and hazardous and remote terrain. No other force or wing of the Government can claim to make so much of sacrifice and do so much of hard work day after day or year after year to ensure peace and order in society. One would expect nothing but total respect and trust by the nation and the public for such police forces. But when we look at the reality, the police do not enjoy the trust and respect of the public for whom they are supposed to serve and for whose benefits they make all the sacrifices.

It is the perceived brutality and rude behaviour on the part of some of the policemen, which is responsible for most of the police having a bad image. There are a few persons in the police force, who have scant regard for human rights and the number of such people is always small compared to the total strength of the force, though their capacity to do damage to the reputation and image of the force is certainly enormous. Most of such violations take place at the hands of grass-root level functionaries of police force, who constitute the vast majority of the police in the whole country. Whatever they do goes by the name of the entire police force.

Custodial violence is a calculated assault on human dignity. In D.K.Basu's case the Supreme Court observed "whenever human dignity is wounded, civilisation takes a step backward. The flag of humanity on each occasion must fly half-mast".

Reasons of Brutality

As the police is the only organisation authorised to use force, it may tend to attract some persons who really like to use it. Policemen see so much of violence and brutality in their day to day work, that it may have the effect of brutalising some of them to some extent. The environment in which the police are required to function may be another contributing factor. The police are also constantly subjected to tremendous pressure and criticism for any increase in crime for which the police is singled out for blame. What is forgotten is that even under the best of the circumstances, the ability of the police to control crime is limited, as crime is a result of various factors over most of which the police have no control. Similarly, the riots or law and order situations are most often created by the omissions and commissions of the various political and administrative authorities and the police are called upon only to deal with the consequences. The politicians use them for their political and personal ends. The policeman's status is low, their resources are meagre, but the expectations of the public are always very high. When the police cannot control crime, it is subjected to tremendous pressure from all sides. The impact of the pressure is felt strongly at the subordinate levels who are required to deliver goods in quick time.

These pressures generate a sub-culture, in which an accused or even a suspect is looked upon by the lower subordinates as a source of major trouble, and an enemy to be fought. War against crime and criminals for them is a war for survival and taking short-cuts to solve cases and making shrift of criminals is a temptation. Even some members of the public including the intelligentsia share this feeling, particularly when they themselves are the relatives of victims of crime. They often complain that the police officers are not taking enough interest in solving the case merely because no third-degree methods are being used.

When the prevailing system of criminal justice fails to give a feeling of security to the people, they seek alternative ways of protecting themselves against crime and criminals. In such an environment, the police is tempted to resort to extra-legal methods and commit violence against the persons in their custody in the belief that such behaviour would have the tacit approval of the public.

No where else in the world is the law of the land so biased against the police as it is in this country. Since the case on hand has not only to be solved, but also made legally foolproof to stand scrutiny in the court of law, investigating officer is tempted to take recourse to extra-legal methods. This actually creates a vicious circle. The police use illegal methods in some cases because of inadequacies in the law, and the law is not reformed on the ground that the behaviour of the policemen does not justify reposing trust in them.

Remedial Measures

Any incident of excessive and unjustified use of force or abuse of power by State authorities weakens the fabric of a democratic set up. Preservation of citizen's rights is as important for survival of democracy and rule of law as maintenance of law and order. The world wide movement for preservation of human rights has resulted in the international community according great importance to a country's rights record. The emphasis should be to ensure that those who are trying to gain an entry into the police forces are emotionally balanced and sensitive. Imbued with right attitudes and an understanding of the broad philosophy of the constitution, which guarantees fundamental rights to the citizens of the country. There is need to prescribe psychological tests and to associate psychologists with the recruitment process so that wrong type of people are not allowed to enter into the forces.

Measures must be taken to improve training standards to improve professional skills and to bring out required changes in the attitudes. Attitudinal transformation in tune with the changing aspirations and needs of the present day democratic society should be brought about. The police personnel at all levels should be sensitised to human rights issues through basic as well as in-service training courses. More important is to ensure that human rights are protected at the level of enforcement and any infringement or violation is viewed seriously. A strict, close and continuous supervision over the work of lower subordinates in the police can play a very important role in checking the incidents of custodial crimes.

When action is not taken on genuine complaints against police personnel for committing unjustified custodial violations, it creates and perpetuates a feeling of injustice in the minds of the public. Action taken against police personnel found guilty in such cases, would strengthen the confidence of the public in the ability of the Police Department itself to deal with such cases effectively.

The police have to perform an extremely difficult task, particularly in view of the deteriorating law and order situation due to various socio-politico-economic factors, increase in organised crimes and drug menace, criminalisation of politics, politicisation of police and administration, near collapse of criminal justice delivery system and the threat posed by insurgency, terrorism and extremism. A balance approach is, therefore, needed to deal with the problems.

There is no law governing the liability of the State for the wrong done to a citizen by a public servant in the course of his employment. However, the National Human Rights Commission and the Courts of Law have been granting compensation to the victims of custodial crimes. What is required is to frame suitable legislation, under which the State should pay adequate compensation to the victims of custodial crimes and to their kith and kin in cases of death.

The National Human Rights Commission is of the view that the upswing in reported deaths in custody is the result of its repeated instructions that information regarding such tragic occurrences must not be suppressed, but must be reported promptly, investigated and acted upon. The issue is of such overriding importance to the Commission that every occasion is seized by it to discuss and to follow up on reports of custodial death, whether this be through visits to individual States, or in discussions at the Commission's Headquarters in New Delhi, when Chief Secretaries and Director Generals of Police are required to be present.

To gain the trust and respect of the public there is only one formula, i.e., to treat the public with dignity, respect and courtesy, they should treat others as they themselves would like to be treated. The police should recognise, respect and protect the human rights of every individual, even that of a criminal. Any other attitude or behaviour will not only diminish the stature, personality and image of the police, but also will render them totally ineffective.

Debate by CPOs

One of the statutory obligation of the NHRC as per the Protection of Human Rights Act 1993, is to create human rights awareness and spread/disseminate human rights literacy/culture throughout the country. In this noble endeavour, the Commission, in order to generate better and clearer consciousness amongst the Central Police Organisations, have been organising an Annual Debate competition, since 1996.

The objective of this annual event is two-fold, firstly to engage their continuing interest in the issues of human rights and secondly to inoculate and sensitise the Force personnel to abide/respect such rights and remain constantly mindful of them despite the difficult, provocating circumstances in which they have to or operate, particularly, in areas facing foreign abetted terrorism and insurgency. The responsibility to organise the debate competition amongst the CPOs is by rotation and this year, the honour in staging it goes to the BSF.

HR Violations (Spheres)

There is no conflict between being a police officer and human rights activist. In fact, if a police officer is conscientious and upright, he would be a staunch defender of human rights.

I do agree that human rights violations are committed by police officers in police stations. But I cannot agree with the view that gross human rights violations take place only in police stations. The task of the police is no doubt difficult and they are always placed in a negative and confrontational role with the people on behalf of the State. The police have to face criminals, extremists and violent mobs, though they are not responsible for the factors that spawn criminality, extremism and violence. They are the consequence of the omissions and commissions of the government and the general degeneration and loss of values in society.

Yet, there are many police stations where upright officers give complete protection to human rights according to the law of the land.

There is a motivated campaign by some sections that human rights violations take place only in police stations. But actually in India most serious violations of human rights take place in the following spheres:

(a) The abject failure of governance which is established by the fact that even after 55 years of independence, 26 per cent of the population (26 crores of people) are still leading a sub-human existence below the poverty line.

(b) The complete inaction of the political leadership and administration in preventing the deaths of thousands of people, mostly children, who are dying of preventable diseases for which treatment is available in the country.

(c) One third of the infants born in this country do not have adequate weight and have just half the brain capacity of normal children. That means, they will never be able to develop the capability to understand matters clearly and retain them in their memory. This is caused by the severe malnourishment of mothers who do not have access to adequate food due to poverty and ignorance.

(d) The failure of the administrators, law makers and law enforcement agencies to prevent child labour and child prostitution, even after 55 years of independence.

(e) The failure of governments to ensure universal education for the nation's children, though the Constitution stipulates that all children aged between 5 and 14 should have been given basic education by 1960.

(f) The total failure of the administration to contain corruption. In fact, corruption has been increasing year after year, sapping the vitals of the economy and society.

(g) The failure to ensure social, political and economic justice and to reduce the disparity between the 'haves' and 'have nots', which is a major source of crime, violence and extremism.

(h) The failure of the government to streamline the criminal justice system due to which hundreds and thousands of crime victims are denied after basic human rights and justice and which also makes crime a low risk, high profit business.

(i) The failure of the governments to ensure adequate development in rural areas has resulted in the violation of the human rights of 70 per cent of the population who are rural.

(j) The failure of the Criminal Justice System which is responsible for the sufferings of the nearly 80 per cent of prisoners who are under trial and who are imprisoned for unduly long periods as their trials are not concluded within a reasonable time.

(k) The failure of the administration to protect the environment and to carry out afforestation and water conservation projects which has resulted in the denial of the basic right to adequate, clean water to millions of citizens.

This is not an attempt in any way to condone or minimise the seriousness of human rights violations by the police. Such violations take place due to antiquated laws and procedures; society not discharging its responsibility in assisting the police to perform its task; improper selection, training and the poor living and working conditions of most policemen. When policemen are subjected to severe stress in a high pressure environment they are likely to indulge in human rights violations.

Over-worked policemen, who are denied the support of society and sufficient legal authority. Many have to face the unpleasant task of tackling violent mobs, who are disappointed with the omissions and commissions on the part of the government on various issues. The policemen at some point or the other are forced to use force to put down violent agitations, though they are in no way responsible for the original cause of the trouble.

Although no violations of human rights by policemen should be tolerated or excused, the fact is that much more serious violations are taking place through the acts of commissions and omissions of various other authorities and agencies.

AUTHORS INTERVIEW PUBLISHED IN A MAGAZINE

You pioneered the system of scientifically investigating crime through the Rajiv Gandhi murder case and set an example, but even today most police officers do not favour scientific methods of investigation. What do you say about this?

While investigating Rajiv Gandhi's assassination, which was a blind case to start with and the first assassination of a world leader by a human bomb, we had to use extensively all methods of investigations. Thousands of witnesses were examined and hundreds of thousands of documents and books were scrutinized. Nearly 500 video cassettes had to be examined and around a hundred thousand photographs were also seized and checked. Yet the most important evidences in the case were secured through scientific methods. All seized material were subjected to scientific examination and the information gathered was utilised for the investigation and the trial.

I do not agree with the view that most police officers do not like scientific investigation. The fact is that we do not have sufficient forensic laboratories in the country. Even where they are available, we do not have all the necessary scientific equipment. Very often trained and qualified forensic experts are not available. Hence there is an enormous backlog of work in our forensic laboratories, resulting in considerable delays in geting expert opinion. This causes undue delay in the investigation and sometimes the very purpose of investigation gets defeated.

We should have more forensic experts, equipment and laboratories so that investigating officers can get expert opinion fast enough.

Can you explain the significance of Interpol especially for a country like India? Has membership in it helped?

The Interpol (International Police Organisation) is headquartered at Lyons in France. It performs the critical role of coordinating police organisations all over the world.

India has gained a lot by being a very important and valued member of the Interpol. Lookout and Red Corner notices are issued to locate absconding criminals. Interpol has helped India in securing many wanted terrorists and criminals. Interpol also collects and disseminates information and intelligence on crime and criminals with particular reference to drug traffickers and terrorists.

Are you on the LTTE's hit list?

I have no personal knowledge on whether I am on the hit list of the LTTE and if so, at what level. We did the investigation fairly and objectively without any prejudice. The most important criminal investigation ever done in this country was based entirely on truth, physical, scientific, oral and documentary evidence. We did not have any personal reasons to hunt down any of the accused or the LTTE as an organisation.

For me, it was just pursuit of truth and discharging my duty to the nation through a fair, impartial, objective and scientific investigation. What came to light was placed before court. Having done my duty without any fear or favour according to the law, facts and truth, I leave the rest to destiny.

Don't you feel that it is the right time for India to effect police and prison reforms?

I entirely agree that for India police and prison reforms should be a high priority matter. There is a widespread opinion among top jurists that the country's criminal justice system is on the verge of collapse. If it deteriorates further, there would be anarchy. The first job of any government is to govern and in governance, the most important duty is to protect the life and property of citizens, maintain law and order and prevent and detect crimes.

Governments are increasingly failing in this *sine qua non* of governance. If society has to be saved from chaos and takeover by mafias, not only police and prison reforms but revamping of the entire criminal justice system must be given the highest priority. Otherwise no government can undertake even development activities.

How do you Assess the Indian Police?

My assessment of the Indian police is that it is an over-worked and much-maligned force. I do not say that the police is always on the right. There are wrong-doers who should be punished severely. But it would be unfair to condemn the entire police force for the arrogance, incompetence and corruption of some. By that standard, no authority, no department, no profession in this country, or for that matter anywhere else in the world can be given a good certificate.

The police is engaged in a very difficult task. They work day and night throughout the year and when others celebrate festivals. In this country over a thousand policemen and women belonging to various organisations sacrifice their lives every year while performing their duties.

I am talking about only those who get killed while fighting organised crime, extremism, insurgency and terrorism. Many more get incapacitated in some form or the other due to the difficult nature of their duties or while dealing with criminals and frustrated sections of society.

If you want to improve the functioning of the police the following steps should be taken immediately:

(i) Proper recruitment and training of police personnel.

(ii) Adequate salary and security.

(iii) Provision of housing and medical facilities.

(iv) Revision of Criminal Laws, Laws of Evidence and Criminal Procedure Code, to make item up-to-date in tune with the revised laws in other democratic countries like the USA and UK.

(v) A charter of citizen's duties which enjoins members of the public to come forward to assist the police and courts by providing information and evidence without any fear or favour.

(vi) Reform of court procedures to ensure that the guilty do not go unpunished in the anxiety of the court to ensure perfect proof of guilt.

(vii) De-politicise and professionalise police forces so that they function as servants of law and society and not as a tool in the hands of the political masters.

What do you say about the Paramilitary Forces?

Our paramilitary forces are responsible for protecting the unity and territorial integrity of this country. Central forces like the Border Security Force, Central Industrial Security Force and the Indo-Tibetan Police Force play a vital role. I am personally aware of the tremendous contributions made by the Central Reserve Police Force. During my association with the CRPF for nearly 10 years, I have seen them fighting terrorism in Punjab, Kashmir, the North-East and in the Naxalite areas of Andhra Pradesh, apart from working with the IPKF in Sri Lanka. For sheer dedication, discipline, competence and dependability they can be compared with the best in the world.

Your Comments on the Implementation of POTA?

Even when I was Director General of the National Human Rights Commission, I have openly argued the case for strong laws to tackle terrorism. I have always said that stringent provisions should be included to prevent the misuse of such laws. All violators who misuse these laws should be summarily dealt with, dismissed and even prosecuted. Even Supreme Court has said that the possibility of misuse is no excuse for not having such a law.It is clear that way every law in this country can be misused and has been misused at some time or the other. To deal with problems like the abuse of such laws the basic solution is to de-politicise the police and other law enforcement agencies. Unfortunately today people perceive the police as a tool in the hands of those in power and not as an instrument of law. If we cannot prevent misuse or abuse of such stringent provisions of anti-terrorist laws, naturally the public will demand scrapping of such laws. Without public approval, such laws will lose their legitimacy even if they are legally valid.

The increasing politicisation of the police and other instruments of governance are eroding their credibility. If such organisations do not enjoy credibility, they will not get public support and trust. Without public support, no agency of the government can effectively perform its duties. So, the first and foremost task is to make the police and other law enforcement agencies politically neutral so that they can function as enforcers of the law and not as tools in the hands of political masters.

I am happy to learn that in Kerala, a serious and sincere effort is being made to keep the police apolitical and in allowing law and order agencies to perform professionally as per the law.

11

Problems of Refugees*

Give to every human being every right that you claim for yourself.

– Robert Ingersoll, American Orator, Lawyer

It is often easier to become outraged by injustice half a world away than by oppression and discrimination half a block from home.

– Carl T. Rowan, Journalist

Refugees are a matter of global concern and it is the responsibility of the entire international community to make sincere efforts to resolve their problems, both legally and politically. In the aftermath of the Second World War, the United Nations was confronted with the tragedy of the uprootedness and exile. This led to the creation of the office of the United Nations High Commission for Refugees (UNHCR) in 1950.

Several significant events in subsequent decades in Europe, Africa and Asia resulted in millions of refugees stagnating in overcrowded camps in countries which had no capacity to absorb these growing numbers. As for the international community, with little hope for pursuing either repatriation or integration of refugees, the best that could be done in most cases was to provide humanitarian assistance to meet basic needs.

The Partition of India resulted in one of the greatest mass migration of modern history. It is estimated that at least 15 million people migrated. Dislocation of population between the two countries following independence from colonial rule is symptomatic of the paradox in which they lived together in tolerance for several centuries. The refugees had to make multiple efforts to deal with new situations and negotiate a new complex arena of societal relations and new initiatives to become self-reliant. Refugees who are outcome of a complex articulation of colonial and national power

* Presentation at a seminar on 'Refugees', convened by the *Institute of Peace and Conflict Studies*, New Delhi.

are inevitable victims of change. Their rehabilitation and assimilation in the national, political, social, economic and cultural mainstream is one of the greatest success stories of modern India.

As civil conflict, political persecution and natural disasters continue to plague many countries, millions of people are forced to live outside their countries of origin. Women and children make up the majority of the world's refugee population.

The challenge is not how to manage the refugee movements so as to balance the rights of the refugees as well as the interests of the host State in a just and humane manner. This delicate balance can best be observed by the eternal vigilance of sensitive and dedicated human rights organisations.

International protection is guaranteed to refugees for reasons of humanity. Basis of protection of refugees is found in the statute of the office of the UNHCR and the Refugee Conventions.

UNHCR was established by General Assembly of United Nations as a subsidiary organ under Article 22 of the United Nations Charter and the body continues to play an active role and expanding the mandate of the office. UNHCR does enjoy international personality. As a subsidiary organ of the General Assembly, its "Personality" can be traced to the United Nations at large. Moreover, its statute shows that the office was entrusted by the General Assembly to act on the international plane.

Its standing in regard to protection has been further re-enforced by successive General Assembly resolutions urging all states to support the High Commissioner's activities. The UNHCR's statute mandates that it has to work with non-government agencies. It works with hundreds of NGOs throughout the world like CARE and Save the Children.

Over the past four decades, UNHCR's traditional protection role has become much broader in scope and significantly more operational. At the same time, its focus is equally on protection in States of asylums of refugees and the activities in countries of origin.

Human instincts undoubtedly propel people to assist others in need since the dawn of civilisation. Today the process of providing humanitarian assistance has became a highly organised enterprise involving law and regulations, defined roles and vested interests, major political implications, international organisations and large sums of money.

Nevertheless, refugee assistance efforts remain heavily imbued with idealism and humanitarian motivation, particularly noticeable in private religions and charitable agencies. The concept of rescuing victims of persecution and violence is central to this motivation.

Magnitude in South Asia

It is estimated that South Asia has over 1.3 million refugees. Though these regions have been following a generous tradition of receiving refugees and looking after them, none of these countries is a party to the 1951 Convention relating to the Status of Refugees or its 1967 Protocol.

At the end of 2000, over 3.6 million Afghans were living as refugees in other countries. Over 13,000 Afghan refugees were in India.

At the end of 2000, Bangladesh hosted over 1,21,600 refugees.

An estimated 1,44,0000 persons from Bhutan were living as refugees in neighbouring countries including 1,29,000 and more than 13,000 in India.

At the end of the year 2000, more than 300,000 refugees were living in India. This included 110,000 from Tibet, 110,000 from Sri Lanka, 42,000 from Bhutan, 30,000 from Afghanistan and more than 300 from another countries. Another 40,000 Afghans were living in India in refugee-like condition.

Over 500,000 people were internally displaced in India because of political violence including 3,50,000 Kashmiris and more than 1,57,000 others in North-East India.

The 17 years conflict between Sri Lanka Sinhalese – Buddhist majority and Tamil-Hindu minority has resulted in over 110,000 Sri Lankan Tamils fleeing into India.

The number of Tibetan refugees in India keeps fluctuating because of deaths, births and arrival of an additional 2000 to 3000 refugees from Tibet each year.

More than 40,000 ethnic Chin and 1000 ethnic Naga refugees from Burma were living in North Eastern States of India.

None of the South Asian countries have any national laws on refugees. Governments have dealt with refugee problems through bilateral negotiations.

Refugees and asylum seekers in the region are treated like any other foreigners and are subjected to the laws and regulations governing the entry, stay and departure of foreigners. Obviously the provisions of the Foreigners Act will not be adequate to meet the humanitarian and basic need of refugees.

The seminar organised by SAARCLAW in collaboration with the UNHCR examined the situation of refugees in the region. Most participants supported the need for refugee laws. They also acknowledged the need for finding a humanitarian solution.

As observed by the Chief of Mission, UNHCR, New Delhi, the fundamental legal issues concerning the rights and obligations of both refugees and governments need to be addressed concurrently with the political aspects of a refugee problem. International refugee law was concerned both with protecting the rights of refugees as well as solving refugee problems.

While the country of asylum had the obligation to protect refugees, the country of origin had the obligation to create conditions so that refugees can return to their homes in safety.

The lack of a legal procedure to distinguish between illegal immigrants and refugees had resulted in increasing confusion of the two in the popular mind, thus straining the tradition of hospitality in the region.

There is a close relationship between the violation of human rights and the refugee situation. In addition to persons who fled their homes because of violation of human rights, others who were forced to leave on account of man-made disasters, conflict situations, and poverty should also be classified as refugees.

India was not a signatory to either 1951 UN Convention or its 1965 Protocol, obviously because these conventions stressed on the rights of refugees only, thus placing disproportionate obligations on refugee-receiving States. India has offered safety and security to hundreds of thousands of victims of ethnic conflict in the last 55 years.

Most of the causes for mass exodus are due to human rights violations and such mass migration gave rise to human rights problems.

Hence, it has to be borne in mind that refugee law was part of the broader spectrum of International Human Rights Law.

Refugee legislation is imperative to avoid adhoc and delayed decisions. Such legal framework has to reconcile the conflicting interests of the receiving countries and the refugees.

As Pandit Jawaharlal Nehru once said, "The Rule of Law must strengthen the Rule of Life."

While asylum may not be a final solution to problems of refugees it was an essential component of refugee protection.

One of the reasons for some Asian countries not being signatory to 1951 convention or its 1961 protocol is that these countries are not in a position to guarantee all the socio-economic rights of refugees as granted by these instruments.

However, India has always supported the basic principles that UNHCR stands for. This is obvious in the way India treated Tibetan, Sri Lankan and Chakma refugees.

The Supreme Court of India has played a singular contribution in extending the rights of both citizens and aliens by imposing corresponding obligation on the state.

A common refugee legislation of SAARC region would also need to be accompanied by clear citizenship laws for the region.

The problem of refugees, as stated by the eminent jurist Justice Shri P.N. Bhagwati, is a global one. It is the developing countries which continue to bear the major share of refugee inflows and are called upon to host large refugees and migrant populations. They find themselves overwhelmed by the burden imposed with scarce resources and energy diverted from their primary responsibilities of meeting the developmental needs of their own people. Their environment stands devastated, resources eroded, economy disrupted, law and order threatened and sometimes even their hospitality abused.

Social, economic and ethnic tension caused by their presence in areas where life is a perpetual struggle for existence by the locals themselves, result in widespread demands for expulsions of refugees and sometimes even for crossing of borders.

India has the problems of Chakma refugees from Bangladesh, Tamil refugees from Sri Lanka, Tibetan refugees, Bhutanese refugees, Arakanese refugees from Myanmar and refugees from some other countries as well. Virtually no country in South Asia has been free from the problem of the refugees.

When large number of people move across an international border, it is not usually possible to ascertain whether every person involved strictly meets the criteria of refugee status. Low-income countries simply do not have the logistical and administrative resources for such demanding and delicate tasks.

Countries of asylum have an obligation to ensure that the refugees are assured of the widest possible exercise of all basic human rights affirmed in the UN Charter, the Universal declaration of human rights and the terms of the 1951 conventions.

The refugees in turn are required to abide by the laws and regulations of the country which has granted them asylum and conform to any measures taken for the maintenance of public order.

The problem of forced displacement has become considerably larger and more complex over the last decade. But the number of refugees has actually declined in recent times; from 18.2 million in 1993 to 213.3 million at the beginning of 1997. Reduction in refugees number can be attributed to the succession of large-scale repatriation movements which have taken place since 1990s.

Article 1 of the statute provides that UNHCR "Shall Assume the function of providing international protection under the auspices of the United Nations to refugees who fall within the scope of the present statute."

Besides the Refugee Convention of 1951 and additional protocol of 1967, there are a number of regional conventions further expanding the definitions and rights of refugees to meet the peculiar regional conditions.

Prevention of migration of refugees does not mean building barriers to stop refugees from entering the country but tackling the causes, which compel people to move. In seeking to prevent refugee movements, equal emphasis must also be placed on the economic and social conditions in which people live. Meeting priority human needs, introducing job criteria, poverty alleviation, education and health, can help to reduce some of the pressures, which lead to unrest, and social upheaval, which in turn may result in refugee flow.

Given the reality, most refugees both originate from and seek refugee status in some of the poorest parts of the world. Neither the country of origin nor the country of asylum can be expected to discharge their respective responsibilities without the political and financial support of the international community.

In the final analysis, refugees are symptoms of the deeper social, economic and political problems. The challenge is not how to keep people away but how to meet the needs of the victims and communities which receive them, how to manage refugees in a way which have all basic human rights while addressing the concerns of the State of asylum.

Solving refugee problem involves aspects of human rights, charity, immigration services, religious services, developments, education, advocacy and a host of support and other functions.

Thus, the NGOs including human rights organisations play a crucial role in understanding, dealing with and solving the refugee problems at every stage. No element has been more vital to the successive conduct of the programmes of the UNHCR in resolving the refugee problem than the close partnership between UNHCR and the voluntary agencies. Such agencies act as agents of private conscience and have become a permanent factor in refugee work since the last eight decades. The growing recognition of the role of NGOs and other human rights organisations in protecting and resolving the refugee problems requires their enhanced participation in dialogue with governments and national and State level Human Rights Commissions.

Internally Displaced Persons

An estimated 1,60,000 persons of various ethnicities were displaced in several parts of North-East India. This geographically and to some extent politically isolated area of India is home to many tribal groups.

The displaced populations include an estimated 87,000 ethnic Santhals in Assam; 3500 Bengalis in Assam; 37,000 ethnics displaced from Mizoram into Tripura; 25,000 Bengalis in Tripura, and 3000 ethnic Chakmas in Arunachal Pradesh.

As many as 3,50,000 Kashmiris, mostly Hindu Pundits, have been displaced since 1990 as a result of long-standing conflict in Kashmir. Nearly 2,50,000 displaced Kashmiris are living near the city in Jammu, both in the camps and in their homes. An estimated 100,000 Kashmiris are displaced elsewhere in India, primarily in the New Delhi areas.

Many displaced pundits receive cash assistance and food aid from the Government of India. Former government workers continue to receive full salaries or retirement benefits. Nevertheles, some displaced Kashmiris complain that the government assistance is inadequate.

According to UNHCR more than 600,000 Sri Lankans were internally displaced. Another 110,000 Sri Lankans have come to India as refugees. Most Sri Lankan refugees and displaced persons were Hindu Tamils, although Muslims and some Buddhist Sinhalese were also displaced. Sri Lanka hosted only 16 refugees, mostly Iraqis and Afghans.

Sri Lankan refugees and displaced persons have been engaged

in a bloody 17 year conflict that has claimed more than 62,000 lives. The conflict is between government forces that primarily represent Sri Lanka's Buddhists, Sinhalese majority and the LTTE.

An estimated 15,000 Lhotshampa ethnic Nepalese refugees from Bhutan are living in India. Most are located in West Bengal and Assam States. Under the terms of the Indo-Bhutan Friendship Treaty of 1950, India allows Bhutanese to live and work freely in India. Therefore, the Government does not acknowledge the Bhutanese as refugees, neither assisting them nor requiring them to live in the camps. Nearly 14,000 UNHCR-recognised refugees lived in urban sectors in India, mostly in New Delhi. At the end of the year 2000, a large majority (13,000) were from Afghanistan, smaller number came from Burma, Iran and Somalia. According to Indian refugee advocates, more than 40,000 other Afghans may be living in India in refugee-like circumstances.

In dealing with refugee problem, the Human Rights Organisations and Human Rights Commissions have a vital role to play. It is both in the sphere of preventing exodus of the refugees from the home state and also in looking after the essential needs and welfare of the refugees in the asylum States.

According to the United Nations High Commission for Refugee (UNHCR)—

"Human Rights violations are a major factor in causing the plight of refugees as well as an obstacle to their safe and voluntary return home. Safeguarding Human Rights in countries of origin is therefore critical both for the prevention and for the solution of refugee problems. Respect for Human Rights is also essential for the protection of refugees in countries of asylum".

Even in the absence of specific legislation refugees are entitled for enjoyment and protection of human rights, a large number of which are enshrined in major International and Regional Human Rights instruments and national constitutions. For instance is the right of religions freedom—the freedom to hold and express opinions—the freedom to organise and participate in public gathering.

Under International Human Rights Law, all of these rights are guaranteed to both citizens and non-citizens. The Human Rights committee has explicitly stated that "Aliens have the right to freedom of thought, conscience and religion and the right to hold opinions and to express them. Aliens receive the benefit of the right of peaceful assembly and of freedom of association. Of course all these rights are subject to certain limitations."

Some of the international instruments constituting International Human Rights Law are—

1. Universal Declaration of Human Rights.
2. International Convention of Civil and Political Rights.
3. Convention on the Right of the Child.
4. European Convention for the Protection of Human Rights.
5. American declaration of the rights and the duties of men.
6. Declaration on the Elimination of All Forms of Intolerance and Discrimination based on Religion and Belief.

India has been a receiving State since centuries and has throughout its history welcomed all to come to its land and absorb them and refugees as part of the people of India. They have mingled, merged and got lost in one common humanity. But all this has been done as a matter of policy without any specific legislation. Even in the absence of legislation, India has always respected the Principle of Non-Refoulment. It is only when the security of the State is threatened or law and order is endangered that India has been compelled to impose some restrictions on refugees. However, bona fide asylum seekers have always been recognised and protected.

India has acceded to or signed most of the major international human rights instruments, many provisions of which are complementary to the protection of refugees. The Convention on the Elimination of all Forms of Racial Discrimination was ratified in 1969. In 1979, India acceded to the International Covenant on Civil and Political Rights and the International Covenant on the Economic, Social and Cultural Rights (1986). In 1992, India acceded to the Convention on the Rights of the Child (1989). The Convention on the Elimination of all Forms of Discrimination against women (1979) ratified in 1993 and in 1997, India signed the Convention against Torture.

However, there is no specific legislation dealing with the problems of refugees. These problems are dealt with by India and all other countries of South Asia on a purely *ad hoc* basis. This is purely due to a growing concern that persons who may have committed crime against humanity, war crimes or other acts which are incompatible with the humanitarian nature of refugee status, may enter and remain on the Indian soil under the pretext of being refugees. There is real concern that persons who may have committed crimes against humanity, war crimes or other acts which are incompatible with the humanitarian nature of refugees status, may be able to enter and remain in an asylum country. It is necessary to emphasize that the absence of specific refugee laws and procedures may put the state at a disadvantage in reaching a proper decision regarding determination.

Role of Judiciary

Despite the absence of a formal legal instrument, the Judiciary in India has played a major role in safeguarding the rights of refugees and asylum seekers. Indeed some Indian Judicial pronouncements have enshrined principles on the right to seek asylum, Non-Refoulment and Voluntary Repatriation. The courts have arrived at their decisions without specifying or entering in a discussion on International Refugee Law. They have relied on applicability. Article 21 (Right to Live and Liberty) of the Indians constitution and have held that Article 21 is applicable to refugees.

The decision of the apex court regarding the treatment of foreigners enunciated that foreigners are entitled to protection under Article 21. Where there was imminent danger to Chakma refugees, the state was directed to ensure the rights and liberty of each and every one of them (*NHRC* vs *State of Arunachal Pradesh* 1996).

Article 51C in Part IV of the Constitution provides that the state was enjoined to foster respect to International law and treatment applications. The apex court does require the governments and courts to apply principles of interpretation that promote further and not hinder the aspirations of Part IV of the Constitution.

The courts in India have laid down guidelines in the area of refugee protection by reading Article 21 in its expansive signification in the light of the Directive Principles of State Policy.

When Chakma refugees were being threatened with deportation, the National Human Rights Commission of India took the case to Supreme Court. National Human Rights Commission also sent its team to examine the conditions in the refugee camps and made appropriate recommendations to the concerned Governments.

As the foundation of the refugee problem rested on human rights violations in the home country, appropriate measures are required to address these problems and to restore normalcy for ensuring effective repatriations. Minimum standards of treatment should be prescribed, a mechanism for redressal should be created. When these standards are not met, the country of origin should be held accountable for any refugee exodus.

There is a need for promoting awareness of international refugee laws and standards. To ensure clarity, certainty and uniformity in substance and procedure, the several refugee related ordinances issued from time to time should be codified, complied by the authorities, the human rights organisations and the public should be sensitized on various issues pertaining to the refugees.

Clear provisions should be included on the protection of refugee women and children as well as their safe and voluntary repatriation.

For a human problem, the solution has to be one of humanism. Hence, the legal framework has to be found from human rights.

In any civilized society, any human problem or any number or group of humanity is a matter of common concern. Hence the problem of refugees cannot be viewed in isolation. Therefore, the legal framework which has got to be built not only should take care and provide for the protection, welfare, rehabilitation and repatriation of the refugees, but also reconcile the conflicting interests of the receiving country. The basic cause for this problem is human rights abuse. Human rights are claims, which every individual has, or should have upon the society in which he or she lives. They are universal and are the due of every human being in every society. They do not differ with the country, culture, ideology or with any political or economic systems. They do not depend on gender, race, class or status. They need not be earned or deserved. They are claims as of rights, not merely appeals to grace or charity or brotherhood or love. They are claims of entitlement and the corresponding obligation is on the political and administrative institutions.

The basic human rights being inherent, they need not specifically be conferred by any constitution or an act or law. What the constitution or any specific law does is merely to recognise its existence and provide the machinery for protection of these rights and enforcement, whenever there is need for it.

The 1951 convention relating to the status of refugees and the 1961 protocol have to be given legal sanction by enacting domestic laws which can be enforced in national courts.

Mere enactment of a law is not enogh. Enactment of a law

which is more readily acceptable is more effective. The existing position is that it is only to the extent that national courts can provide relief that it has been possible to do it.

The premise on which the judiciary has been acting to protect the interest of the refugees so far is that the basic human rights are supposed to be implied in every civilized system, and therefore unless there is an inconsistent provision in the domestic laws, basic human rights have been read into the provisions of the constitution and other enacted laws.

Therefore, it is as a result of judicial creativity, certain basic rights of the refugees have been taken care of through the medium of the courts.

In India the apex court has held that certain basic rights like the right to equality (Article 14), right to life and liberty (Article 21), and freedom to practice and propagate in own religion (Article 25), are available to non-citizen refugees as well.

Due to the creativity and humanistic interpretation, the rights of citizens as well as non-citizens have been expanded by the courts.

Role of NHRC

In the North-East frontier states when quit notices were issued to refugees by an activist students organisation, the Supreme Court granted relief when NHRC approached the Supreme Court under Article 32.

The National Alliance of People's Movement submitted a petition before the NHRC seeking its intervention in the matter relating to alleged human rights violations of the Bargi Dam Ousties in Madhya Pradesh. Later the Commission sent a team for an on-the-spot study. The Commission recommended to the Ministry of Rural Development, Government of India, that at policy level the Central and State governments should re-examine and appropriately amend laws, regulations and practices in order to ensure that when it comes to acquisition of land for purposes related to national economic development, the provisions of the Constitution, pronouncements of the Supreme Court and as contained in International Instruments in which India is a party, should be fully respected. The government has reported to the Commission that a National Policy on Resettlement and Rehabilitation for displaced persons was under consideration at the highest levels of the Government. The Human Rights organisations brought to the notice of the Commission that the Land Acquisition Act 1984, which is still in force today, does not contain any provision for rehabilitation and therefore, this is a grave violation of the human rights of the displaced persons who depend for their livelihood on the land and other resources. The Commission considered the issue in depth and recommended that adequate provisions for resettlement and rehabilitation of persons displaced in land acquisition for various projects should be incorporated in the Land Acquisition Act itself. Ministry of Rural Development was advised to incorporate the rehabilitation and resettlement package in the Land Acquisition Act itself for the following reasons:

1. I.L.O. Convention to which India is a party, provides for the protection of rights of indigenous and tribal people;
2. Incorporation of rehabilitation and resettlement (R&R) package in the law will ensure R&R of Project Affected People in a systematic manner;
3. The provisions of R&R in the law will avoid litigation, at times frivolous, in the manner, which would help in avoidance of delays and cost overrun of the projects;
4. Once the R&R package is provided in the law, there will be uniformity in dealing with the cases by the Court and would avoid lack of uniformity in interference by the Courts;
5. The R&R facilities should be provided in advance before actual acquisition of land takes place;
6. The Commission had noted in a number of cases that excess land is being acquired and no consultation takes place with the people likely to be affected by the acquisition of land. A properly drawn project document with estimates of expenditure involved in R&R would avoid acquisition of excess land.
7. For the purpose of transparency and information of the people likely to be affected by the Project, a Committee consisting of representatives of Government, the industry/agency for which land is proposed to be acquired and the project affected people, as is the practice in USA, may have detailed consultations before acquisition of land.

The NHRC has done valuable work in addressing the plight of refugees in specific cases like Chakmas and the Srilankan Tamils. The Commission has also made several recommendations to the

Central and State governments to relieve distress and plight of internally displaced persons like Kashmiri Pandits and also those who were displaced and dislocated by major irrigation projects.

I myself conducted an investigation as Director General in the National Human Rights Commission into the enormous problems faced by thousands of persons who were dislocated and uprooted due to the huge naval project called SEABIRD on the Karwar coast. I reported several inadequacies in the rehabilitation arrangements. The Commission directed the Government of India and Karnataka Government to pay adequate compensation to every displaced person and also adopt several other measures to improve the lives of the displaced persons and their families.

Where necessary, the NHRC has taken the issue to Supreme Court as was done in *NHRC* Vs *State of Arunachal Pradesh*.

The important role which can be played by the Human Rights Commissions and Organisations need to be appreciated and encouraged. Of course, the role of institutions like the Human Rights Commission and the Judiciary are basically remedial. However, when NHRC and State Human Rights Commissions lay down guidelines, they are also for the benefit of the authorities for strict implementation to prevent suffering by such displaced persons in future.

12

Constitutional Safeguards to Human Rights*

The Framers of the Bill of Rights did not purport to "create" rights. Rather, they designed the Bill of Rights to prohibit our Government from infringing rights and liberties presumed to be preexisting.

—Justice William J. Brennan, Judge US Supreme Court (1956-1990)

Several aspects of human rights are covered by Parts III and IV of the Indian Constitution. It is considered as a Social Document. Some of the Articles are worth mentioning.

Article 14 states that "the State shall not deny to any person equality before the law and equal protection of the laws within the territory of India." Article 15 states, "(1) The State shall not discriminate against any citizen on grounds only of religion, race, caste, sex, place of birth or any of them. (2) No citizen shall on grounds only of religion, race, caste, sex, place of birth or any of them be subject to any disability, liability, restriction or condition with regard to (a) access to shops, public restaurants, hotels and places of public entertainment." Article 16 states that "(1) there shall be equality of opportunity for all citizens in matters relating to employment or appointment to any office under the State."

Article 19 states that "(1) All citizens shall have the right—

(a) to freedom of speech and expression;
(b) to assemble peacefully and without arms;
(c) to form associations or unions;
(d) to move freely throughout the territory of India;
(e) to reside and settle in any part of the territory of India; and
(f) to practice any profession or to carry on any occupation, trade or business."

* From a talk at the seminar organised by Human Rights Organisation at Pondicherry.

Article 20 states, "No person shall be convicted of any offence except for violation of a law in force at the time of the commission of the act charged as an offence, nor be subjected to a penalty greater than that which might have been inflicted under the law in force at the time of the commission of the offence." Article 21, the most important article of all in the Fundamental Rights section, states that "no person shall be deprived of his life or personal liberty except according to the procedure established by law."

All of the above-mentioned Articles of the Indian Constitution come under the Fundamental Rights guaranteed by the State. Article 32 provides that, if any of the above Fundamental Rights are violated, one has the right to call on the Supreme Court directly. Thus the above-mentioned articles form the bedrock of human rights, guaranteed by the Indian Constitution.

In addition there are a number of other rights, which come under the "Directive Principles of the State Policy." Though these rights are not enforceable like the Fundamental Rights, they provide guidelines for the States to follow these principles in legislating and implementing laws. These rights focus on the following:

- Providing adequate means of livelihood. [Article 39(A)];
- Equal pay for equal work for both men and women. [Article 39(d)];
- Adequate protection of the health and strength of workers, men and women [Article 39(e)];
- Equal justice and free legal aid [Article 39(a)]
- Living wage, conditions of work ensuring a decent standard of life and full enjoyment of leisure and social and cultural opportunities. [Article 43];
- Free and compulsory education for children [Article 45];
- Increasing the level of nutrition and the standard and the improvement of public health. [Article 47];
- Prohibiting the slaughter of cows and calves and other milk and draught cattle [Article 48].

Main categories of Human Rights abuses are social-untouchability, dowry, atrocities against women etc. While the Hindu religion at its inception has no such discrimination or distinction, over a period of time these distortions crept in a physically and economically male dominated society. The second category is economic—child labour, violence related to economic factors, for example, the naxal violence, etc, are the result of economic subjugation and exploitation of the dominant classes in the society over the weaker sections. The third major category is political—denial and/or abrogation of fundamental rights. These rights are denied by the politically dominant sections to perpetuate their suzerainty and to enslave the weaker sections of the society.

All these and related abuses can be remedied in various degrees in different parts of the country by enactment of laws, by making the procedure simpler and by enhancing the punishments; by granting financial relief to the victims; and by creating awareness among the society on the nature of human rights violations.

Colonial mindset still exists in certain sections of bureauracy, law enforcing agencies and even among the civil society. Loopholes exist in law and procedure. Powerful elements do exploit the existing ineffective investigation and undue delay in judicial trials. Political power and ill gotten wealth sometimes impedes the course of investigation of rendering justice. Poverty and ignorance on the part of victims very often disables them from seeking relief.

With the increase in literacy, even in rural areas and with the reduction of poverty and hunger, with changes being brought in laws and procedures in investigation, trials of human rights violations, with decentralisation and devolution of economic and political power from centre to the state, from state to districts and from district to villages—there will be reduction of human rights in all forms.

It is obvious, though this process is slow—but steady and before long the society will reach a situation where there will be "All Human Rights For All."

13

Institutional Safeguards to Human Right*

No man is above the law and no man below it.

– Theodore Roosevelt

In India, the Judiciary plays a leading role in protecting and enhancing human rights. Broadly speaking, the judiciary plays the following major functions in protecting human rights. First, it ensures that the human rights are not violated legally. Article 32 of the Indian Constitution confers the enforcement of fundamental rights on the Supreme Court. Under Article 32, every citizen has a right to request the Supreme Court directly to enforce the Fundamental Rights. The Supreme Court has the power to issue orders or writs in the nature of *habeas corpus, mandamus,* prohibition and certiorari, whichever may be appropriate. This power to issue writs has been used extensively by both the Supreme Courts and the High Courts.

Second, the Judiciary has interpreted the Constitution in various cases, expanding the scope of human rights in India. Some of the cases and their judgment are worth mentioning. In *Francis Coralis Mullin v Administrator, Union Territory of Delhi* (1981), the Supreme Court of India observed that,

"The right to life includes the right to live with human dignity and all that goes alongwith it, namely the bare necessaries of life such as adequate nutrition, clothing and shelter and facilities for reading, writing and expressing oneself in diverse forms, freely moving about and mixing and commingling with fellow human beings."

In *Bandhuva Mukti Morcha* v *Union of India* (1984), the Supreme Court expressed that,

"... Right to life with human dignity... must include protection

---

Gist of a Memorial Lecture by AJ Coimbatore Bar Association.

> of the health and strength of workers, men and women, and of the tender age of children against abuse, opportunities and facilities for children to develop in a healthy manner and in conditions of freedom and dignity, educational facilities, just and humane conditions of work and maternity relief. These are the minimum requirements which must exist in order to enable a person to live with human dignity and no state—neither the Central Government nor any State government—has the right to any action which will deprive a person of the enjoyment of basic essentials."

The governments do face problems in achieving these ideals due to social and economic backwardness of the nation and its huge population. Though these are ideals and the state is attempting to reach that ideal, like any society, there are always some shortfalls which need to be taken into consideration.

In another judgment in *Consumer Education and Research Centre v Union of India,* the Supreme Court held that,

"'Right to life' in Article 21 includes protection of health and the strength of the worker. The expression 'life' in Article 21 does not connote mere animal existence. It has a much wider meaning, which includes right to livelihood, better standard of life, hygienic conditions in workplace and leisure."

Fighting Human Rights Violations in India

Human rights violations, whether perpetrated by state actors or non-state entities, are being countered by three major agencies; the National Human Rights Commission and the State Human Rights Commissions funded by the State, Non-Governmental Organisations and the Judiciary.

The National Human Rights Commission (NHRC)

The National Human Rights Commission (NHRC) was established by legislation—the Protection of Human Rights Act 1993. The main objective of the NHRC is to protect human rights by inquiring into specific complaints of human rights violations and to provide human rights education. Though the NHRC is instituted by the government, its autonomy has been ensured through the following provisions. First, the Chairperson and the members of the NHRC are appointed by the President of India from persons recommended by a committee, which consists of the Prime Minister, Speaker of the House of the People, Leader of the Opposition in the

Lower and Upper Houses, Minister of Home Affairs and the Deputy Chairman of the Council of States. Second, the member of the NHRC can be removed only by the order of the President of India on the grounds of proved misbehaviour or incapacity. Third, the members have a fixed tenure – they are elected for a period of five years.

The main functions of the NHRC include the following:

- Inquiring *suo moto* or on petition presented to it by a victim or any person on behalf of victims on complaints of human rights violations;
- Reviewing factors that curtail the enjoyment of human rights acts such as terrorism and giving recommendations;
- Reviewing the provisions in the Indian Constitution that protect Human Rights;
- Studying international treaties and documents and ensuring their effective implementation;
- Undertaking research to promote human rights in India;
- Promoting human rights awareness.

In the last eight years of its existence, the NHRC has issued a number of directives and guidelines to the government, especially in the following areas:

- Misuse of police power, especially arbitrary arrests;
- Elimination of child labour;
- Compulsory education;
- Setting up human rights cells in state and city police headquarters;
- Prison reforms;
- Caste and communal violence.

One of the major limitations of the NHRC has been that its scope of investigation does not include human rights violations by the armed forces. Besides, the success of the governments in applying the recommendations made by the NHRC is varying, due to economic and social factors that have been discussed before.

State Human Rights Commissions

The Protection of Human Rights Act, 1993 also provides for the establishment of State Human Rights Commissions (SHRC). The SHRC is to consist of a Chairperson, who has been a Chief Justice of a High Court, one member who is/has been a Judge of a High Court, one member who is/has been a district judge in that State and two members from persons having knowledge of human rights. The SHRCs are to inquire into matters related with List II and III of the Seventh Schedule to the Indian Constitution.

Like that of the NHRC, the members of the SHRCs are appointed by a committee consisting of the Chief Minister of the State, Speaker of the Legislative Assembly, Minister of Development of Home, Leaders of the Opposition in the Legislative Council and Assembly and Chairman of the Legislative Council. The Governor appoints the members. The members are appointed for a fixed period of five years and can be removed by the Governor only on the grounds of misbehaviour or incapacity. This strengthens the autonomy of the SHRCs. The effectiveness of the SHRC depends upon its structure, its chairman and the members. The responsibilities of the Chief Minister, who heads the State governments, also play a crucial part in making the SHRC effective. Besides the success of a SHRC also depends on the public awareness and the role that society could play led by the media and voluntary organisations.

At present only 12 of 28 states in India have established SHRCs.

Other Human Rights Commissions

Besides the NHRC and the SHRCs, there are other commissions, whose functions involve protecting human rights in India.

National Commission for Women (NCW)

Set up in January 1992 under the National Commission for Women Act, 1990, the National Commission for Women consists of a Chairman and five other members. The main functions of the NCW include the following:

- Examining issues relating to the safeguards provided for women under the Constitution and other laws;
- Providing reports to the Central Government on the working of safeguards provided for women under the Constitution;
- Recommending measures to implement the safeguards effectively by the Union or any state;
- Taking up cases of violation of the provisions of the Constitutions and of other laws relating to women with the appropriate authorities;
- Looking into complaints relating to the deprivation of women's rights; non-implementation of laws enacted to provide protection to women and also to achieve the

objectives of equality and development; and non-compliance of policy decisions, guidelines or instructions aimed at mitigating hardship and ensuring the welfare of and providing relief to women.

National Commission for Minorities (NCM)

The National Commission for Minorities was set up in 1992 under the National Commission for Minorities Act. The objectives of the NCM include:

- Evaluating the progress of the development of minorities in India;
- Monitoring the working of the safeguards in regard to minorities provided in the Constitution and in laws enacted by Parliament and the State Legislatures;
- Recommending effective implementation of safeguards for the protection of the interests of minorities by the Central Government or the State Governments;
- Focusing on specific complaints regarding deprivation of rights and safeguards of minorities;
- Suggesting appropriate measures in respect of any minority to be undertaken by the Central Government or the State Governments.

National Commission for Scheduled Castes and Scheduled Tribes

The National Commission for Scheduled Castes and Scheduled Tribes was originally formed as the Commission for Scheduled Castes and Scheduled Tribes in 1978. Its functions include the following:

- Monitoring issues related to the safeguards provided for SC/STs under the Constitution;
- Enquiring into specific complaints with respect to the deprivation of rights and safeguards of SC/STs;
- Reporting to the President regarding the working of these safeguards;
- Recommending measures that should be taken by the Union or any state for the effective implementation of these safeguards and other measures for the protection, welfare and socio-economic development of SC/STs.

Non-Governmental Organisations

Besides commissions established by the government at the Union and State levels, a number of NGOs function at the national and regional levels to protect human rights and protest against their violations. There are at least three major NGOs – People's Union for Civil Liberties (PUCL), People's Union for Democratic Rights (PUDR) and Citizens for Democracy.

People's Union for Civil Liberties (PUCL)

The PUCL was originally founded as the People's Union for Civil Liberties and Democratic Rights (PUCLDR) in 1976 by Jayprakash Narayanan. The objective was to make the PUCLDR free from political ideologies, so that people belonging to different groups and parties would come together to fight for civil liberties and human rights. PUCL, in its present form, came into existence after a conference held in November 1980. A new Constitution was drafted and adopted at the conference. This made the PUCL a membership-based organisation, aiming to have branches all over the country.

The PUCL had set up units in various states, for example in Delhi, Bombay, Bihar, Madhya Pradesh, Allahabad, etc., and efforts are being undertaken to establish units in other states.

The PUCL is actively involved in fighting human rights violations, whether by the state or non-state actors. It has constituted a number of Fact-Finding Missions to investigate human rights violations. The PUCL has published the following reports, which are mostly based on its fact-finding missions.

- The Banjhi Massacre: Report of Fact Finding Team;
- Fact Finding Report: Kidnapping in Bihar;
- Who are the guilty? Report of a joint inquiry into the causes and impact of the anti-Sikh violence in Delhi from 31 October to 10 November 1984;
- Black Laws – 1984-85;
- Death in Ranchi Mental Asylum;
- Report on Police Firing on workers at Abhanpur;
- Brutal Attacks on Social Workers by Jungle Mafia in Chhattisgarh, 1995;
- Report on Police Firing in Mahendragarh, Haryana, 1997;
- "Democratic" Elections in Bihar: Report to the Nation on Banka By-election 1986;

- Justice Denied: Report on communal incidents in Meerut, UP, 1987;
- Kashmir: A Report to the Nation, 1993;
- Status of Human Rights in India: Report on Charaar-e-Shareef;
- Report on Communal Incidents at Meerut, April-May, 1987.

People's Union for Democratic Rights (PUDR)

PUDR is another offshoot of People's Union for Civil Liberties and Democratic Rights (PUCLDR). Like the PUCL, the PUDR has also been involved in a number of fact-finding missions and reports related to social, economic and political issues. In particular, the PUDR focuses on police atrocities and encounter deaths. [Encounter deaths refer to those deaths that occur in clashes with the police. While the police claims all such deaths due to self-defence, very often the NGOs claim that such deaths are "false encounters" meaning that innocent, unarmed persons were killed unjustifiably by the police. Very often a judicial or administrative enquiry is ordered by the government to establish whether the death is due to "genuine encounter" which is justified under the law.]

The PUDR reports include the following:

- Dead. Hence Guilty. *"Encounter" at Bhawanipur and its Aftermath,* April 2001;
- Not Another Terrorist Law Please: A Critique of the Proposed Prevention of Terrorism Bill, Delhi, July 2000;
- The Company They Keep: A Report on Workers of Jhalani Tools Ltd., Faridabad, November 1997;
- Bloody Sunday: Brutal Attack on Jamia Students, May 2000;
- Report of the All India Fact-Finding Team into the Human Rights Situation in Jammu and Kashmir, June 2001.

14
Judicial Activism*

I would remind you that extremism in the defense of liberty is no vice! And let me remind you also that moderation in the pursuit of justice is no virtue.
- Barry Goldwater, Former five time US Senator.

The Magna Carta says "Justice delayed is Justice denied." If regular courts showed urgency, special ones would be unnecessary. Judicial activism has to be matched by judicial accountability. The extent of judicial activism, how far the court should go in interfering the executive decisions, is a critical factor in determining the success of democracy. There have been instances where the executive did not have the political courage to take a decision and passed on the issue with both its limitation and strong points to the Supreme Court.

The most remarkable effect of PIL has been upon the judicial process itself. Access to justice has been made far easier.

The Supreme Court set the parameters for judicial action in these words:

> "It is only when Courts are apprised of gross violation of fundamental rights by a Court or cross section or when basic human rights are invaded or when there are complaints, such acts have to shock the judicial conscious that the Courts, should leave aside procedural shutters and hear such petitions and extend its jurisdiction and under all available provisions for rewarding the hardships and misery of the needy, the underdog and the neglect. It will be significant to none for extending help when such help is required. But this does not mean that the doors of this Court are always opened for anyone to walk in. It is necessary to have some self-imposed restraints of public interest litigants."

There is no more cruel tyranny than that which is perpetuated under the shield of law and in the name of justice (Barron - De

* Gist of Talk at a gathering of Judges and Lawyers at Coimbatore.

Montesque). Activism, as is commonly understood connotes a policy of vigorous action in pursuit of a cause.

In such case there is a Legislative entry so as to implement a special directive for taking action in support of the cause. Though the directives cannot override the fundamental rights, in determining the scope and ambit of the fundamental rights, the court should adopt the principle of harmonious construction so as to give effect to both as much as possible - reading the Directive Principles into the Fundamental Rights.

Law is meant to render justice and hence it has to be dynamic and change with the needs of the society. In the words of Justice O. Chennappa Reddy, "the Judiciary assiduously upheld Fundamental Rights and would not even look on the Directive Principles of the State Policy on the ground that they were not justiciable. Later, they would look at them and lament that they were not justiciable. They would occasionally refer to the Directive Principles of State Policy. In recent times, the judicial attitude has changed enormously. The Supreme Court has not only expanded the scope of various Articles but also expanded the 'locus standi' and made it possible for any genuinely interested person to approach the Apex Court, on behalf of people who otherwise could not approach the court for remedy or redress. The Court has expanded the concept of right to life and right to liberty.

A heavy responsibility is cast upon courts to evolve law in consonance with the changing needs and aspirations of the society and to serve the cause of social justice.

The judges broadened the concept of 'locus standi' and permitted well-meaning NGOs like Common Cause and individuals to gain excess to the court on behalf of the victims. Even letters written by humble people ventilating legal grievances were taken seriously for remedies. Victimology attained a new status and realistic and immediate reliefs were granted.

Industries which caused pollution were directed to be removed and bonded labour was ordered to be released and rehabilitated. Prisoners were humanised and compensation granted to victims of executive excesses.

Equality and equal protection of the laws received a dynamic meaning, incorporating International Covenants and UN Instruments as long as they are not in conflict with domestic laws. The concept of right to life was expanded to include the right to livelihood, shelter, health, dignity, free and compulsory education.

When the legislature failed to bring in the laws or amendments that are badly needed and the Executive failed to discharge its responsibilities, the Judiciary has effectively stepped in to fill the vacuum and grant relief to the citizens.

Justice is the foremost human right and the court is chosen instrument in this behalf. However, the, courts are dynamic and accountable, functioning as they do for the people. They have to give complete relief, enforce remedies and fulfil rights and ensure social justice.

The courts declare—as Thomas Fuller did centuries ago "be you ever so high, the law is above you".

As the Supreme Court observed in the case of High Court of Judicature at Bombay V. Shirishkumar Rangarao Patil, "In times of grave danger, it is the constitutional duty of Judiciary to poise the scales of justice unmoved by the powers (actual or perceived), undisturbed by the clamour of the multitude".

Justice V.R. Krishna lyer observed: "We are governed by the Constitution but a Constitution is what judges say it is. So, judicature is the most strategic instrument. What it declares as law binds all, what it decrees or directs as "necessary for doing complete justice for any cause or any matter pending before it" shall be enforceable. All are duty bound to assist the Supreme Court in the discharge of its function. Being a court of record, it has powers to punish any one for contempt of court.

Fundamental Rights, give the right to every citizen to get social, economic, political and cultural justice are directly enforceable by the Supreme Court.

The late K.P.S. Menon, in his delectable style, related a story of three masons. The first one, when asked what he was doing, stated that he was earning a living. The second said in reply to same question that he was chiseling bricks. The third, with a higher level of consciousness, answered: I am building a Cathedral. We have counterparts in every other profession. Some Judges dispose of dockets; other judges maintain the status quo based on the established order; and the third creative category, sharing the vision of the Constitution and its commitment, generates a humanist jurisprudence vitalizing the values of the supreme lex.

It was Lord Denning who said, "the judges will always be

vigilant in guarding our freedom. Someone must be trusted. Let it be the judges."

The rule of law with equal eye and even hand is categorical, imperative and inviolable feature of constitutional order. The central role of the Judiciary in arresting absolutism of the Executive and Legislative organs is obvious. "Justice without power is inefficient, power without justice is tyranny." According to the text of the Preamble, the supreme or fundamental constitutional values in which the founding fathers believed, which they wanted the future citizens of the Republic to foster among themselves and which they hoped, would guide all those who, from generation to generation, would be called upon to work the Constitution were:

- Sovereignty
- Socialism
- Secularism
- Democracy
- Republic character
- Justice
- Liberty
- Equality
- Fraternity
- Dignity of the Individual, and
- Unity and Integrity of the Nation

The Constitution of India visualises development of a pluralist society based on the principles of equality and social justice. It indicates the nation's resolve to develop a State which is socialistic, secular and democratic in nature. The education system will have to consciously reflect the constitutional obligations through process. It will have to play an important role in preparing the younger generations, in particular, for assuming their roles as constructive and responsible citizens.

Framers of the Indian Constitution were such visionaries as had practised values in life discharging their societal and national obligations and had followed noble ideals which had inspired our national struggle for freedom and the need to defend the country, promote harmony, secularism and preserve the rich heritage of the composite Indian culture. To the framers of the Constitution, these were basic and inherent values to be practised by each and every one. Initially nurtured in the home through tradition and subsequently by education in schools, colleges and universities, these were integral part of the way of life in India and it was taken for granted that aberrations in the practice of these will not be acceptable in the society. As such no need was felt to incorporate Fundamental Duties specifically in the Constitution. It was also presumed that these would be covered under basic values inherent in the constitutional promise in the Preamble to the Constitution of India.

Constitutional amendment concerning Fundamental Duties indicated the urgency to act, as Article 51A comprises such aspects as cannot be ignored any more. These have to be paid immediate and urgent attention by the systems in existence as well as by the individuals in the society. Essentially all that is contained in the Fundamental Duties is just a codification of tasks integral to the Indian way of life. A close scrutiny of the clauses of Article 51A would indicate that a number of these clauses basically refer to such values as have been a part of the Indian tradition, mythology, religions and practices. At this juncture of history, the nation realises an urgent need to re-emphasise these in a manner that would be acceptable to and be imbibed by all generations. To achieve these objectives, it would be essential to create public awareness of the need to appreciate and internalise the concept and practice of Fundamental Duties with particular emphasis on the necessity of creating a harmonious society with a scientific outlook, free from tensions and turmoils.

Human Rights and Responsibilities

An eminent Australian Judge Justice Michael Kirby, while delivering Bar Association of India Lecture, in 1997, had dealt with the subject admirably. I cannot do any better than quote a few sentences from that lecture.

"The Indian Courts, particularly the Supreme Court have a respected reputation for creativity and ingenuity in the development and adaptation of the common law to the enormous contemporary problems and opportunities of this country. Those who travelled to examine the law of India carefully soon came to an understanding of the way in which the Supreme Court has, by a series of landmark judgements described by some as "judicial activism", established basic principles which would repay study in other parts of the common law world. I refer in this regard to decisions on such matters as right to go abroad; the right to privacy; the right to protection against solitary confinement; the right not to be held in fetters; the right of an indigent person to have legal aid; the right to speedy trial; the right against handcuffing; the right against custodial violence; the right against public hanging; the right in certain circumstances to critical assistance; and the right in certain cases to the provision of physical shelter.

Within India, as in my own and every country, there are different views about judicial activism. Anxiety about social justice and the removal of discrimination are all irrational grounds has caused judges like Krishna Iyer to become exemplars of a kind of "judicial activism", that is often in tune with the deeply felt emotions of ordinary citizens. It is concerned about the rights of children. It is concerned about torture, cruel, inhuman and degrading treatment of punished. It is concerned about the struggle of citizens with the bureaucracy.

Judicial experience teaches me that, in all of them, there would be another point of view. For every litigant demanding judicial activism there is ordinarily another urging judicial restraint. In India, the special features of society and its institutions and urgency of the problem presented to the courts, doubtlessly help to explain the demands for "judicial activism".

Soli Sorabji has pointed out that "indignant critics forget that it is the Executive failure to perform its duty and the notorious tardiness of legislatures that impels judicial activism and provides its motivation and legitimacy. When gross violation of human rights are brought to its notice, the judiciary cannot procrastinate. It must respond."

In India, from the highest level of judiciary, there has been a recognition that excessive ill-judged activism may damage the very institution which gives birth to it. Thus, the Chief Justice of India has suggested that the phenomenon of judicial activism, evident in India today, may be seen as a temporary one, responding to the peculiar needs of the nation at this time.

The law abhors a vacuum. Into a vacuum left by the failure of the other branches of Government to respond to urgent legal and social needs, the courts have sometimes stepped in.

15

Custodial Justice : Guidelines to Police Commissioners and District Magistrates

"Safeguarding the rights of others is the most noble and beautiful end of a human being."

— *Kahlil Gibran*

Custodial violence,including torture and death in the lock ups, strikes a blow at the Rule of Law, which demands that the powers of the executive should not only be derived from law but also that the same should be limited by law. Custodial Violence is a matter of concern. It is aggravated by the fact that it is committed by persons who are supposed to be the protectors of the citizens. It is committed under the shield of uniform and authority in the four walls of a police station or lock-up, the victim being totally helpless. The Protection of an individual from torture and abuse by the police and other law enforcing officers is a matter of deep concern in a free society. "Torture " of a human being by another human being is essentially an instrument to impose the will of the "strong" over the "Weak" by Suffering. The word "torture" today has become synonymous with the darker side of human civilization. It is a calculated assault on human dignity and whenever human dignity is wounded, civilization takes a step backward – the flag of humanity must on each such occasion fly half-mast. - Supreme Court of India in D.K.Basu v Union of India, 1996

---

* Compiled by the author for the National Institute of Administrative Research – Lal Bahadur Shastri National Academy of Administration, Mussorie.

I
General Guidelines

Role of a District Magistrate in Custodial Justice

- *Effective monitoring.* This is a method of improving protection of human rights in general, and ensuring custodial justice in particular. The principal objective of custodial justice monitoring is to reinforce State responsibility to protect human rights. One should also perform a preventive role. When a law enforcement official is monitored, he/she becomes more careful about his/her conduct. District Magistrates and Police Commissioners exercising magisterial powers must relate their work to the overall objective of human rights protection. A District Magistrate can record observations and collect information for immediate action and later use. He/she can communicate the information to appropriate authorities and/or bodies like Government of the day, National Human Rights Commission, State Human Rights Commission etc. A District Magistrate should not only observe developments, collect information, and perceive patterns of conduct, but should, as far as his/her mandate allow and competence permits, identify problems, diagnose their causes, consider potential solutions, and assist in problem solving. While exercising good judgement at all times, District Magistrates should take initiative in solving problems and should not wait for a specific instructions or expressed permission before acting to prevent Human rights violation.
- *Do not harm.* The actions and/or inactions of a District Magistrate should not jeopardize the safety of victims, witnesses or other individuals with whom they come into contact, or the sound functioning of custodial justice system.
- *Respect the limitations.* A District Magistrate should always work strictly within the broad parameters indicated in the respective jail manual or any other law for the time being in force and decide and determine his/her level of intervention accordingly.
- *Know the standards.* A District Magistrate should be fully familiar with the requirements of custodial justice system, which are relevant to his/her role and the responsibility of State in a given circumstance.
- *Exercise good judgement.* Whatever their precision, rules

cannot substitute for the good personal judgement and common sense of the District Magistrate. He/she should exercise good judgement at all times and in all circumstances.

- ***Seek consultation.*** Wisdom springs from discussion and consultation. When a District Magistrate is dealing with a difficult case, a case on the borderline of the role or a case which could be doubtful, it is always wise to consult other officers, experts and, whenever possible, superiors.
- ***Respect the authorities.*** District Magistrates should keep in mind that their objective and the principal role is to encourage the law enforcement officials to improve their behaviour. Hence they should respect proper functioning of the law enforcement agencies, should welcome improvements, should seek ways to encourage policies and practices which will continue to implement appropriate standards for all times to come.
- ***Credibility.*** District Magistrate's credibility is crucial for ensuring custodial justice. He/she should be sure not to make any promises they are unlikely or unable to keep and follow through on any promise that he/she makes. When interviewing detainees/prisoners and witnesses of violence, the District Magistrate should introduce himself/herself, briefly explain the purpose of his/her visit, should also briefly describe what can and cannot be done by him/her, emphasize the confidentiality of the information received, and stress the importance of obtaining as many details as possible to establish the facts (for example, whether there has been a human rights violation).
- ***Confidentiality.*** Respect for the confidentiality of information is essential because any breach of this principle could have very serious consequences: (a) for the person interviewed and for the victim; (b) for the District Magistrate's credibility and safety; (c) for the level of confidence enjoyed by the visit/inspection in the minds of inmates of the prison; and thus (d) for the effectiveness of the inspection/visit.
- ***Security.*** District Magistrate should always bear in mind the security of the people who provide information. They should obtain consent of witnesses for interviews and assure them about confidentiality. If need be, security measures should be put in place to also protect the identity of informants, interviewees, witnesses, etc.

- ***Understanding the local problems.*** District Magistrate should endeavour to understand the place where he/she works, including its people, history, administrative structure, culture, customs, language.
- ***Evaluation of the information received.*** District Magistrate should carefully, sometimes critically, examine information received and have it compared and verified before acting upon the same.
- ***Accuracy and precision.*** Written communication is always essential to avoid lack of precision, rumours and misunderstandings.
- ***Impartiality.*** It should always be remembered that a District Magistrate has to carryout his/her work and/or discharge his/her role with complete impartiality. He/she should not only be impartial but also should seem to be impartial.
- ***Sensitivity.*** While inspecting/visiting a place of detention or jail or custody, the District Magistrate should be sensitive to the suffering which an individual may have experienced, as well as to the need to take the necessary steps to protect the security of the individual.
- ***Integrity.*** District Magistrate should treat all informants, interviewees and the staff with decency and respect. He/she should carryout the visit in an honest and honourable manner.
- ***Visibility.*** A District Magistrate should be sure that both the law enforcement officials and inmates of the prison are aware of his/or her presence. The presence and visibility of District Magistrate can deter human rights violation.

A Law Enforcement Official Should Know

(i) He/she is a representative of, and responsive and accountable to, the community as a whole.

(ii) Effective maintenance of ethical standards among law enforcement officials depends on identification of well-conceived, popularly accepted and human system of laws and subsequent implementation thereof.

(iii) Every law enforcement official is a part of the criminal justice system, the aim of which is to prevent and control crime, and the conduct of every official has an impact on the entire system.

(iv) Every law enforcement agency should discipline itself to uphold human rights standards and actions of law enforcement officials should be open to public scrutiny.

(v) Standards for humane conduct of law enforcement official lack practical value unless their content and meaning become part of the creed of every law enforcement official, through education, training and monitoring.

II

Ten Basic Rules to Ensure "Custodial Justice"

These rules are intended as a quick reference, and not as full explanation of or commentary on the applicability of human rights standards vis-a-vis custodial justice relevant to law enforcement. Fairness, Accountability, Commitment, Excellence, Integrity and Trust are the essentials for strict implementation of this set of rules.

It is hoped that all concerned with enforcement of law will be able to use these Ten Basic Rules as a starting point to develop detailed guidance for the training and monitoring of the conduct of police personnel. Certainly, it is the duty of all officers to ensure that their colleagues/ sub ordinates uphold the ethical standards of their profession—the rules outlined here are essential for exercising that responsibility.

Basic Rule 1. Everyone is entitled to equal protection of the law, without discrimination on any ground, and especially against violence or threat. Be especially vigilant to protect potentially vulnerable groups such as children, the elderly, women, refugees, displaced persons and members of minority groups.

This rule requires recognising;

1.1. Every one has the right to liberty and security of the person;

1.2. No one should be subjected to arbitrary arrest, detention or exile;

1.3. All persons deprived of their liberty have the right not to suffer torture or cruel, inhuman or degrading treatment;

1.4. Everyone is entitled without any discrimination to equal protection of the law; and

1.5. Everyone has the right to a fair trial.

Basic Rule 2. Treat all detainees in custody or under detention with compassion and respect, and in particular protect their safety and privacy.

This rule demands:

2.1. Ensure that, if needed, measures are taken to ensure the protection and safety to detainees/arrestees from intimidation and retaliation;

2.2. Inform detainees/arrestees without delay of the availability of health and social services and other relevant assistance;

2.3. Provide without delay specialist care for women who have suffered violence;

2.4. Develop investigative techniques that do not degrade/disgrace women who have been arrested/detained;

2.5. Give particular attention to detainees/arrestees who have special needs because of the nature of the harm they have sustained because of factors such as race, colour, gender, sexual orientation, age, language, religion, nationality, political or other opinion, disability, ethnic or social origin, etc.

Basic Rule 3. Do not use force except when strictly necessary and to the minimum extent required under the circumstances.

This rule mandates:

3.1. Exercise restraint in such use and act in proportion to the seriousness of the offence and the legitimate objective to be achieved;

3.2. Minimise damage and injury, and respect and preserve human life and personal liberty;

3.3. Ensure that all possible assistance and medical aid are rendered to any injured or affected detainee/arrestee at the earliest possible moment;

3.4. Ensure that relatives or close friends of the injured or affected detainee are notified at the earliest possible moment;

3.5. Where injury or death is caused by the use of force by police officers/jail official, they shall report the incident promptly to their superiors, who should ensure that proper investigation of all such incidents are carried out;

3.6. In all cases of custodial death a magisterial inquiry should be conducted for fact finding.

Basic Rule 4. Avoid using force when policing unlawful but non-violent assemblies. When dispersing violent assemblies, use force only to the minimum extent necessary.

This rule warrants:

4.1. In policing of assemblies that are unlawful but non-violent, police officers must avoid the use of force. If force is indispensable, for example to secure the safety of others, they must restrict such force to the minimum extent necessary and in compliance with the requirements of Rule 3;

4.2. Firearms shall not be used in the policing of non-violent assemblies. The use of firearms is strictly limited to the objectives mentioned in Rule 5;

4.3. In the dispersal of violent assemblies police officers may use force only if other means remain ineffective or without any promise of achieving the intended result. When using force police officers must comply with the requirements of Rule 3;

4.4. In the dispersal of violent assemblies police officers may use firearms only when use of less force is not practicable and only to the minimum extent necessary to achieve one of the objectives mentioned in Rule 5 and in accordance with the provisions of Rule 3 and Rule 5.

Basic Rule 5. Lethal force should not be used except when strictly unavoidable in order to protect your life or the lives of others.

This rule sets the following objectives and strictly warns against use of lethal force excepting in following situations:

5.1. In self-defence or in defence of others against the imminent threat of death or serious injury;

5.2. To prevent the perpetration of a particularly serious crime involving grave threat to life;

5.3. To arrest a person presenting such a danger and resisting the police officer's authority;

5.4. In any event, intentional lethal use of firearms may only be made when strictly unavoidable in order to protect life;

5.5. Police officers must identify themselves as such and give a clear warning of their intent to use firearms, with sufficient time for the warning to be observed, unless to do so would unduly place the officers at risk or would creat a risk of death or serious harm to other persons, or would be clearly inappropriate or pointless in the circumstances of the incident;

5.6. Use of firearms by police officers should be strictly in accordance with the Rules and regulations on the use of firearms.

Basic Rule 6. Arrest no person unless there are legal grounds to do so, and the arrest is carried out in accordance with lawful arrest procedures.

This rule directs:

6.1. Arrest or detention shall only be carried out strictly in accordance with provisions of the law and guidelines formulated by judiciary and NHRC, and only by competent officials or persons authorised for that purpose;

6.2. Police or other authorities which arrest a person shall exercise only the powers explicitly granted to them under the law;

6.3. Anyone arrested must be informed at the time of arrest of the reasons for the arrest;

6.4. The time of the arrest, the reasons for the arrest, precise information identifying the place of custody, and the identity of the law enforcement officials concerned must be recorded; in addition, the records must be communicated to the detained person or to his or her lawyer;

6.5. Officials carrying out arrest should identify themselves to the person arrested and, on demand, to others witnessing the event;

6.6. Police officers and other officials who make arrests should wear name tags or numbers so that they can be clearly identified. Other identifying markings such as the insignia of soldiers' battalions or detachments should also be visible;

6.7. Police and military vehicles should be clearly identified as such. They should carry number plates at all times;

6.8. A person should not be kept in detention without being given an effective opportunity to be heard promptly by a judicial or other officer authorized by law to exercise judicial power, and be entitled to a trial within a reasonable time.

6.9. Persons awaiting trial need not be detained in custody, but their release on bail may be subject to reasonable guarantees of their appearance for trial;

6.10. All detainees should only be kept in recognised places of detention. Such places of detention should be visited regularly by qualified and experienced persons appointed by, and responsible to, a competent authority distinct from the authority directly in charge of the administration of the place of detention;

6.11. The detention of refugees and asylum seekers should normally be avoided. No asylum-seeker should be detained unless it has been established that detention is necessary, is lawful and complies with one of the grounds recognised as legitimate by international standards. In all cases, detention should not last longer than is strictly necessary;

6.12. All asylum-seekers should be given adequate opportunity to have their detention reviewed by a judicial or similar authority.

Reference regarding the detention of refugees and asylum-seekers should be made to the competent authorities, as well as to the office of the United Nations High Commissioner for Refugees (UNHCR) and other refugee assistance organisations.

Basic Rule 7. Ensure all detainees have access promptly after arrest to their family and legal representative and to any necessary medical assistance.

This rule postulates:

7.1. Detainees should be promptly told of their rights, including the right to lodge complaints about their treatment;

7.2. A detainee who does not understand or speak the language used by the authorities responsible for his or her arrest is entitled to receive information and have the assistance, free of charge if necessary, of an interpreter in connection with the legal proceedings subsequent of his or her arrest;

7.3. A detainee who is a foreigner should be promptly informed of his or her right to communicate with the relevant consular post or diplomatic mission;

7.4. All detained refugees and asylum-seekers should be allowed to access the local representative of the UNHCR and to refugee assistance organisations, regardless of why they are being detained. If a detainee identifies himself/herself as a refugee or an asylum-seeker, or otherwise indicates their fear at being returned to their counry, it is incumbent on the detaining officials to facilitate contact with these organisations.

7.5. Police officers or other competent authorities must ensure that all detainees are fully able in practice to avail themselves of the right to notify family members or others immediately of their whereabouts;

7.6. Police officers or other competent authorities must ensure that accurate information on the arrest, place of detention, transfer of detainees is available promptly in a place where relatives and others concerned can obtain it;

7.7. They must ensure that relatives are not obstructed from obtaining this information, and that they know or are able to find out where the information can be obtained.

7.8. Relatives and others should be able to visit a detainee as soon as possible after he or she is taken into custody. Relatives and others should be able to correspond with the detainee and make further visits regularly to verify the detainee's continued well-being;

7.9. Every detainee must be informed promptly after the arrest of his or her right to a legal counsel and be helped by the authorities to exercise this right. Moreover, every detainee must be able to communicate regularly and confidentially with their lawyer, including having meetings with their lawyer within sight but not within hearing of a guard or police officer, in order to help prepare the detainee's defence and to exercise his or her rights.

7.10. An independent doctor should promptly conduct a proper medical examination of the detainee after taking into custody in order to ascertain that the detainee is healthy and not suffering from torture or ill-treatment, including rape and sexual abuse. Thereafter, medical care and treatment shall be provided whenever necessary;

7.11. Every detainee or his or her legal counsel has the right to request a second medical examination or opinion. Detainees must never be subjected to medical or scientific experimentation;

7.12. Female detainees should be entitled to medical examination by a female doctor. They should be provided with all necessary pre-natal and post-natal care and treatment. Restraints should only be used on pregnant as a last resort and should never put the safety of a woman or foetus at risk. Women should never be restrained during labour.

Basic Rule 8. All detainees must be treated humanely. Do not inflict, instigate or tolerate any act of torture or ill-treatment, in any circumstances, and refuse to obey any order to do so.

This Dule Demands:

8. 1. Detainees are inherently vulnerable because they are under the control of law enforcement officials who therefore have a duty to protect detainees from any violation of their right to life by strictly observing procedures designed to respect the inherent dignity of the

human person. Accurate record-keeping is an essential element of the proper administration of places of detention;

8.2. The existence of official records which are open for consultation helps to protect detainees from ill-treatment including torture. The implementation of Basic Rule 8 requires, among other things, that:

8.3. No person under any form of detention may be subjected to torture, or to cruel, inhuman or degrading treatment or punishment, and law enforcement officers have a right and a duty to disobey orders to carry out such acts;

8.4. No law enforcement official may inflict, instigate or tolerate any act of torture or other cruel, inhuman or degrading treatment or punishment, nor may they invoke superior orders or exceptional circumstances such as a state of war or threat of war, or political instability or other public emergency, as a justification for such acts;

8.5. Law enforcement officials should be instructed that molestation or rape of women in their custody constitutes grave crime that will not be tolerated. Similarly, they should be instructed that any other forms of sexual abuse may constitute torture or cruel, inhuman or degrading treatment and that offenders will also be brought to justice;

8.6. The term "cruel, inhuman or degrading treatment or punishment" should be interpreted so as to extend the widest possible protection against abuses, whether physical or mental, including holding a detainee in conditions which deprive him or her, even temporarily, of the use of any of his or her natural senses, such as sight or hearing, of his or her awareness of place of passing of time. Compliance with other basic rules for law enforcement are also essential safeguards against torture and ill-treatment;

8.7. A detainee may not be compelled to confess, to otherwise incriminate himself or herself or to testify against any other person. While being interrogated, no detainee may be subject to violent threats or methods which impair his or her capacity of decision or judgement. Female guards should be present during the interrogation of female detainees and should be solely responsible for carrying out any body searches of female detainees;

8.8. Children should be detained only as a last resort and for the shortest possible time. They should be given immediate access to relatives, legal counsel and medical assistance and relatives or guardians should be informed immediately of their whereabouts;

8.9. Juvenile detainees should be kept separate from adults and detained in separate institutions. They should be protected from torture and ill-treatment, including rape and sexual abuse, whether by officials or other detainees;

8.10. Refugees and asylum-seekers detained for non-criminal reasons should never be detained together with common law prisoners. Conditions and treatment should be humane, and appropriate to their status as refugees;

8.11. Detainees should be kept separate from imprisoned persons. All detainees should if possible wear their own clothing if it is clean and suitable, sleep singly in separate rooms, be fed properly and be allowed to buy or receive books, newspapers, writing materials and other means of occupation as are compatible with the interests of justice;

8.12. Registers of detainees should be kept in all places of detention including police stations and military bases. The register should consist of a bound book with numbered pages which cannnot be tampered with. Information to be entered in them should include:

- The name and identity of each person detained;
- The reasons for his or her arrest or detention;
- The names and identities of officials who arrested the detainee or transported him or her;
- The date and time of the arrest and of the transportation to a place of detention;
- The time, place and duration of each interrogation and the name of the persons conducting it;
- The time of the detainee's first appearance before a judicial authority, and;
- Precise information concerning the place of custody, the date, time and circumstances of the detainee's release or transfer to another place of detention.

Basic Rule 9. Do not carry out, order or cover up extrajudicial executions or disappearances, and refuse to obey any order to do so. There are several important elements in the concept of an extrajudicial execution:

- It is deliberate, non accidental;
- It violates national laws such as those which prohibit murder, and/or international standards forbidding the arbitrary deprivation of life;
- Its unlawfulness distinguishes an extrajudicial execution from:

- A justifiable killing in self-defrence,
- A death resulting from use of force by law enforcement officials which is neverthless consistant with criminal law standards,
- A killing in an armed conflict situation which is not prohibited by criminal law jurisprudence.

This rule strictly requires:

9.1. In an armed conflict, armed officers and soldiers of the Government are prohibited from carrying out arbitrary and summary executions. This would constitute violation of basic principles of criminal law;

9.2. All police officers and all other law enforcement. personnel should be aware of their right and duty to disobey orders the implementation of which might result in serious human rights violations. Since those violations are unlawful, police officers and others must not participate in them. The need to disobey an unlawful order should be seen as a duty, taking precedence over the normal duty to obey orders. The duty to disobey an unlawful order entails the right to disobey it;

9.3. The right and duty to disobey an order to participate in "disappearances" and extrajudicial killings are implicit from the constitutional guarantees;

9.4. To implement Basic Rule-9, it is important that the use of force and firearms by the police strictly complies with all the provisions in Basic Rule-3, 4 and 5.

Basic Rule 10. Report all breaches of these Basic Rules to your senior officers and to the office of the District Magistrate. Do everything within your power to ensure steps are taken to investigate these breaches.

III
COMMENTARY ON VARIOUS ASPECTS OF "CUSTODIAL JUSTICE"

Introduction

District Magistrate being overall in-charge of law and order in the district, he has a crucial role to play. He should be very well aware of his direct responsibilities as District Magistrate and also as supervisory officer responsible to the Government for all that happens in his jurisdiction.

The custodial justice system has to operate within an ethical framework. Without a strong ethical context, one group of people when given considerable power over another group can easily become abusers of power. The ethical context is not just a matter of the behaviour of an individual officer towards detainees. A sense of the ethics of imprisonment needs to pervade the management process from the top downwards. A demand for operational efficiency, or pressure to meet management targets without prior consideration of ethical imperatives can lead to great inhumanity. Administration of custodial justice is primarily about the management of human beings in custody. This further involves ensuring justice to men and women who have been deprived of their liberty, some of whom may be mentally disturbed, suffer from addictions, have poor social and educational skills and belong to marginalised groups in society. Some of them could be a threat to the society; some may be dangerous and aggressive, while others may try their best to escape. None wants to be in prison.

In a democratic society like India the law underpins and protects the fundamental values of the society. There has to be respect for the inherent dignity of all human beings, whatever their personal or social status. One of the greatest tests of this 'respect for humanity' lies in the way in which a society treats those who have broken, or are accused of having broken the criminal law. These are people who themselves may well have shown a lack of respect for the dignity and rights of others. All involved in administration of criminal justice system have a special role on behalf of the rest of society in respecting their human dignity, despite any crime that they may have committed. Senior administrators, law enforcement officials and others concerned with custodial justice system may always be conscious of this imperative. Applying it in very difficult circumstances requires commitment. First line law enforcement officials will be able to maintain this commitment only if they get a clear and consistent message from those in charge of the system that this is an imperative.

Principles of Custodial Justice

Persons who are detained or imprisoned retain all their rights as human beings with the exception of those that have been lost as a specific consequence of deprivation of liberty. All concerned with custodial justice need to have a clear understanding of the implications of this principle. Some issues are very clear. There is, for example, a total prohibition on torture and deliberately inflicted cruel, inhuman or degrading treatment. There has to be an understanding that this prohibition does not merely apply to direct physical or mental abuse. It also applies to the totality of conditions in which prisoners are held. In other words "prisoners are kept in prison as a punishment and not for punishment".

While handling with detainees, particularly while imposing restrictions on them one should know which specific rights are forfeited. These are summed up as follows:

(i) The right of freedom of movement is obviously restricted by the nature of detention, as is that of free association. Even these rights are not completely removed since detenues are rarely held in total isolation and, where they are, there has to be very good and specific reason.

(ii) The right to family contact is not taken away but its exercise may be restricted. A father, for example, does not have unrestricted access to his children, nor they to him, while under imprisonment.

(iii) The rights of mothers and children to family life require special consideration. Mere imprisonment cannot be a ground to deprive the detainees from the natural love and affection of their families.

Constitutional Scheme

From judicial perspective 'the right to life and personal liberty' contained in Article 21 of Indian Constitution encompasses all basic conditions for a life with dignity and liberty. Such an approach allows it to come down heavily on the system of administration of criminal justice; custodial justice in particular, and law enforcement. It also brings into the fold of Article 21, all those directive principles of State policy that are essential for a 'life with dignity'. The right to life guaranteed by Article 21 of the Constitution of India is not merely a fundamental right but is the basic human right from which all other human rights stem. It is basic in the sense that the enjoyment of the right to life is a necessary condition for the enjoyment of all other human rights.

The right existed even prior to the commencement of Indian Constitution. In *A.D.M. Jabalpur Vs. Shivakant Shukla* case, Justice H.R. Khanna rightly observed, '...sanctity of life and liberty was not something new when the Constitution was drafted. It represented a facet of higher values which mankind began to cherish in its evolution from a state of tooth and claw to a civilised existence. Likewise, the principle that no one shall be deprived of his life and liberty arbitrarily without the authority of law was not the gift of the Constitution. It was a necessary corollary of the concept relating to the sanctity of life and liberty which existed and was in force before the coming into force of the Constitution..."

The Court adopted an annotation of Article 21, in *Kharak Singh Vs. State of U.P.* and expanded the connotation of the term 'life' and said "...life is something more than mere animal existence. The inhibition against its deprivation extends to all those limbs and faculties by which life is enjoyed. The provision equally prohibits the mutilation of the body by the amputation of an arm or leg, of the putting out of an eye, or the destruction of any other organ of the body through which the soul communicates with the outer world...". In *Maneka Gandhi Vs. Union of India,* Bhagawati J. opined that "the fundamental right of life and personal liberty has many attributes and it covers a variety of rights which go to constitute the personal liberty of man and some of them have been raised to the status of distinct fundamental rights and given additional protection under Article 19" and in the same case it was held that the procedure contemplated under Article 21 is a right, just and fair procedure, not an arbitrary or oppressive procedures. The procedure which is reasonable and fair must now be in confirmity with the rest of Article 14. In other words, the Supreme Court while considering the ambit of Article 21 in a number of cases established that Article 21 does not exclude Article 19 and that even if there is a law prescribing a procedure for depriving a person of 'personal liberty' and there is consequently no infringment of the fundamental right conferred by Article 21, such law in so far as it abridges or takes away any fundamental right under Article 19 would have to meet the requirements of that Article. Further any procedure contemplated by State to curtail 'life and personal liberty' of an individual should meet the requirement of Article 14.

Death Penalty

India has not abolished death penalty, but as a rule laid down by the Supreme Court, it is to be awarded by the competent courts only in the 'rarest of the rare cases, in which the crime committed is so heinous that it shook the conscience of mankind'. Under the present criminal law, imposition of death sentence is an exception rather than the rule. Even in those exceptional cases, special reasons have to be given in justification of the imposition of death penalty. Section 416 of Cr. P.C. requires the High Court to postpone the execution of a capital sentence on pregnant women and may, if it thinks fit, commute the sentence to imprisonment for life. In *Rajendra Prasad Vs. State of U.P.* Krishna Ayer J. expressed his view by stating that the Criminal law of Raj vintage has lost some of it's vitality, notwithstanding its formal persistance in print of the Penal Code so far as Section 302 of IPC is concerned. In the post Constitution period, Section 302 of IPC and Section 354(3) of Cr.P.C. have to be read in the light of Parts III and IV of the Constitution. He further went ahead in saying that the death sentence would not be justified unless it was shown that the criminal was dangerous to the society. In *Bachan Singh's* case the Supreme Court elaborated 'special reasons' for awarding capital punishment and established that when the conviction is for an offence punishable with death, the judgment should state the special reasons for such a sentence.

Constitutional provisions apart, the Supreme Court has evolved a number of safeguards to protect the dignity and personal liberty of persons awarded life sentence while waiting for execution of the sentence. These include their right to worship, right to see family members, right to remorse etc. In *Attorney General of India Vs. Lachman Devi* case the Court opined that the execution of death sentence by public hangng is barbaric and violative of Article 21 of the Constitution. The Court held that although the crime of which the accused have been found to be guilty was barbaric, however, a barbaric crime does not have to be visited with a barbaric penalty such as public hanging.

Torture

Convention against Torture explicitly states that "No exceptional circumstances whatsoever, whether a state of war or a threat of war, internal political instability or any other public emergency, may be invoked as justification of torture". The Supreme Court of India and the National Human Rights Commission have upheld this view in their various judgements/recommendations and have jointly and individually established that the prohibition of torture is absolute and may not be suspended no matter how heinous the crime for which someone has been arrested. It is a right from which the Government is not permitted to derogate, even in situations of emergency. 44th amendment of the Indian Constitution declares Article 20 and 21 as non derogable even in emergency situations.

The term 'torture' is defined in the Convention against torture and other cruel, inhuman or degrading treatment or punishment. Article 1.1 of the same defines torture as "any act by which severe pain or suffering, whether physical or mental, is intentionally inflicted on a person for such purposes as obtaining from him or a third person information or a confession, punishing him for an act he or a third person has committed or is suspected of having committed, or intimidating or coercing him or a third person, or for any reason based on discrimination of any kind, when such pain or suffering is inflicted by or at the instigation of or with the consent or acquiescence of a public official or other person acting in an official capacity. It does not include pain or suffering arising from, inherent in or incidental to lawful sanctions". Article 21 of Constitution only provides "no person shall be deprived of his life or personal liberty except according to procedure established by law". The term 'life' or personal liberty has been held to include the right to live with human dignity and, therefore, includes within its ambit a guarantee against torture and assult by the state or its functionaries. Any person subjected to torture or to cruel, inhuman or degrading treatment or punishment can move the higher Courts for various judicial remedies under Article 32 and 226 of the Constitution.

Arrest and Detention

The Supreme Court initiated the development of "Custodial Jurisprudence" in *D.K. Basu Vs. State of West Bengal.* The case came up before the Court through a writ petition under Article 32 of the Constitution by an NGO. In this case the Chief Justice of India's notice was drawn to a news published in *The Telegraph* regarding deaths in police lock-ups and in jail in the State of West Bengal. It was requested in this petition to examine in depth and to develop custodial jurisprudence. In this case the Court outlined the following requirements which should be followed in all cases of arrest or detention as preventive measures:

1. The police personnel carrying out the arrest and handling the interrogation of the arrestee should bear accurate, visible and clear identification and name tags with their designations. The particulars of all such police personnel

who handle interrogation of the arrestee must be recorded in a register.

2. The police officer carrying out the arrest of the arrestee shall prepare a memo of arrest at the time of arrest and such memo shall be attested by at least one witness, who may be either a member of the family of the arrestee or a respectable person of the locality from where the arrest is made. It shall also be countersigned by the arrestee and shall contain the time and date of arrest.
3. A person who has been arrested or detained and is being held in custody in a police station or interrogation centre or other lock-up, shall be entitled to have one friend or relative or other person known to him or having interest in his welfare being informed, as soon as practicable, that he has been arrested and is being detained at the particular place, unless the arresting witness of the memo of the arrest is himself such a friend or relative of the arrestee.
4. The time, place of arrest and venue of custody of an arrestee must be notified by the police where the next friend or relative of the arrestee lives outside the district or town through the Legal Aid Organisation in the District and the Police station of the area concerned telegraphically within a period of 8 to 12 hours after the arrest.
5. The person arrested must be made aware of his right to have one informed of his arrest or detention as soon as he is put under arrest or is detained.
6. An entry must be made in the diary at the place of detention regarding the arrest of the person which shall also disclose the name of the next friend of arrestee and the name and particulars of the police officials in whose custody the arrestee is.
7. The arrestee should, where he so requests, be also examined at the time of his arrest and major and minor injuries, if any present on his/her body, must be recorded at that time. The "Inspection Memo" must be signed both by the arrestee and the police officer effecting the arrest and its copy provided to the arrestee.
8. The arrestee should be subjected to medical examination

by a trained doctor every 48 hours during his detention in custody by a doctor on the panel of approved doctors appointed by Director, Health Services of the concerned State or Union Territory. Director, Health Services should prepare such a panel for all Tehsils and Districts as well.

9. Copies of all the documents including the memo of arrest, referred to above, should be sent to the Magistrate for his record.
10. The arrestee may be permitted to meet his lawyer during interrogation, though not throughout the interrogation.
11. A police control room should be provided to all district and State Headquarters, where information regarding the arrest and place off custody of the arrestee shall be communicated by the officer causing the arrest. Within 12 hours of effecting the arrest and at the police control room it should be displayed on a conspicuous board.

The Court observed that the requirements, referred to above flow from Articles 21 and 22(1) of the Constitution and need to be strictly followed.

In *Nilabati Behera* Vs. *State of Orissa,* the Court observed that prisoners and detainees are not denuded of their fundamental rights under Article 21 and that it is only such restrictions as are permitted by law, which can be imposed on the enjoyment of the fundamental rights of the arrestees and detainees. It was further observed "...there is a great responsibility on the police or prison authorities to ensure that the citizen in its custody is not deprived of his right to life. His liberty is in the very nature of things circumscribed by the fact of his confinement and therefore his interest in the limited liberty left to him is rather precious. The duty of care on the part of the State is strict and admits of no exceptions. The wrongdoer is accountable and the State is responsible if the person in custody of the police is deprived of his life except according to procedure established by law..." In this case Court awarded a sum of Rs. 1.5 lakhs to the mother as her son had died in police custody. The Court's judgement also referred to Article 9(5) of the International Covenant on Civil and Political Rights, which indicates that an enforceable right to compensation is not alien to the concept of enforcement of a guaranteed right. Anyone who has been the victim of unlawful arrest or detention shall have an enforceable right to compensation.

Human Dignity

The Latin maxims *salus populi est suprema lex* (the safety of the people is the supreme law) and *salus republicae est suprema lex* (safety of the State is the supreme law) co-exist and are not only important but lie at the heart of the doctrine that the welfare of an individual must yield to that of the community. However, the action of the State must be "right, just and fair". Practising any form of torture for extracting any kind of information would neither be right nor just nor fair and therefore would be impermissible, being offensive to Article 21.

The Court noted in the *Basu* case that 'there is no express provision in the Constitution of India for the grant of compensation for violation of a fundamental right to life, in spite of this lacuna the Court has judiciously evolved a right to compensation in case of established unconstitutional deprivation of personal liberty'. In *Sunil Batra Vs. Delhi Administration,* the Court was called upon to determine the validity of solitary confinement and keeping a prisoner in fetters. Justice Desai, speaking for the majority, admitted that there was no provision in the Indian Constitution like the Eighth Amendment of American Constitution which forbids cruel and unusual punishment. But, he pointed out that conviction did not degrade the convict to be non-person, vulnerable to major punishments imposed by the jail authorities without observance of due procedural safeguards. He also emphasised a Court's duty towards a prisoner as he was in prison under its order and direction. He held "We cannot be oblivious to the fact that the treatment of a human being which offends human dignity imposes avoidable torture and reduces the man to the level of a beast would certainly be arbitrary and can be questioned under Article 14". In the same case another fact was brought to the notice of the Court that undertrials were kept alongwith the convicts. Justice Iyer observed: "The undertrials who are presumably innocent until convicted are being sent to jail, by contamination, made criminals—a custodial perversity which violates the test of reasonableness in Article 19 and of fairness in Article 21. How cruel would it be if one went to a hospital for a check-up and by being kept alongwith contagious cases came home with a new disease". The learned judge drew the picture of Tihar prison thus: "Tihar prison is an arena of tension, trauma, tantrums and crimes of violence, vulgarity and corruption. And to cap it all, there occurs the contamination of pre-trial accused with habitual, and 'injurious prisoners of international gangs'. The crowning piece is that the jail officials themselves are allegedly in league with the criminals in the cell. That is, there is a large network of criminals, officials, and non-officials, in the house of correction. Drug racket, alcoholism, smuggling, violence, theft, unconstitutional punishment by way of solitary cellular life, and transfer to other jails are not uncommon".

The Court held in this case that personal liberty of the person who is incarcerated is to a great extent curtailed by punitive detention. The liberty to move, mix, mingle, talk, share company with co-prisoners, if substantially curtailed would be a violation of Article 21 unless the curtailment has the backing of law. In another important judgement delivered by the Supreme Court in *Francis Corallie Mullin Vs. the Administrator, Union Territory of Delhi,* Bhagawati J. observed "the right to life enshrined in Article 21 cannot be restricted to mere animal existence. It means something much more than just physical survival. The right to life includes the right to live with human dignity and all that goes along with it, namely, the bare necessaries of life such as adequate nutrition, clothing and shelter over the head and facilities for reading, writing and expressing oneself in diverse forms, freely moving out and mixing and comingling with fellow human beings".

In a number of cases the Supreme Court held that handcuffing of prisoners is against human dignity and violative of Article 21. In *Prem Shankar Shukla Vs. Delhi Administration,* while delivering the judgement Justice Krishna Iyer drew attention to Article 5 of the Universal Declaration of Human Rights and held that handcuffing of a prisoner was unconstitutional if there was any other reasonable way of preventing the escape of the prisoner. He reiterated the Article 21, now the sanctuary of human values, prescribes fair procedure and forbits barbarities, punitive as well as procedural. In *State of Maharashtra Vs. Ravikant,* the Court came down heavily on the Government for handcuffing an undertrial prisoner and making him parade in streets in a procession by the police. In this case the Court directed the Government for paying a sum of Rs. 10,000 to the victim for the humiliation he had suffered.

Interrogation

Provision innumerated in Chapter XII of Criminal Procedure Code confers power on the Police to examine accused person and witnesses. However, while carrying out such job it is of utmost importance to follow all other provisions of the code as well as Constitution to ensure human dignity and personal liberty of the person under examination. While examining an accused/witness for the purposes of fact finding the following legal provisions should be paid heed to:

(i) Section 54 of the Cr. P.C. confers upon an arrested person the right to have himself medically examined.

(ii) A confession made to police officer is not admissible in evidence under Section 25 and 26 of the Indian Evidence Act.

(iii) Section 162 of Cr.P.C., also provides that no statement of a witness recorded by a police officer can be used for any purpose other than that of contradicting his statement before the Court.

(iv) Section 24 of Indian Evidence Act also provides that when admissible, confession must be made voluntarily. If it is made under any inducement, threat or promise, it is inadmissible in criminal proceedings.

(v) An additional safeguard is that under Section 164 of the Cr.P.C., it is for the Magistrate to ensure that a confession or statement being made by an accused person is voluntary.

There are a few constitutional safeguards provided to a person to protect his personal liberty against any unjustified assault by the State. Article 22 guarantees protection against arrest and detention in certain cases and declares that no person who is arrested shall be detained in custody without being informed of the grounds of such arrest and he shall not be denied the right to consult and defend himself by a legal practitioner of his choice. Article 22(2) directs that the person arrested and detained in custody shall be produced before the nearest Magistrate within a period of 24 hours of such arrest, excluding the time necessary for the journey from the place of the arrest to the Court of the Magistrate. Article 20(3) of the Constitution lays down that a person accused of an offence shall not be compelled to be a witness against himself. Manner in which examination of accused should be conducted is elaborated under the head 'confession'.

Confession

Article 20(3) of the Constitution provides that no person accused of any offence shall be compelled to be a witness against himself; and Section 161(2) Cr.P.C., enjoins that any person supposed to be acquainted with the facts and circumstances of the case shall be bound to answer truly all questions relating to such case put to him by any police officer making an investigation under Chapter XII of the Code, other than questions the answers to which would have the tendency to expose him to a criminal charge or to a penalty or forfeiture.

Case of *Nandini Satpathy Vs. P.L. Danis,* is the classic example in this context, wherein the Supreme Court held that Section 161 of Cr.P.C. enables the police to examine the accused during investigation. The prohibitive sweep of Article 20(3) goes back to the stage of police interrogation-not, as contended, commencing in Court only. In our judgement, the provisions of article 20(3) and Section 161(1) substantially covers the same area, so far as police investigations are concerned. The ban on self-accusation and the right to silence, while one investigation or trial is under way, goes beyond that case and protects the accused in regard to other offences pending or imminent, which may deter him from voluntary disclosure of criminatory matter. We are disposed to read 'compelled testimony' as evidence procured not merely by physical threats or violence but psychic torture, atmospheric pressure, environmental coercion, tiring interrogative prolixity, overbearing and intimidatory methods and the like—not legal penalty for violation. So, the legal perils following upon refusal to answer, or answer truthfully, cannot be regarded as compulsion within the meaning of Article 20(3). The prospect of prosecution may lead to legal tension in the exercise of a constitutional right, but then, a stance of silence is running a calculated risk. On the other hand, if there is any mode of pressure, subtle or crude, mental or physical, direct or indirect, but sufficiently substantial, applied by the policemen for obtaining information from an accused strongly suggestive of guilt, it becomes 'compelled testimony', violative of Article 20(3).

Legal penalty for refusing to answer or answer truthfully may by itself not amount to duress. It cannot be regarded as compulsion under Article 20(3). But frequent threats of prosecution if there is failure to answer may take on the complexion of undue pressure violating Article 20(3). The manner of mentioning it to the victim of interrogation may introduce an element of tension and tone of command perilously hovering near compulsion.

Lawyer's presence is a constitutional claim in some circumstances in our country also, and, in the context of Article 20(3), is an assurance of awareness and observance of the right to silence. The *Miranda* decision has insisted that if an accused person asks for a lawyer's assistance, at the stage of interrogation, it shall be granted before commencing or continuing with the questioning. We think that Article 20(3) and Article 22(1) may, in a way, be telescoped by making it prudent for the police to permit the advocate of the accused, if there be one, to be present at the time he is examined. Overreaching Article 20(3) and Section 161(2) will be obviated by this requirement. In the same case it was categorically stated that if an accused person expresses the wish to have his lawyer by his side when his examination goes on, this facility shall not be denied, without being exposed to the serious reproof that involuntary self-incrimination secured in secrecy and by coercing the will. The police need not wait more than for a reasonable while for an advocate's arrival. But they must invariably warn—and record that fact—about the right to silence against self-incrimination; and where the accused is literate take his written acknowledgement.

The symbiotic need to preserve the immunity without stifling legitimate investigation persuaded the court to indicate that after an examination of the accused, where lawyer of his choice is not available, the police official must take him to a magistrate, doctor or other willing and responsible non-partisan official or non-official and allow a secluded audience where he may unburden himself beyond the view of the police and tell whether he has suffered duress, which should be followed by judicial or some other custody for him where the police cannot reach him. That collocutor may briefly record the relevant conversation and communicate it—not to the police—but to the nearest magistrate. Pilot projects on this pattern to guide the practical processes of implementing Article 20(3) was strongly suggested in the case.

It was further observed that: above all, long run recipes must be innovated whereby fists are replaced by wits, ignorance by awareness, 'third degree' by civilised tools and technology. Special training, special legal courses, technological and other detective updating are important. An aware policemen is the best social asset towards crimelessness. The consciousness of the official as much as of the community is the healing hope for a crime-ridden society. Judge-centred remedies don't work in the absence of community-centred rights. Investigatory personnel must be separated from the general mass and given in-service specialisation on a scientific basis.

The policeman must be released from addiction to coercion and sensitized to constitutional values.

Considering the statutory safeguards to protect this right in *Sarvan Singh Vs. State of Punjab,* the Court held that "act of recording confession under Section 164 Cr.P.C. is very solemn act and, in discharging his duties under the said Section, the Magistrate must take care to see that the requirements of sub-section (3) of Section 164 are fully satisfied. It would of course be necessary in every case to put the questions prescribed by the High Court circulars but the questions intended to be put under sub-section (3) of Section 164 should not be allowed to become a matter of mere mechanical enquiry. No element of casualness should be allowed to creep in and the Magistrate should be fully satisfied that the confessional statement which the accused wants to make is in fact and in substance voluntary.

Emphasising the importance of Section 164 of the Cr.P.C. the court observed that: "the whole object of putting questions to an accused person who offers to confess is to obtain an assurance of the fact that the confession is not caused by any inducement, threat or promise having reference to the charge against the accused person as mentioned in Section 24 of the Indian Evidence Act. There can be no doubt that, when an accused person is produced before the Magistrate by the investigating officer, it is of utmost importance that the mind of the accused person should be completely freed from any possible influence of the police and the effective way of securing such freedom from fear to the accused person is to send him to jail custody and give him adequate time to consider whether he should make a confession at all. It would naturally be difficult to lay down any hard and fast rule as to the time which should be allowed to an accused person in any given case. However, speaking generally, it would, we think, be reasonable to insist upon giving an accused person at least 24 hours to decide whether or not he should make a confession. Where there may be reason to suspect that the accused has been persuaded or coerced to make a confession, even longer period may have to be given to him before his statement is recorded".

In the same case it was further held that "even if the confession is held to be voluntary, it must also be established that the confession is true and for the purpose of dealing with this question it would be necessary to examine the confession and compare it with the rest of the prosecution evidence and probabilities in the case". The Court reiterated its view in *Davendra Prasad Vs. State of U.P.* by saying that before a confessional statement made under S. 164 of the Code of Criminal Procedure can be acted upon, it must be shown to be voluntary and free from police influence.

While determining the Magistrate's role, Supreme Court in *Shivappa Vs. State of Karnataka* held: From the plain language of Section 164 of Cr.P.C. and the rules and guidelines framed by the High Court regarding the recording of confessional statements of an accused under Section 164 Cr.P.C., it is manifest that the said provision emphasise an inquiry by the Magistrate to ascertain the involuntary nature of the confession. This inquiry appears to be the most significant and important part of the duty of the Magistrate recording the confessional statement of an accused under Section 164 Cr.P.C. the failure of the Magistrate to put such questions from which he could ascertain the voluntary nature of the confession detracts so materially from the evidentiary value the confession of an accused that it would not be safe to act upon the same. Full and adequate compliance not merely in form but in essence with the provisions of Section 164 of Cr.P.C. and the rules framed by the High Court is imperative and its non-compliance goes to the root of the Magistrate's jurisdiction to record the confession and render the confession unworthy of credence. Before proceeding to record the confessional statement, a searching enquiry must be made from the accused as to the custody from which he was produced and the treatment he had been receiving in such custody in order to ensure that there is no scope for doubt of any sort of extraneous influence proceeding from a source interested in the prosecution still lurking in the mind of an accused. In case the Magistrate discovers on such enquiry that there is ground for such supposition he should give the accused sufficient time for reflection before he is asked to make his statement and should assure himself that during the time of reflection, he is completely out of police influence. An accused should particularly be asked the reason why he wants to make a statement which would surely go against his self-interest in course of the trial, even if he contrives subsequently to retract the confession. Besides administrating the caution, warning specifically provided for in the first part of sub-section (2) of Section 164 namely, that the accused is not bound to make a statement and that if he makes one it may be used against him as evidence in relation to his complicity in the offence at the trial, that is to follow, he should also, in plain language, be assured of protection from any sort of apprehended torture or pressure from such extraneous agents as the police or the like in case he declines to make a statement and be given the assurance that even if he declined to make the confession, he shall not be remanded to police custody.

The Magistrate who is entrusted with the duty of recording confession of an accused coming from police custody of jail custody must appreciate his function in that behalf as one of a judicial officer and he must apply his judicial mind to ascertain and satisfy his conscience that the statement accused makes is not on account of any extraneous influence on him. That indeed is the essence of a 'voluntary' statement within the meaning of the provisions of Section 164 Cr.P.C. and the rules framed by the High Court for the guidance of the subordinate courts. Moreover, the Magistrate must not only be satisfied as to the voluntary character of the statement, he should also make and leave such material on record in proof of the compliance with the imperative requirements of the statutory provisions, as would satisfy the court that sits in judgment in the case, that the confessional statements was made by the accused voluntarily and the statutory provisions were strictly complied with.

Even though an accused makes a confession and pleads guilty, the Magistrate should examine him under Section 313 Cr.P.C. to enable him to explain the circumstances under which the offence was committed.

The confession of a co-accused is not a substantive evidence. It can be used in service when the Court is inclined to accept other evidence and feels the necessity of seeking for an assurance in support of his conclusion deductible from other evidence. When there is no substantive evidence about a fact or circumstance, the previous statement of the accused to prove the fact or circumstances cannot be relied upon, and no conviction can be based solely on such a statement.

Information Leading to Discovery

While investigating into an offence, it is obvious for the investigative agency to seek information related to weapons of offence, stolen property, dead body of the victim and other similar vital constituents of the offence from the accused/suspect. However, it is very important to remember that while eliciting such information from the accused, the investigating official should not resort to torture or any other similar methods. All requirements elaborated under head 'confession' is equally applicable while seeking information from the accused for the purposes of discovery.

Bail

The innovative interpretation of constitutional provisions by the Supreme Court and High Courts have developed bail as a human right. The Code of Criminal Procedure contains provisions for bail. Section 57 of the Code provides:

"No police officer shall detain in custody a person arrested without warrant for a longer period than under all the circumstances of the case is reasonable, and such period shall not, in the absence of a special order of a Magistrate under Section 167, exceed twenty four hours exclusive of the time necessary for the journey from the place of arrest to the Magistrate's Court."

The Supreme Court observed that the right to bail is an invaluable right available to a person and that this right should not be denied arbitrarily, and that denial of this contravenes the fundamental right to personal liberty. As it is established in the Indian Judicial system, law presumes and accused to be innocent until his guilt is established, and as an innocent person he is entitled to defend his freedom. Relying on this principle in *Vidya Sagar Vs. State of Punjab,* the Court observed: "though the stage for raising the presumption of innocence in favour of the accused person does not arise till the conclusion of the trial and appreciation of entire evidence on the record, yet the matter of granting bail has to be considered in the background of the fact that in the criminal jurisprudence, which guides the Courts, there is a presumption in favour of the accused".

In *Kashmira Singh Vs. State of Punjab,* Justice Bhagawati observed: "it would be indeed a travesty of justice to keep a person in jail for a period of five to six years for an offence which is ultimately found not to have been committed by him. Can the Courts ever compensate him for his incarceration which is found to be unjustified?". Krishna Iyer J. expressing his view in *Godikanti Vs. Public Prosecutor* case observed: "Bail or Jail? At the pretrial or post conviction stage belongs to the blurred area of the criminal justice system and largely hangs on the hunch of the bench, otherwise called judicial discretion".

In the same judgement it was emphasised that "personal liberty, deprived when bail is refused, is too precious a value of our Constitution recognised under Article 21 and that the crucial power to negate it is a great trust exercisable, not casually but judicially, with likely concern for the cost to individual and the community. To glamorise impressionistic orders as discretionary may, on occasions, make a litigative gamble decisive of a fundamental right. After all, personal liberty of an accused or convict is fundamental, suffering lawful eclipse only in terms of 'procedure established by law'. The last four words of Article 21 are the life of that human right". In another case Krishna Iyer, J. stressed, "reasonableness postulates intelligent care and predicates the deprivation of freedom by refusal of bail is not for punitive purpose but for the bi-focal interest of justice to the individual involved and society affected".

It has been notified in several cases that an acused is not able to furnish bail bond because of his poverty. This important aspect was dealt in *Moti Ram Vs. State of Madhya Pradesh*. In this case the Court held that there is a need for liberal interpretation of social justice, individual freedom and indigent's rights and while awarding bail covers release on one's own bond, with or without surities. When surities should be demanded and what sum should be insisted on are dependent on variables.

In *Hussainara Khatoon Vs. State of Bihar,* Bhagawati J., while effectively raising the inherent weaknesses of monetary bond said: "the bail system, as we see it administered in the criminal courts today, is extremely unsatisfactory and needs drastic change. In the first place it is virtually impossible to translate risk of non-appearance by the accused into precise monetary terms and even its basic premise that risk of financial loss is necessary to prevent the accused from fleeing is of doubtful validity. There are several considerations which deter an accused from running away from justice and risk of financial loss is only one of them and that too not a major one. The experience of enlightened projects in the United States such as Manhattan Bail Project and D.C. Bail Project shows that even without monetary bail it has been possible to secure the presence of the accused at the trial in quite a large number of cases. Moreover, the bail system causes discrimination against the poor would not be able to furnish bail on account of their poverty while the wealthier persons otherwise in similar situation would be able to secure their freedom because they can afford to furnish bail. This discrimination arises even if the amount of the bail as fixed by the Magistrate is not high, for a large majority of those who are brought before the courts in criminal cases are so poor that they would find it difficult to furnish bail even in a small amount".

Justice Bhagawati suggested that, under the law as it stands today the Court must abandon the antiquated concept under which pre-trial release is ordered only against bail with sureties. The concept is outdated and experience has shown that it has done more harm than good. The new insight into the subject of pre-trial release which has been developed in socially advanced countries and particularly the United States should now inform the decisions of our Courts in regard to pre-trial release. If the Court is satisfied, after taking into account, on the basis of information placed before the Court, that the accused has his roots in the community and is not likely to abscond, the Court can safely release the accused on his personal bond. To determine whether the accused has his roots in the community which would deter him from fleeing, the Court should take into account the following factors concerning the accused:

(i) The length of his residence in the community.
(ii) His employment status, history and his financial condition.
(iii) His family ties and relationships.
(iv) His reputation, character and monetary condition.
(v) His prior criminal record including any record of prior release on recognisance or on bail.
(vi) The identity of responsible members of the community who would vouch for his reliability.
(vii) The nature of the offence charged and the apparent probability of conviction and the likely sentence in so far as these factors are relevant to the risk of non-appearance, and
(viii) Any other factors indicating the ties of the accused to the community or bearing on the risk of wilful failure to appeal.

Guidelines

1. Arrests without substantial grounds need to be avoided.
2. While recording First Information Report it should be ensured that the same is in accordance with established procedures and names of innocent uninvolved persons are not unnecessarily placed in the report.
3. If 'caution', 'fine' or any thing similar will serve the purpose then the same should be used instead of arrest.
4. Procedures of arrest need to be followed meticulously; offenders being duly informed of their rights and their relatives being informed of the offender's arrest and

whereabouts.

5. Procedures carried out at the Police stations should be transparent.
6. Women arrestees should be handled with special care and attention to their gender.
7. Proper records of cases brought before each police station should be maintained and should be readily available for examination by those who are entitled to examine the same.
8. Officers who are in charge of the investigation of cases should not be part of the prosecuting agency to avoid tough stances against arrested person to justify arrest.
9. Where police have the power to grant bail the power should be exercised.
10. Extension of remand should not be sought for automatically or mechanically.

Standards particularly applicable to pre-trial detainees

Detention pending trial should be an exception rather than the rule. There are several issues to be considered to assess pre-trial detention is necessary in a given case, including:

- Are there reasonable grounds to believe that the person has committed the offence?
- Would the deprivation of liberty be disproportionate to the alleged offence and expected sentence?
- Is there a danger of that the suspect will abscond?
- Is there a danger that the suspect will commit further offence?
- Is there a danger of serious interference with the course of justice if the suspect is released?
- Would bail or release on condition be sufficient?

Trial

Trial is the process through which judiciary determines criminal liability of an accused. During trial it is the duty/burden of the prosecution to prove charges against the accused beyond any reasonable doubt. It is established criminal law that a person shall be presumed innocent till finally convicted by a competent court. It is the duty of all concerned with 'custodial justice system' to conduct themselves in accordance with the Criminal Procedure Code.

(a) Fair Trial

In the determination of any criminal charge, every person shall be equally entitled to the following minimum guarantees necessry for defence.

(i) to be informed promptly of any charges upon arrest; to be brought promptly before a judicial officer for an assessment of the legality of an arrest;
(ii) to equal treatment before courts; to a fair and usually public hearing by a competent, independent and impartial court established by law; to be presumed innocent;
(iii) to be informed promptly and in detail in a language one understands the nature of charges; to have adequate time and facilities for the preparation of a defence; to communicate with counsel of one's own choice;
(iv) to be tried without undue delay;
(v) to be tried in one's presence;
(vi) to defend one's self in person or through legal assistance of one's choice;
(vii) to be informed that counsel will be appointed if one does not have sufficient funds and the interests of justice require such appointment;
(viii) to examine or have examined witnesses;
(ix) to obtain the attendance and examination of witnesses on the same conditions as adverse witnesses;
(x) to have the assistance of an interpreter if one cannot understand the language used in court;
(xi) not to be compelled to testify against one's self or to confess guilt;
(xii) to have a conviction reviewed by a higher court according to law;
(xiii) to be compensated for any punishment which is conclusively shown to be a miscarriage of justice;
(xiv) not to be convicted for any offence for which one has been finally convicted or acquitted (double-jeopardy);
(xv) not to be convicted for any act which did not constitute a criminal offence under criminal law at the time of the conduct (retrospective application of criminal law); and
(xvi) to benefit from any subsequent decrease in punishment.

(b) Remand and Custody

The whole spirit of the Constitution and the Criminal Procedure Code is that the custody and liberty of the accused/

detainee is entirely governed by the authority and sanction of a court of law beyond the initial 24 hours between the first arrest and production before the Magistrate thereafter. By no twisted interpretation can this power in actual fact and practice be passed on into the mere discretion of the investigating agency. Once an accused is produced before the court, it is the Court's responsibility and power as to whether he is to be remanded to further custody or granted bail or released altogether. To seek remand the investigation agency has to prefer an application stating therein weighty reasons for the same. Under no circumstances remand order can be passed mechanically and the Magistrate passing an order of the remand ought, as far as possible, to see that the detainee is produced before the court when remand order is passed.

Speedy Trial

Article 14(3)(c) of the International Covenant for Civil and Political Rights provides for the right "to be tried without undue delay". The right to speedy trial is incorporated under the Indian Constitution as part of personal liberty. However, there is no specific provision under the Indian Constitution which deals specifically with speedy trial. In spite of this, there is no dearth of judicial decisions which have given new dimensions to speedy trial, and made it almost a fundamental right.

The landmark case is *Hussainara Khatoon* Vs. *State of Bihar*. Justice Bhagawati observed in this case that although speedy trial is not specifically enumerated as a fundamental right, it is implicit in the broad sweep and content of Article 21. The Supreme Court had held in *Maneka Gandhi* Vs. *Union of India* that Article 21 confers a fundamental right on every person not to be deprived of his life or liberty except in accordance with the procedure prescribed by law. If a person is deprived of his liberty under a procedure which is not 'reasonable, fair or just', such deprivation would be violative of his fundamental right under Article 21 and he would be entitled to enforce such fundamental right and secure his release. Obviously a procedure established by law for depriving a person of his liberty cannot be reasonable, fair or just unless that procedure ensures a speedy trial for determination of the guilt of such person. "Any procedure which does not ensure a reasonably quick trial cannot be regarded 'reasonable, fair or just' and would fall foul of Article 21". Therefore, by speedy trial we mean reasonable expeditious trial which is an intrinsic and essential part of the fundamental right to life and liberty enshrined in Article 21. The Supreme Court further observed that speedy trial was the essence of criminal justice system and delay in trial by itself constitutes a denial of justice.

In *Kadra Pahadiya* Vs. *State of Bihar,* four young boys who were designated as petitioners who were lodged in Pakur sub-jail in Santhal Parganas for a period of eight years without trial. They all belonged to the Paharia tribe, a backward tribe. Out of four, two of them were arrested on 26th November 1978 while the other two, on 19th December 1972. The jail record showed the ages of the petitioners being between 18 to 22 years at the time of their arrest, but the writ petition stated that they could not have been more than 9 to 11 years old when they were arrested. Bhagawati J. said, on behalf of the Court, "We hoped that after the anguish expressed and the severe strictures passed by us, the justice system in the State of Bihar would improve and no one shall be allowed to be confined in jail for more than a reasonable period of time, which we think cannot and should not exceed one year for a sessions trial, but we find that the situation has remained unchanged and these four petitioners, who entered the jail as young lads of 12 to 13 have been languishing in jail for over eight years for a crime which perhaps ultimately they may be found not to have committed". The position continues to be very disappointing and still a large number of prisoners languish in jail without their trial having commenced.

This issues related to speedy trial again came before the Supreme Court in *Raghuvir Singh* Vs. *State of Bihar,* wherein the Court held "...the Constitutional position is now well settled that the right to speedy trial is one of the dimensions of the fundamental right to life and liberty..." In *Madhu Mehta* Vs. *Union of India,* the Supreme Court reiterated that speedy trial is implicit in the broad sweep and content of Article 21. This principle has no less importance for the disposal of mercy petitions than to trial in the Court.

Appeal

In a number of cases the Supreme Court upheld the right to appeal. Considering the difficulties of the prisoners in exercising this invaluable right in *M.H. Hoskot Vs. State of Maharashtra,* the Court declared that the Constitutional mandates under Article 21 read with Article 19(1)(d) prescribes:

(a) Courts shall forthwith furnish a free transcript of the judgment when sentencing a person to a prison term.
(b) In the event of any such copy being sent to the jail authorities for delivery to the prisoner by the appellate, revisional or other court, the official concerned shall, with quick despatch, get it delivered to the sentencee and obtain written acknowledgement thereof from him.
(c) where the prisoner seeks to file an appeal or revision, every facility for exercise of that right shall be made available by the jail administration.
(d) where the prisoner is disabled from engaging a lawyer on reasonable grounds such as indigence or because of difficulty in communication with outsiders, the court shall, if circumstances of the case, or the gravity of the sentence and the ends of justice so require, assign competent counsel for the prisoner's defence provided the party does not object to that lawyer.
(e) The State which prosecuted the prisoner and set in motion the process so to deprive him of his liberty shall pay to the assigned counsel such sum as the court may equitably fix.
(f) These benign prescriptions operate from the lowest to the highest court where a deprivation of life and personal liberty is in substantial peril.

Under Article 21 no person shall be deprived of his life or personal liberty except according to procedure established by law. 'Procedure established by law' are words of deep meaning for all lovers of liberty and judicial sentinels. Amplified activist fashion 'procedure' means 'fair and reasonable procedure' which confirms with civilised norms like natural justice rooted firm in community consciousness—not primitive processual barbarity nor legislated normative mockery. Generally speaking, and subject to just exceptions at least a single right of appeal on facts where criminal conviction is fraught with long loss of liberty, is basic to civilised jurisprudence. It is integral to fair procedure, natural justice and normative universality save in special cases like the Original Tribunal being a high bench sitting on a collegiate basis. Every step that makes a right of appeal fruitful is obligatory and every action or inaction which stultifies it is unfair and hence unconstitutional. In a sense, Article 19 joins hand with Article 21 necessitating the two requirements: (1) service of a copy of the judgment in time to the prisoner intending to file an appeal, and (2) provision for the free legal services to a prisoner who is indigent or otherwise disabled from securing legal assistance where the ends of justice call for such service. With the aforesaid guidelines the Court directed that the jail manuals will have to be suitably amended to ensure that the prisoner receives the copy of the judgment in time.

The Indian socio-legal mileu makes free legal service at trial and higher levels an imperative processual piece of criminal justice where deprivation of life or personal liberties hangs in the judicial balance. If a prisoner sentenced to imprisonment is virtually unable to exercise his constitutional and statutory right of appeal inclusive of special appeal to appeal for want of legal assistance, there is implicit in the Supreme Court under Article 142 read with Articles 21 and 39A, power to assign counsel for such imprisoned individuals for doing 'complete justice'. It is State's duty and not merely Government's charity. Equally affirmative is the implication that while legal services must be free to the beneficiary, the lawyer himself has to be reasonably remunerated for his services. There is a right to counsel, not in the permissive sense of Article 22(1), but in its wider amplitude in the peremptory sense of Article 21.

Release on Probation

Granting of probation is a discretionary power with the court. Such powers of the court are governed under Section 360 and 361 of Cr.P.C. These provisions state under what circumstances probation can be granted. Generally when the accused is neither a habitual offender nor a previous convict, courts grant probation. Under Section 562(1), Cr.P.C. an offender can be released on probation only before he is sentenced to any punishment. If the court convicts the accused and sentences him to any punishment, it's power to make an alternative order is exhausted. While granting probation the court has to take the age, character, nature of the offence, mental and physical condition and antecedents of the accused/ offender and all other extenuating circumstances associated with the offence into consideration apart from other conditions stipulated in the aforesaid provisions.

Health and Well-Being

Good health is important to everyone. It affects how people behave and their ability to function as members of the community. It has a particular significance in the closed community of a prison. By its nature the condition of imprisonment can have a damaging effect on both the physical and mental wellbeing of prisoners. Prison administrations have a responsibility, therefore, not simply to provide medical care but also to establish conditions which promote the wellbeing of both prisoners and prison staff. Prisoners should not leave prison in a worse condition than how they entered. This applies to all aspects of prison life, but especially to health care.

Those who are imprisoned retain their fundamental right to enjoy good health, both physical and mental, and they retain their entitlement to a standard of medical care which is at least the equivalent of that provided in the wider community. Alongside these fundamental rights of all human persons, prisoners have additional safeguards as a result of their status. When a state deprives people of their liberty it takes on a responsibility to look after their health in terms both of the conditions under which it detains them and of the individual treatment which may be necessary as a result of those conditions. While dealing with this aspect special attention should be given to factors like age, gender, mental condition, etc, of a prisoner. It is unethical to classify prisoners as a single group for proving medical facilities. Each prisoner should be given adequate medical care as his/her body demands.

Whenever possible prisoners should have full access to the medical facilities which are available to the public at large. However, for management reasons presently this access is limited to specialist care while general medical care is provided within the individual prison or in specific prison medical facilities. Any medical treatment or nursing care provided by the prison administration should be atleast comparable to what is available in the outside community.

There is an absolute obligation on the State to preserve and, if necessary, restore the health of those individuals for whom it takes responsibility by depriving them of their liberty. The conditions under which prisoners are detained will have a major impact on their health and well-being. In order to meet their responsibilities therefore, prison administration should ensure appropriate standards in all those areas which may affect the health and hygiene of prisoners. The physical conditions of the accommodation, the food and the arrangement for hygiene and sanitation should all be designated in such a way as to help those who are unwell to recover and to prevent the spread of infection to the healthy.

The conditions of imprisonment will have a serious impact on the mental well-being of prisoners. Prison administrations should seek to reduce the extent of that impact and should also establish procedures to monitor its effects on individual prisoners, steps should be taken to identify those prisoners who might be at risk of self harm or suicide. Staff should be properly trained in recognising the indicators of potential self-harm. Health care staff have an important role in establishing the concept that health care embraces not simply treatment but all aspects of creating a healthy environment and that this requires the cooperation of everyone in the prison. This will be particularly challenging when resources are limited.

The foregone requirements apart there are a number of issues in which medical staff need to distinguish between the demands of the prison administration and the ethics of professional health care. Prisoners' right to privacy and confidentiality are amongst such considerations, which have to be adequately taken care of by the prison medical staff.

Guidelines for medical care in prisions

As a minimum, the prison administration should provide in each prison:

1. Initial medical screening on admission to the prison;
2. Regular out-patient consultations;
3. Emergency treatment;
4. Suitably equipped premises for consultation with and the treatment of prisoners;
5. An adequate supply of appropriate medicines dispensed by qualified pharmacists;
6. Facilities for physiotherapy and post-treatment rehabilitation;
7. Any special diets which may be identified as medically necessary;
8. Prison administration will need to ensure that access to general medical care is available at any time without delay in cases of urgency;
9. Necessary medical care and treatment should be provided free of charge.
10. Where prisoners are diagnosed as mentally ill they should not be held in prison but should be transferred to a suitably equipped psychiatric facility;
11. The treatment provided as a result of consultation and diagnosis should be that which is in the best interests of the individual prisoner. Decisions should not be based on the

relative cost or convenience to the prison administration.

12. Any diagnosis made or advice offered by prison medical staff should be based on professional judgement and in the best interests of the prisoner.

Wages in Prison

The Supreme Court in the case of *State of Gujarat* Vs. *Hon'ble Court of Gujarat* examined the question of minimum wages of prisoners and in its order dated 24th September 1998 held that it was 'lawful to employ prisoners sentences to rigorous imprisonment whether he consents to do it or not'. The apex court also held:

- it is open to the jail officials to permit other prisoners also to do the work which they chose to do, provided such prisoners make a request for the purpose;
- it is imperative that the prisoners should be paid equitable wages for the work done by them. In order to determine the quantum of equitable wages payable to prisoners the State concerned shall constitute a wage fixation body for making recommendations. Each State is directed to do so as early as possible;
- until the State Government takes any decision on such recommendations every prisoner must be paid wages for work done by him at such rates or revised rates as the Government concerned fixes in the light of the observations made above. For this purpose all the State Governments are directed to fix the rate of such interim wages within six weeks (from 24th September 1998) and report to the Court compliance with the direction.

This direction of the Supreme Court was reiterated by the National Human Rights Commission, which insisted strict implementation of the same at the earliest possibility. Following such directions, most of the State Governments have made upward revision of the paltry wages being paid to the prisoners. However, it is important to take the health of the prisoner in to consideration while assigning him/her work. Health is of paramount importance and under no circumstances a prisoner can be forced to do work that is not permitted by his/her health.

Preventive Detention

After the commencement of the Constitution, the liberty of a citizen of India has to be zealously guarded and preserved. Article 21 of the Constitution enjoins 'no person shall be deprived of his life or personal liberty except according to procedure established by law. Once a person is arrested and detained the executive has to justify its action in the sense that the detention is either for violation of some law or for preventive purpose, as prescribed by law. In both the cases, the justification for detention has to be only under the authority of law. It is an established principle that before a person is deprived of his liberty the procedure established by law must be strictly followed and must not be departed from to the disadvantage of the person affected.

Preventive detention differs from imprisonment on conviction or during investigation of the crime of an accused which permits separate classification of the detainees under preventive detention. Preventive detention is to prevent breach of law while imprisonment or conviction or during investigation subsequent to the commission of the crime. The executive derives its authority to resort to preventive detention from specific legislations like National Security Act specifically designed with an object like 'to cope with situations of communal disharmony, social tensions, extremist activities, industrial unrest and increasing tendency on the part of various interested parties to engineer agitations on different issues.

It is imperative to follow the law meticulosly while resorting to preventive detention. The executive cannot exercise such powers unless the same is clearly and expressedly stipulated in the respective legislation. Further, it is very important to facilitate review of the order of detention. The detainee should be provided with all relevant information so as to enable him/her to prepare an effective representation against his/her detention. And such representation should be processed and considered expeditiously. While a detainee is under preventive detention he/she is entitled to all rights corresponding to his/her human dignity.

Custodial Death

In *Nilabati Behera Vs. State of Orissa,* the Supreme Court observed that "...there is a great responsibility on the police or prison authorities to ensure that the citizen in its custody is not deprived of his right to life. His liberty is in the very nature of things circumscribed by the very fact of his confinement and therefore his interest in the limited liberty left to him is rather precious. The duty of care on the part of the State is strict and admits of no exceptions. The wrongdoer is accountable and the State is responsible if the person in custody of the police is deprived of his life except according to procedure established by law..."

Article 9(5) of the International Covenant on Civil and Political Rights indicates that an enforceable 'right to compensation' is not alien to the concept of enforcement of a guaranteed right. Anyone who has been the victim of unlawful arrest or detention shall have an enforceable right to compensation. Following this principle in *Nilabati Behera Vs. State of Orissa* the Court awarded a sum of Rs. 1.5 lakhs to the mother as her son had died in police custody.

For determining whether State is responsible for 'custodial death' or not the National Human Rights Commission has issued strict instructions to all concerned from time to time, which are as follows:

(i) custodial death should be reported by the District Magistrate and the Superintendent of Police of the respective district to the Secretary General of the National Human Rights Commission within 24 hours of occurrence or of these officers having come to know about such incidents.

(ii) The expression 'custodial death' encompasses deaths in police custody as well as in judicial custody.

(iii) Post-mortem examination is a must for all cases of custodial deaths. All post-mortem examinations done in respect of deaths in police custody and in jails should be video filmed and cassets be sent to the Commission alongwith the post-mortem report, as prescribed by the Commission.

(iv) In all cases of custodial death a magisterial inquiry should be conducted for fact finding

[***Remember***—failure to report promptly would give rise to presumption that there was an attempt to suppress the incident]

Conclusion

District Magistrate and every authority who has something to do with custodial justice should know that today how civilised a society, is judged by the international community by the standard of recognition and protection of human rights of even those in custody.

It is the paramount duty of everyone to ensure that human dignity shall not be violated under any circumstances.

If all the instructions and guidelines given are followed, District

Magistrate can ensure effective custodial justice.

Glossary of Terms and Definitions

Administrative detention: deprivation of liberty by Government action, but outside the process of the police arresting suspects and bringing them into the criminal justice system.

Administration of Custodial justice: it includes the functioning and independence of the Courts, the role of prosecutors, the role of lawyers; the role of law enforcement officials; human rights during criminal investigations, arrest and detention; the right to a fair trial; standards for the protection of prisoners; non-custodial measures; the administration of juvenile justice; the rights of minorities, non-nationals and refugees; women's human rights in legal system; protection and redress for victims of crime and abuses of power, the adrninistration of Justice under state of' emergency, the right to habeas corpus.

Administration of juvenile justice: a system/protocol which ensures that juvenile persons are entitled to procedures that can take account of their age and the desirability of promoting their rehabilitation. Further it requires, any child alleged to have committed a criminal offence shall be treated in a manner consistent with the child's dignity and worth as well as the desirability of promoting the child's reintegration in society. Such a child alleged to have infringed the penal law is entitled to the presumption of innocence, to be informed promptly of the charges; to have the matter determined without delay by a competent, independent and impartial judicial authority in a fair hearing according to law, in the presence of legal or other appropriate assistance, and usually in the presence of the child's parents or legal guardians. In addition to the said rights the child will have all other rights conferred on an accused in general.

Arbitrary detention: when a public official or any other person acting in an official capacity or with official instigation, consent or acquiescence, deprives a person, without a valid reason, of his/her liberty by confining him/her in a prison or any other detention facility or compels him/her to stay in an assigned place.

Arbitrary execution: killing of a person perpetrated by an agent of the State or any other person acting under Government authority or with its complicity, tolerance, or acquiescence, but without any or due judicial process. Executions resulting from a death sentence issued by a court, are also arbitrary executions if the fair trials guarantees provided in Constitution and judicial authority are not respected.

Bail: conditional release of an accused person; in principle it shall not be the general rule that persons awaiting trial shall be detained in custody, but release may be subject to guarantees to appear for trial, at any other stage of the judicial proceedings and, should occasion arise, for execution of the judgement.

Derogation of rights: permissible limitation on rights. Under certain specific conditions set forth in the Constitution of India, limitations can be imposed by the State on exercise of some fundamental rights. It should be clear, however, that limitations on rights should be seen as exception, rather than the rule. Limitations on rights, where they are permitted, are specified in the various provisions of Constitution. In general, such limitations and restrictions must be those which are determined by law and necessary in a democratic society to: (i) Ensure respect for the rights and freedoms of others; and (ii) Meet the just requirements of public order, public health or morals, national security or public safety. Derogation imposed outside or beyond the above-mentioned conditions are not tolerated by human rights law, more specifically custodial justice system. And for derogation of rights declaration of state of emergency is a must.

Disappearance: an action of' taking persons into custody by agents of' the state, yet whose whereabouts and fate are concealed. It is a grave violation of human rights to carry out disappearances.

Extrajudicial execution: an unlawful and deliberate killing carried out by, or on the order of, someone at some level of government, whether national, state or local, or with acquiescence.

Enforced disappearance: when persons are arrested, detained or abducted against their will or otherwise deprived of their liberty by officials of different branches or levels of Government, or by organised groups or private individuals acting on behalf of, or with the support-direct or indirect- consent or acquiescence of the Government, and followed by the Government's refusal to disclose the fate or whereabouts of the persons concerned or a refusal to acknowledge the deprivation of their liberty.

Fair trial: with regard to a criminal case, it includes the rights to be informed promptly of any charges upon arrest, to be brought promptly before a judicial officer for an assesssment of the legality of an arrest; to equal treatment before courts; to a fair and usually public hearing by a competent, independent and impartial court established by law; to be presumed innocent; to be informed promptly and in detail in a language one understand the nature of charges, to have adequate time and facilities for the preparation to communicate with counsel of one's own choice; to be tried without undue delay, to be tried in one's presence; to defend one's self in person or through legal assistance of one's choice; to be informed that counsel will be appointed if one does not have sufficient funds and the interests of justice require such appointment; to examine or have examined witnesses; to obtain the attendence and examination of witnesses on the same conditions as adverse witnesses; to have the assistance of an interpretor if one cannot understand the language used in court; not to be compelled to testify against one's self or to confess guilt; to have a conviction reviewed by a higher court according to law; to be compensated for any punishment which is conclusively shown to be a miscarriage of justice; not to be convicted for any offence for which one has already been finally convicted or acquitted (double-jeopardy); not to be convicted for any act which did not constitute a criminal offence under criminal law at the time of the conduct (retrospective application of criminal law); to benefit from any subsequent decrease in punishment.

Habeas corpus writ: anyone who is deprived of his liberty by arrest or detention shall be entitled to take proceedings before a court, in order that court may decide without delay on the lawfulness of his detention and order his release if the detention is not lawful.

Human Rights: *(special characteristics)*: inherent, universal, inalienable, indivisible and interdependent.

Human Rights violation: the expression includes governmental transgressions of the rights guaranteed by national, regional and international human rights law and acts and ommissions directly attributable to the State involving the failure to implement human rights standards. Violations occur when a law, policy or practice deliberately contravenes or ignores obligations held by the State concerned or when the State fails to achieve a required standard of conduct or result. Additional violations occur when a State withdraws or removes existing human rights protections.

Human Rights abuses: it is a broader term than "violations", which includes violative conduct committed by non-State actors.

Human rights of children: the general thrust behind national and international action on behalf of children is the moral and legal recognition of their emotional, physical and psychological vulnerability, their need for special care, and recognition of the obligation to respect and to ensure respect for their rights, including having their views respected.

Internally displaced persons: persons or groups of persons who have been forced or obliged to flee or to leave their homes or places of habitual residence, in particular as a result of or in order to avoid the effects of armed conflict, situations of generalised violence, violations of human rights or natural or human-made disasters, and who have not crossed any internationally recognised State border. Such persons are entitled to a treatment with due respect to their plight.

Interview: process of obtaining information through the use of planned but informal dialogue in a cordial atmosphere where a person interviewed is more comfortable physically and psychologically.

Judicial access: the right to be brought promptly before a judicial authority, whose function it is to assess whether a legal reason exists for a person's arrest and whether detention until trial is necessary. Also the right to challenge one's detention before a competent judicial authority.

Just treatment to women: prohibits any acts of gender-based violence which have the potential to result in physical, sexual or psychological harm or suffering to women, whether occurring in public or in private life. This further prohibits, in addition to violence or condoned by the State, violence occurring within the family (domestic violence), and within the community. It is the duty of law enforcement agency to prevent, investigate and punish all acts of violence against women, whether by the State or by private persons, to provide women who are subjected to violence with access to the mechanisms of justice and to just and effective remedies, and to ensure that law enforcement officers and public officials concerned are sensitive enough to the specific needs of women.

Law enforcement officials: it includes all officers of the law, whether appointed or elected, who exercise police powers, especially the powers of arrest and detention. This should be given the widest possible interpretation, and includes military and other security personnel as well as immigration officials where they exercise such powers.

Non-derogable rights: the rights which can never be restricted, suspended or subjected to any limitation or curtailment even under emergency situation. Article 20 and 21 of the Constitution are declared as non-derogable by 44th amendment of the Constitution of India.

Non-discrimination: the practice of respecting and ensuring all rights recognised by a civil society, without distinction of any kind, such as race, colour, sex, language, religion, political or other opinion, place of birth or other status.

Presumption of innocence: an accused/suspect should be presumed as innocent till his/her conviction by a competent court.

Protection of minorities: it requires absolute non-discrimination. All persons are equal before the law and are entitled without any discrimination to the equal protection of law. In this respect, it should be practiced to prohibit any discrimination and guarantee all persons equal and effective protection against discrimination on any ground such as race, colour, sex, language, religion, political or other opinion, place of birth, property or any other status.

Returnee: this term is used by the international community to identify a person who was a refugee, but who has recently returned to his/her country of origin.

Self-incrimination: making a confession or, giving testimoney against one's own self: forced self incrimination is prohibited by the Constitution of India.

Torture: any act by which severe pain or suffering, whether physical or mental, is intentionally inflicted on a person for such purposes as obtaining from him or a third person information or a confession, punishing him for an act he or a third person has committed or is suspected of having committed, or intimidating of coercing him or a third person, or for any reason based on discrimination of any kind, when such pain or suffering is inflicted by or at the instigation of or with consent or acquiescence of a public official or other person acting in an official capacity. It does not include pain or suffering arising from, inherent in or incidental to lawful sanctions.

16

Custodial Justice : Standard Minimum Rules for the Treatment of Prisoners*

I am the inferior of any man whose rights I trample under my foot.

—*Horace Greeley , Journalist*

Conditions in Indian Prisons, Rights of Prisoners and Speedy Trial

Of the issues related to conditions in Indian prisons, rights of prisoners and speedy trials need to be highlighted, as they involve human rights violations.

First, prisons in India are overcrowded. According to a survey, there were around 9000 prisoners against a capacity of a mere 2500 in Tihar jail in New Delhi, and 3000 against a capacity of a mere 650 in Meerut. Invariably, the conditions are the same all over India. The reasons for overcrowding are mainly an administrative failure to provide adequate jails and the slow investigation process and trial resulting in the presence of a number of under trials. The term under trials refer to those prisoners who are detained in prison and awaiting trial or undergoing trial. These overcrowded prisons "do not have space, facility and resources to provide prisoners their normal work, training and other educational opportunities."

Second, the medical facilities in jails in India are very poor. 308 cases of deaths in 1995-96 and 700 deaths in 1996-97 were reported to the National Human Rights Commission (NHRC). One of the reasons for the high incidence of death in jail custody is the utter inadequacy of treatment facilities in jails.

The Judiciary of India has played a leading role in prison reforms and the rights of the prisoners and their conditions. In *Sunil Batra v Delhi Administration,* the Court expressed,

* From U.N. documents

> "To fetter prisoners in irons is an inhumanity unjustified save where safe custody is otherwise impossible. The routine resort to handcuffs and irons bespeaks a barbarity hostile to our goal of human dignity and social justice."

In yet another judgment in *Kishore v State of Rajasthan*, it was observed that,

> "...the State must reducate the constabulary out of their sadistic acts and inculcate a respect for human person—a process which must begin more by example than precept if the lower rungs are really to emulate... Nothing is more cowardly and unconscionable than a person in police custody being beaten up and nothing inflicts a deeper wound on our constitutional culture than a state official running berserk regardless of human rights."

Third, the cases pending trial, the slow process of prosecution (both deliberately and by chance), and the attitude of the administration (both State and Centre), need to be discussed. Confinement without trial for a long period is against the spirit and principles of the Indian Constitution and its commitment to the 1948 Universal Declaration of Human Rights. As Sharma argues,

> "The distributive justice demands that the criminal justice should be swift and sure, that the guilty should be punished while the events are still fresh in public mind and that the innocent should be absolved as early as is consistent with a fair and impartial trial. A criminal trial, which drags on for an unreasonably long time, is not a fair trial. Sometimes, the offences with which the accused is charged are so trivial that even if prove, would not warrant punishment for more than few months, but the accused has to suffer detention because of the protracted nature of the trial."

According to Article 9(3) of the International Covenant on Civil and Political Rights, 1966, to which India is a party, "Anyone arrested or detained on a criminal charge shall be brought promptly before a judge or other officer authorised by law to exercise judicial power and shall be entitled to a trial within a reasonable time or to release." The Covenant also mentions [Article 14(3c)], which states that "In the determination of any criminal charge against him, every one shall be entitled ... (c) to be tried without undue delays."

Although the judiciary in India has condemned the delay in trials repeatedly, nothing much has happened in actual terms. Justice

Krishna Iyer in *Babu Singh v State of UP* mentions this problem:

"Our justice system, even in grave cases, suffers from slow motion syndrome, which is lethal to fair trial whatever the ultimate decision. Speedy justice is a component of social justice. Since the community as a whole is concerned in the criminal being in police custody and finally punished within a reasonable time and the innocent being absolved from the inordinate ordeal of criminal proceedings."

In another case—*Nimeon Sangma v Home Secretary, Govt. of Meghalaya,* it was observed that "It is unfortunate, indeed pathetic, that there should have been such considerable delay in investigation by the police in utter disregard of the fact that a citizen has been deprived of his freedom on the ground that he is accused of an offence."

Prof. Upendra Baxi explains the problem facing an under trial very clearly. He says :

"If I am locked up in 'protective custody' without even a charge against me or if I am not produced before the magistrate periodically, I could remain under trial for an indefinite period of time. The state is under no duty to render me legal assistance; nor is it under any liability to pay me compensation for illegal or wrongful confinement."

Standard Minimum Rules for the Treatment of Prisoners

The original idea for universal standards related to the treatment of prisoners was conceived by the International Penal and Penitentiary Commission, which prepared a set of rules endorsed by the League of Nations in 1934. The Commission was dissolved in 1951, when the United Nations assumed leadership for the promotion of international work in the Commission's field. Before transferring its responsibilities to the United Nations, however, the Commission revised the text of the rules, for submission to the First United Nations Congress on the Prevention of Crime and the Treatment of Offenders, held in Geneva in 1955. The Congress unanimously adopted the new rules on 30 August, and recommended their approval by the Economic and Social Council.

After further discussion, the council approved the Standard Minimum Rules for the Treatment of Prisoners (resolution 663 CI (XXIV) of 31 July 1957), as adopted by the First Congress. The Rules set out what is accepted to be good general principle and practice in the treatment of prisoners. They represent the minimum conditions which are accepted as suitable by the United Nations and, as such, are also intended to guard against mistreatment, particularly in connection with the enforcement of discipline and the use of instruments of restraint in penal institutions. The first part of this write-up contains the text of the Standard Minimum Rules.

When approving the Rules, the Council recommended that Governments give favourable consideration to adopting and applying them in the administration of their penal and correctional institutions. It also recommended that they inform the Secretary-General every five years of the progress made in applying the Rules.

The General Assembly has also recommended that Member States make all possible efforts to implement the Rules in the administration of their penal institutions, and that they take them into account in framing their national laws.

The Secretary-General publishes in the *International Review of Criminal Policy*, the *Yearbook on Human Rights*, the *Crime Prevention and Criminal Justice Newsletter* and other United Nations documents any information sent by Governments in compliance with those recommendations. He is also authorized to ask States and various inter- and non-governmental organizations for supplementary information.

On a recommendation by the Fifth United Nations Congress on the Prevention of Crime and the Treatment of Offenders, held in 1975, the Economic and Social Council (resolution 1993 (LX) of 12 May 1976) asked its Committee on Crime Prevention and Control to study the range of application of the Standard Minimum Rules—in effect, what kinds of detainees were covered by the Rules—and to draw up a set of implementing procedures, i.e., recommendations on how the Rules should be made known and applied in the administration of national penal law, including procedures for reporting to the United Nations on their application.

That Committee subsequently recommended that the scope of several provisions should be extended to protect persons arrested or imprisoned without charge. Thus the Council (resolution 2076 (LXII) of 13 May 1977) approved the addition of rule 95 to the Standard Minimum Rules. In essence, the new rule provides that persons arrested or imprisoned without charge are to be accorded the same protection as persons under arrest or awaiting trial and prisoners under sentence, without any undue imposition of rehabilitative measures.

The Committee completed and submitted its final text on implementing procedures for the Rules to the Economic and Social Council in 1984. On 25 May of that year (resolution 1984/47), the Council approved the procedures for the effective implementation of the Standard Minimum Rules for the Treatment of Prisoners, and invited Member States to take them into consideration when implementing the Rules and when preparing their periodic reports to the United Nations. The Secretary-General was asked to assist Governments, if they requested it, in implementing the Rules in accordance with the new procedures. These 13 procedures are set out in the Annex to this write-up.

Preliminary Observations

1. The following rules are not intended to describe in detail a model system of penal institutions. They seek only, on the basis of the general consensus of contemporary thought and the essential elements of the most adequate systems of today, to set out what is generally accepted as being good principle and practice in the treatment of prisoners and the management of institutions.

2. In view of the great variety of legal, social, economic and geographical conditions of the world, it is evident that not all of the rules are capable of application in all places and at all times. They should, however, serve to stimulate a constant endeavour to overcome practical difficulties in the way of their application, in the knowledge that they represent, as a whole, the minimum conditions which are accepted as suitable by the United Nations.

3. On the other hand, the rules cover a field in which thought is constantly developing. They are not intended to preclude experiment and practices, provided these are in harmony with the principles and seek to further the purposes which derive from the text of the rules as a whole. It will always be justifiable for the central prison administration to authorize departures from the rules in this spirit.

4. (i) Part I of the rules covers the general management of institutions, and is applicable to all categories of prisoners, criminal or civil, untried or convicted including prisoners subject to "security and sures" or corrective measures ordered by the judge.

(ii) Part II contains rules applicable only to the special categories dealt with in each section. Nevertheless, the rules under Section A, applicable to prisoners under sentence, shall be equally applicable to categories of prisoners dealt with in Sections B, C and D, provided they do not conflict with the rules governing those categories and are for their benefit.

5. (i) The rules do not seek to regulate the management of institutions set aside for young persons such as Borstal institutions or correctional schools, but in general Part I would be equally applicable in such institutions.

(ii) The category of young prisoners should include at least all young persons who come within the jurisdiction of juvenile courts. As a rule, such young persons should not be sentenced to imprisonment.

PART I

Rules of General Applications

Basic Principle

6. (i) The following rules shall be applied impartially. There shall be no discrimination on grounds of race, colour, sex, language, religion, political or other opinion, national or social origin, property, birth or other status.

(ii) On the other hand, it is necessary to respect the religious beliefs and moral precepts of the group to which a prisoner belongs.

Register

7. (i) In every place where persons are imprisoned there shall be kept a bound registration book with numbered pages in which shall be entered in respect of each prisoner received.

(a) Information concerning his identity;

(b) The reasons for his imprisonment and the authority thereof;

(c) The day and hour of his admission and release.

(ii) No person shall be received in an institution without a valid commitment order of which the details shall have been previously entered in the register.

Separation of Categories

8. The different categories of prisoners shall be kept in separate institutions or parts of institutions taking account of their sex, age, criminal record, the legal reason for their detention and the necessities of their treatment. Thus,

(a) Men and women shall as far as possible be detained in separate institutions; in an institutions which receives both men and women the whole of the premises allocated to women shall be entirely separate;

(b) Untried prisoners shall be kept separate from convicted prisoners;

(c) Persons imprisoned for debt and other civil prisoners shall be kept separate from persons imprisoned by reason of a criminal offence;

(d) Young prisoners shall be kept separate from adults.

Accommodation

9. (1) Where sleeping accommodation is in individual cells or rooms, each prisoner shall occupy by night a cell or room by himself. If for special reasons, such as temporary overcrowding, it becomes necessary for the central prison administration to make an exception to this rule, it is not desirable to have two prisoners in a cell or room.

(2) Where dormitories are used, they shall be occupied by prisoners carefully selected as being suitable to associate with one another in those conditions. There shall be regular supervision by night, in keeping with the nature of the institution.

10. All accommodation provided for the use of prisoners and in particular all sleeping accommodation shall meet all requirements of health, due regard being paid to climatic conditions and particularly to cubic content of air, minimum floor space, lighting, heating and ventilation.

11. In all places where prisoners are required to live or work,

(a) The windows shall be large enough to enable the prisoners to read or work by natural light, and shall be so constructed that they can allow the entrance of fresh air whether or not there is artificial ventilation.

(b) Artificial light shall be provided sufficient for the prisoners to read or work without injury to eyesight.

12. The sanitary installations shall be adequate to enable every prisoner to comply with the needs of nature when necessary and in a clean and decent manner.

13. Adequate bathing and shower installations shall be provided so that every prisoner may be enabled and required to have a bath or shower, at a temperature suitable to the climate, as frequently as necessary for general hygiene according to season and geographical region, but at least once a week in a temperate climate.

14. All parts of an institution regularly used by prisoners shall be properly maintained and kept scrupulously clean at all times.

Personal Hygiene

15. Prisoners shall be required to keep their persons clean, and to this end they shall be provided with water and with such toilet articles as are necessary for health and cleanliness.

16. In order that prisoners may maintain a good appearance compatible with their self-respect, facilities shall be provided for the proper care of the hair and beard, and men shall be enabled to shave regularly.

Clothing and Bedding

17. (i) Every prisoner who is not allowed to wear his own clothing shall be provided with an outfit or clothing suitable for the climate and adequate to keep him in good health. Such clothing shall in no manner be degrading or humiliating.

(ii) All clothing shall be clean and kept in proper condition. Under-clothing shall be changed and washed as often as necessary for the maintenance of hygiene.

(iii) In exceptional circumstances, whenever a prisoner is removed outside the institution for an authorized purpose, he shall be allowed to wear his own clothing or other inconspicuous clothing.

18. If prisoners are allowed to wear their own clothing, arrangements shall be made on their admission to the institution to ensure that it shall be clean and fit for use.

19. Every prisoner shall, in accordance with local or national standards, be provided with a separate bed, and with separate and sufficient bedding which shall be clean when issued, kept in good order and changed often enough to ensure its cleanliness.

Food

20. (i) Every prisoner shall be provided by the administration at the usual hours with food of nutritional value adequate for health and strength, of wholesome quality and well prepared and served.

(ii) Drinking water shall be available to every prisoner whenever he needs it.

Exercise and Sport

21. (i) Every prisoner who is not employed in outdoor work shall have at least one hour of suitable exercise in the open air daily if the weather permits.

(ii) Young prisoners, and others of suitable age and physique, shall receive physical and recreational training during the period of exercise. To this end, space, installations and equipment should be provided.

Medical Services

22. (i) At every institution there shall be available the services of at least one qualified medical officer who should have some knowledge of psychiatry. The medical services should be organized with close relationship to the general health administration of the community or nation. They shall include a psychiatric service for the diagnosis and, in proper cases, the treatment of states of mental abnormality.

(ii) Sick prisoners who require specialist treatment shall be transferred to specialized institutions or to civil hospitals. Where hospital facilities are provided in an institution, their equipment, furnishings and pharmaceutical supplies shall be proper for the medical care and treatment of sick prisoners, and there shall be a staff of suitably trained officers.

(iii) The services of a qualified dental officer shall be available to every prisoner.

23. (1) In women's institutions there shall be special accommodation for all necessary pre-natal and post-natal care and treatment. Arrangements shall be made wherever practicable for children to be born in a hospital outside the institution. If a child is born in prison, this fact shall not be mentioned in the birth certificate.

(2) Where nursing infants are allowed to remain in the institution with their mothers, provision shall be made for a nursery staffed by qualified persons, where the infants shall be placed when they are not in the care of their mothers.

24. The medical officer shall see and examine every prisoner as soon as possible after his admission and thereafter as necessary, with a view particularly to the discovery of physical or mental illness and the taking of all necessary measures; the segregation of prisoners suspected of infectious or contagious conditions; the noting of physical or mental defects which might hamper rehabilitation, and the determination of the physical capacity of every prisoner for work.

25. (i) The medical officer shall have the care of the physical and mental health of the prisoners and should daily see all sick prisoners, who complain of illness, and any prisoner to whom his

attention is specially directed.

(ii) The medical officer shall report to the director whenever he considers that a prisoner's physical or mental health has been or will be injuriously affected by continued imprisonment or by any condition of imprisonment.

26. (1) The medical officer shall regularly inspect and advise the director upon :

(a) The quantity, quality, preparation and service of food;

(b) The hygiene and cleanliness of the institution and the prisoners;

(c) The sanitation, heating, lighting and ventilation of the institution;

(d) The suitability and cleanliness of the prisoners' clothing and bedding;

(e) The observance of the rules concerning physical education and sports, in cases where there is no technical personnel in charge of these activities.

(2) The director shall take into consideration the reports and advice that the medical officer submits according to rules 25 (2) and 26 and , in case he concurs with the recommendations made, shall take immediate steps to give effect to those recommendations; if they are not within his competence or if he does not concur with them, he shall immediately submit his own report and the advice of the medical officer to higher authority.

Discipline and Punishment

27. Discipline and order shall be maintained with firmness, but with no more restriction than is necessary for safe custody and well-ordered community life.

28. (1) No prisoner shall be employed, in the service of the institution, in any disciplinary capacity.

(2) This rule shall not, however, impede the proper functioning of systems based on self-government, under which specified social, educational or sports activities or responsibilities are entrusted, under supervision, to prisoners who are formed into groups for the purposes of treatment.

29. The following shall always be determined by the law or by the regulation of the competent administrative authority :

(a) Conduct constituting a disciplinary offence;

(b) The types and duration of punishment which may be inflicted;

(c) The authority competent to impose such punishment.

30. (1) No prisoner shall be punished except in accordance with the terms of such law or regulation, and never twice for the same offence.

(2) No prisoner shall be punished unless he has been informed of the offence alleged against him and given a proper opportunity of presenting his defence. The competent authority shall conduct a thorough examination of the case.

(3) Where necessary and practicable the prisoner shall be allowed to make his defence through an interpreter.

31. Corporal punishment, punishment by placing in a dark cell, and all cruel, inhuman or degrading punishments shall be completely prohibited as punishments for disciplinary offences.

32. (1) Punishment by close confinement or reduction of diet shall never be inflicted unless the medical officer has examined the prisoner and certified in writing that he is fit to sustain it.

(2) The same shall apply to any other punishment that may be prejudicial to the physical or mental health of a prisoner. In no case may such punishment be contrary to or depart from the principle state in rule 31.

(3) The medical officer shall visit daily prisoners undergoing such punishments and shall advise the director if he consider the termination or alteration of the punishment necessary on grounds of physical or mental health.

Instruments of Restraint

33. Instruments of restraint, such as handcuffs, chains, irons and strait-jackets, shall never be applied as a punishment. Furthermore, chains or irons shall not be used as restraints. Other instruments of restraint shall not be used except in the following circumstances :

(a) As a precaution against escape during a transfer, provided that they shall be removed when the prisoner appears before a judicial or administrative authority;

(b) On medical grounds by direction of the medical officer;

(c) By order of the director, if other methods of control fail, in order to prevent a prisoner from injuring himself or others or from damaging property; in such instances the director shall at once consult the medical officer and report to the higher administrative authority.

34. The patterns and manner of use of instruments of restraint shall be decided by the central prison administration. Such instruments must not be applied for any longer time than is strictly necessary.

Information to and Complaints by Prisoners

35. (1) Every prisoner on admission shall be provided with written information about the regulations governing the treatment of prisoners of his category, the disciplinary requirements of the institution, the authorized methods of seeking information and making complaints, and all such other matters as are necessary to enable him to understand both his rights and his obligations and to adapt himself to the life of the institution.

(2) If a prisoner is illiterate, the aforesaid information shall be conveyed to him orally.

36. (1) Every prisoner shall have the opportunity each week day of making requests or complaints to the director of the institution or the officer authorized to represent him.

(2) It shall be possible to make requests or complaints to the inspector of prisons during his inspection. The prisoner shall have the opportunity to talk to the inspector or to any other inspecting officer without the director or other members of the staff being present.

(3) Every prisoner shall be allowed to make a request or complaint, without censorship as to substance but in proper form, to the central prison administration, the judicial authority or other proper authorities through approved channels.

(4) Unless it is evidently frivolous or groundless every request or complaint shall be promptly dealt with and replied to without undue delay.

Contact with the Outside World

37. Prisoners shall be allowed under necessary supervision to communicate with their family and reputable friends at regular intervals, both by correspondence and by receiving visits.

38. (1) Prisoners who are foreign nationals shall be allowed reasonable facilities to communicate with the diplomatic and consular representatives of the State to which they belong.

(2) Prisoners who are nationals of States without diplomatic or consular representation in the country and refugees or stateless persons shall be allowed similar facilities to communicate with the diplomatic representative of the State which takes charge of their

interests or any national or international authority whose task it is to protect such persons.

39. Prisoners shall be kept informed regularly of the more important items of news by the reading of newspapers, periodicals or special institutional publications, by hearing wireless transmissions, by lectures or by any similar means as authorized or controlled by the administration.

Library

40. Every institution shall have a library for the use of all categories of prisoners, adequately stocked with both recreational and instructional books, and prisoners shall be encouraged to make full use of it.

Religion

41. (1) If the institution contains sufficient number of prisoners of the same religion, a qualified representative of that religion shall be appointed or approved. If the number of prisoners justifies it and conditions permit, the arrangement should be on a full-time basis.

(2) A qualified representative appointed or approved under paragraph (i) shall be allowed to hold regular services and to pay pastoral visits in private to prisoners of his religion at proper times.

(3) Access to a qualified representative of any religion shall not be refused to any prisoner. On the other hand, if any prisoner should object to a visit of any religious representative, his attitude shall be fully respected.

42. So far as practicable, every prisoner shall be allowed to satisfy the needs of his religious life by attending the services provided in the institution and having in his possession the books of religious observance and instruction of his denomination.

Retention of Prisoners' Property

43. (1) All money, valuables, clothing and other effects belonging to a prisoner which under the regulation of the institution he is not allowed to retain shall on his admission to the institution be placed in safe custody. An inventory thereof shall be signed by the prisoner. Steps shall be taken to keep them in good condition.

(2) On the release of the prisoner all such articles and money shall be returned to him except in so far as he has been authorised to spend money or send any such property out of the institution, or it has been found necessary on hygienic grounds to destroy any article of clothing. The prisoner shall sign a receipt for the articles and

money returned to him

(3) Any money or effects received for a prisoner from outside shall be treated in the same way.

(4) If a prisoner brings in any drugs or medicine, the medical officer shall decide what use shall be made of them.

Notification of Death, Illness, Transfer, etc.

44. (1) Upon the death or serious illness of , or serious injury to a prisoner, or his removal to an institution for the treatment of mental affections, the director shall at once inform the spouse, if the prisoner be married, or the nearest relative and shall in any event inform any other person previously designated by the prisoner.

(2) A prisoner shall be informed at once of the death or serious illness of any near relative. In case of the critical illness of a near relative, the prisoner should be authorised, whereas the circumstances allow, to go to visit the person under escort or alone.

(3) Every prisoner shall have the right to inform at once his family of his imprisonment or his transfer to another institution.

Removel of Prisoners

45. (1) When prisoners are being removed to or from an institution, they shall be exposed to public view as little as possible, and proper safeguards shall be adopted to protect them from insult, curiosity and publicity in any form.

(2) The transport of prisoners in conveyances with inadequate ventilation or light, or in any way which would subject them to unnecessary physical hardship, shall be prohibited.

(3) The transport of prisoners shall be carried out at the expense of the administration and equal conditions shall obtain for all of them.

Institutional Personnel

46. (1) The prison administration shall provide for the careful selection of every grade of the personnel, since it is on their integrity, humanity, professional capacity and personal suitability for the work that the proper administration of the institutions depends.

(2) The prison administration shall constantly seek to awaken and maintain in the minds both of the personnel and of the public the conviction that this work is a social service of great importance, and to this and all appropriate means of informing the public should be use.

(3) To secure the foregoing ends, personnel shall be appointed on a full-time basis as professional prison officers and have civil status with security of tenure subject only to good conduct, efficiency and physical fitness. Salaries shall be adequate to attract and retain suitable men and women employment benefits and conditions of service shall be favourable in view of the exacting nature of the work.

47. (1) The personnel shall possess an adequate standard of education and intelligence.

(2) Before entering on duty, the personnel shall be given a course of training in their general and specific duties and be required to pass theoretical and practical tests.

(3) After entering on duty and during their career, the personnel shall maintain and improve their knowledge and professional capacity by attending courses of in-service training to be organized at suitable intervals.

48. All members of the personnel shall at all times so conduct themselves and perform their duties as to influence the prisoners for good by their examples and to command their respect.

49. (1) So far as possible, the personnel shall include a sufficient number of specialists such as psychistrists, psychologists, social workers, teachers and trade instructors.

(2) The services of social workers, teachers and trade instructors shall be secured on a permanent basis, without thereby excluding part-time or voluntary workers.

50. (1) The director of an institution should be adequately qualified for his task by character, administrative ability, suitable training and experience.

(2) He shall devote his entire time to his official duties and shall not be appointed on a part-time basis.

(3) He shall reside on the premises of the institution or in its immediate vicinity.

(4) When two or more institutions are under the authority of one director, he shall visit each of them at frequent intervals. A responsible resident official shall be in charge of each of these institutions.

51. (1) The director, his deputy, and the majority of the other personnel of the institution shall be able to speak the language of the greatest number of prisoners, or a language understood by the greatest number of them.

(2) Whenever necessary, the services of an interpreter shall be used.

52. (1) In institutions which are large enough to require the services of one or more full-time medical officers, at least one of them shall reside on the premises of the institution or in its immediate vicinity.

(2) In other institutions the medical officer shall visit daily and shall reside near enough to be able to attend without delay in cases of urgency.

53. (1) In an institution for both men and women, the part of the institution set aside for women shall be under the authority of a responsible woman officer who shall have the custody of the keys of all that part of the institution.

(2) No male member of the staff shall enter the part of the institution set aside for women unless accompanied by a woman officer.

(3) Women prisoners shall be attended and supervised only by women officers. This does not, however, preclude male members of the staff, particularly doctors and teachers, from carrying out their professional duties in institutions or parts of institutions set aside for women.

54. (1) Officers of the institutions shall not, in their relations with the prisoners, use force except in self defence or in cases of attempted escape, or active or passive physical resistance to an order based on law or regulations. Officers who have recourse to force must use no more force than is strictly necessary and must report the incident immediately to the director of the institution.

(2) Prison officers shall be given special physical training to enable them to restrain aggressive prisoners.

(3) Except in special circumstances, staff performing duties which bring them into direct contact with prisoners should not be armed. Furthermore, staff should in no circumstances be provided with arms unless they have been trained in their use.

Inspection

55. There shall be a regular inspection of penal institutions and services by qualified and experienced inspectors appointed by a competent authority. Their task shall be in particular to ensure that these institutions are administered in accordance with existing laws and regulations and with a view to bringing about the objectives of penal and correctional services.

PART II

Rules Applicable to Special Categories

A. Prisoners Under Sentence

Guiding Principles

56. The guiding principles hereafter are intended to show the spirit in which penal institutions should be administered and the purposes at which they should aim, in accordance with the declaration made under Preliminary Observation 1 of the present text.

57. Imprisonment and other measures which result in cutting off an offender from the outside world are afflictive by the very fact of taking from the person the right of self-determination by depriving him of his liberty. Therefore the prison system shall not, except as incidental to justifiable segregation or the maintenance of discipline, aggravate the suffering inherent in such a situation.

58. The purpose and justification of a sentence of imprisonment or a similar measure deprivative of liberty is ultimately to protect society against crime. This end can only be achieved if the period of imprisonment is used to ensure, so far as possible, that upon his return to society the offender is not only willing but able to lead a law-abiding and self-supporting life.

59. To this end, the institution should utilize all the remedial, educational, moral, spiritual and other forces and forms of assistance which are appropriate and available, and should seek to apply them according to the individual treatment needs of the prisoners.

60. (1) The regime of the institution should seek to minimize any differences between prison life and life at liberty which tend to lessen the responsibility of the prisoners or the respect due to their dignity as human beings.

(2) Before the completion of the sentence, it is desirable that the necessary steps be taken to ensure for the prisoner a gradual return to life in society. This aim may be achieved, depending on the case, by a pre-release regime organized in the same institution or in another appropriate institution, or by release on trial under some kind of supervision which must not be entrusted to the police but should be combined with effective social aid.

61. The treatment of prisoners should emphasize not their

exclusion from the community, but their continuing part in it. Community agencies should, therefore, be enlisted wherever possible to assist the staff of the institution in the task of social rehabilitation of the prisoners. There should be in connexion with every institution social workers charged with the duty of maintaining and improving all desirable relations of a prisoner with his family and with valuable social agencies. Steps should be taken to safeguard, to the maximum extent compatible with the law and the sentence, the right relating to civil interests, social security rights and other social benefits of prisoners.

62. The medical services of the institution shall seek to detect and shall treat any physical or mental illnesses or defects which may hamper a prisoner's rehabilitation. All necessary medical, surgical and psychiatric services shall be provided to that end.

63. (1) The fulfillment of these principles requires individualization of treatment and for this purpose a flexible system of classifying prisoners in groups; it is therefore desirable that such groups should be distributed in separate institutions suitable for the treatment of each group.

(2) These institutions need not provide the same degree of security for every group. It is desirable to provide varying degrees of security according to the needs of different groups. Open institutions, by the very fact that they provide no physical security against escape but rely on the self-discipline of the inmates, provide the conditions most favourable to rehabilitation for carefully selected prisoners.

(3) It is desirable that the number of prisoners in closed institutions should not be so large that the individualization of treatment is hindered. In some countries it is considered that the population of such institutions should not exceed five hundred. In open institutions the population should be as small as possible.

(4) On the other hand, it is undesirable to maintain prisons which are so small that proper facilities cannot be provided.

64. The duty of society does not end with a prisoner's release. There should, therefore, be governmental or private agencies capable of lending the released prisoner efficient after-care directed towards the lessening of prejudice against him and towards his social rehabilitation.

Treatment

65. The treatment of persons sentenced to imprisonment or a similar measure shall have as its purpose, so far as the length of the

sentence permits, to establish in them the will to lead law-abiding and self-supporting lives after their release and to fit them to do so. The treatment shall be such as will encourage their self-respect and develop their sense of responsibility.

66. (1) To these ends, all appropriate means shall be used, including religious care in the countries where this is possible, education, vocational guidance and training, social casework, employment counselling, physical development and strengthening of moral character, in accordance with the individual needs of each prisoner, taking account of his social and criminal history, his physical and mental capacities and aptitudes, his personal temperament, the length of his sentence and his prospects after release.

(2) For every prisoner with a sentence of suitable length, the director shall receive, as soon as possible after his admission, full reports on all the matters referred to in the foregoing paragraph. Such reports shall always include a report by a medical officer, wherever possible qualified in psychiatry, on the physical and mental condition of the prisoner.

(3) The reports and other relevant documents shall be placed in an individual file. This file shall be kept up-to-date and classified in such a way that it can be consulted by the responsible personnel whenever the need arises.

Classification and Individualization

67. The purposes of classification shall be :

(a) To separate from others those prisoners who, by reason of their criminal records or bad characters, are likely to exercise a bad influence.

(b) To divide the prisoners into classes in order to facilitate their treatment with a view to their social rehabilitation.

68. So far as possible separate institutions or separate sections of an institution shall be used for the treatment of the different classes of prisoners.

69. As soon as possible after admission and after a study of the personality of each prisoner with a sentence of suitable length, a programme of treatment shall be prepared for him in the light of the knowledge obtained about his individual needs, his capacities and dispositions.

Privileges

70. Systems of privileges appropriate for the different classes of prisoner and the different methods of treatment shall be established at every institution, in order to encourage good conduct, develop a sense of responsibility and secure the interest and co-operation of the prisoners in their treatment.

Work

71. (1) Prison labour must not be of an afflictive nature.

(2) All prisoners under sentence shall be required to work, subject to their physical and mental fitness as determined by the medical officer.

(3) Sufficient work of a useful nature shall be provided to keep prisoners actively employed for a normal working day.

(4) So far as possible the work provided shall be such as will maintain or increase the prisoners' ability to earn an honest living after release.

(5) Vocational training in useful trades shall be provided for prisoners able to profit thereby and especially for young prisoners.

(6) Within the limits compatible with proper vocational selection and with the requirements of institutional administration and discipline, the prisoners shall be able to chose the type of work they wish to perform.

72. (1) The organization and methods of work in the institutions shall resemble as closely as possible those of similar work outside institutions, so as to prepare prisoners for the conditions of normal occupational life.

(2) The interests of the prisoners and of their vocational training, however, must not be subordinated to the purpose of making a financial profit from an industry in the institution.

73. (1) Preferably institutional industries and farms should be operated directly by the administration and not by private contractors.

(2) Where prisoners are employed in work not controlled by the administration, they shall always be under supervision of the institution's personnel. Unless the work is for other departments of the government the full normal wages for such work shall be paid to the administration by the persons to whom the labour is supplied, account being taken of the output of the prisoners.

74. (1) The precautions laid down to protect the safety and health of free workmen shall be equally observed in institutions.

(2) Provision shall be made to indemnify prisoners against industrial injury, including occupational disease, on terms not less favourable than those extended by law to free workmen.

75. (1) The maximum daily and weekly working hours of the prisoners shall be fixed by law or by administrative regulation, taking into account local rules or custom in regard to the employment of free workmen.

(2) The hours so fixed shall leave one rest day a week and sufficient time for education and other activities required as part of the treatment and rehabilitation of the prisoners.

76. (1) There shall be a system of equitable remuneration of the work of prisoners.

(2) Under the system prisoners shall be allowed to spend at least a part of their earnings on approved articles for their own use and to send a part of their earnings to their family.

(3) The system should also provide that a part of the earnings should be set aside by the administration so as to constitute a savings fund to be handed over to the prisoner on his release.

Education and Recreation

77. (1) Provision shall be made for the further education of all prisoners capable of profiting thereby, including religious instruction in the countries where this is possible. The education of illiterates and young prisoners shall be compulsory and special attention shall be paid to it by the administration.

(2) So far as practicable, the education of prisoners shall be integrated with the educational system of the country so that after their release they may continue their education without difficulty.

78. Recreational and cultural activities shall be provided in all institutions for the benefit of the mental and physical health of prisoners.

Social Relations and After-care

79. Special attention shall be paid to the maintenance and improvement of such relations between a prisoner and his family as are desirable in the best interests of both.

80. From the beginning of a prisoner's sentence consideration shall be given to his future after release and he shall be encouraged and assisted to maintain or establish such relations with persons or agencies outside the institution as may promote the best interests of his family and his own social rehabilitation.

81. (1) Services and agencies, governmental or otherwise, which assist released prisoners to re-establish themselves in society shall ensure, so far as is possible and necessary, that released prisoners be provided with appropriate documents and identification papers, have suitable homes and work to go to, are suitably and adequately clothed having regard to the climate and season and have sufficient means to reach their destination and maintain themselves in the period immediately following their release.

(2) The approved representatives of such agencies shall have all necessary access to the institution and to prisoners and shall be taken into consultation as to the future of a prisoner from the beginning of his sentence.

(3) It is desirable that the activities of such agencies shall be centralized and co-ordinated as far as possible in order to secure the best use of their efforts.

B. Insane and Mentally Abnormal Prisoners

82. (1) Persons who are found to be insane shall not be detained in prisons and arrangements shall be made to remove them to mental institutions as soon as possible.

(2) Prisoners who suffer from other mental diseases or abnormalities shall be observed and treated in specialized institutions under medical management.

(3) During their stay in a prison, such prisoners shall be placed under the special supervision of a medical officer.

(4) The medical or psychiatric service of the penal institutions shall provide for the psychiatric treatment of all other prisoners who are in need of such treatment.

83. It is desirable that steps should be taken, by arrangement with the appropriate agencies, to ensure if necessary the continuation of psychiatric treatment after release and the provision of social-psychiatric after-care.

C. Prisoners under Arrest or Awaiting Trial

84. (1) Persons arrested or imprisoned by reason of a criminal charge against them, who are detained either in police custody or in prison custody (jail) but have not yet been tried and sentenced, will be referred to as "untried prisoners" hereinafter in these rules.

(2) Unconvicted prisoners are presumed to be innocent and shall be treated as such.

(3) Without prejudice to legal rules for the protection of individual liberty or prescribing the procedure to be observed in respect of untried prisoners, these prisoners shall benefit by a special regime which is described in the following rules in its essential requirements only.

85. (1) Untried prisoners shall be kept separate from convicted prisoners.

(2) Young untried prisoners shall be kept separate from adults and shall in principle be detained in separate institutions.

86. Untried prisoners shall sleep singly in separate rooms, with the reservation of different local custom in respect of the climate.

87. Within the limits compatible with the good order of the institution, untried prisoners may, if they so desire, have their food procured at their own expense from the outside, either through the administration or through their family or friends. Otherwise, the administration shall provide their food.

88. (1) An untried prisoner shall be allowed to wear his own clothing if it is clean and suitable.

(2) If he wears prison dress, it shall be different from that supplied to convicted prisoners.

89. An untried prisoner shall always be offered opportunity to work, but shall not be required to work. If he chooses to work, he shall be paid for it.

90. An untried prisoner shall be allowed to procure at his own expense or at the expense of a third party such books, newspapers, writing materials and other means of occupation as are compatible with the interests of the administration of justice and the security and good order of the institution.

91. An untried prisoner shall be allowed to be visited and treated by his own doctor or dentist if there is reasonable ground for his application and he is able to pay any expenses incurred.

92. An untried prisoner shall be allowed to inform immediately his family of his detention and shall be given all reasonable facilities for communicating with his family and friends, and for receiving visits from them, subject only to such restrictions and supervision as are necessary in the interests of the administration of justice and of the security and good order of the institution.

93. For the purposes of his defence, an untried prisoner shall be allowed to apply for free legal aid where such aid is available,

and to receive visits from his legal adviser with a view to his defence and to prepare and hand to him confidential instructions. For these purposes, he shall if he so desires be supplied with writing material. Interviews between the prisoner and his legal adviser may be within sight but not within the hearing of a police or institution official.

D. Civil Prisoners

94. In countries where the law permits imprisonment for debt or by order of a court under any other non-criminal process, persons so imprisoned shall not be subjected to any greater restriction or severity than is necessary to ensure safe custody and good order. Their treatment shall be not less favourable than that of untried prisoners, with the reservation, however, that they may possibly be required to work.

E. Persons Arrested or Imprisoned without Charge

95. Without prejudice to the provisions of Article 9 of the International Covenant on Civil and Political Rights, persons arrested or imprisoned without charge shall be accorded the same protection as that accorded under Part I and Part II, Section C, Relevant provisions of Part II, Section A, shall likewise be applicable where their application may be conducive to the benefit of this special group of persons in custody, provided that no measures shall be taken implying that re-education or rehabilitation is in any way appropriate to person not convicted of any criminal offence.

Annexure

Procedures for the Effective Implementation of the Standard Minimum Rules for the Treatment of Prisoners

Procedure 1

All States whose standards for the protection of all persons subjected to any form of detention or imprisonment fall short of the Standard Minimum Rules for the Treatment of Prisoners shall adopt the Rules.

Commentary. *The General Assembly, in its resolution 2858 (XXVI) of 20 December 1971, invited the attention of Member States to the Standard Minimum Rules and recommended that they should be effectively implemented in the administration of penal and correctional institutions and that favourable consideration should be given to their incorporation in national legislation. Some States may have* *standards that are more advanced than the Rules, and the adoption of the Rules is therefore not requested on the part of such States. Where States feel that the Rules need to be harmonized with their legal system and adapted to their culture, the emphasis is placed on the substance rather than the letter of the Rules.*

Procedure 2

Subject, as necessary, to their adaptation to the existing laws and culture but without deviation from the spirit and purpose of the Rules, the Standard Minimum Rules shall be embodied in national legislation and other regulations.

Commentary. *This procedure emphasizes that it is necessary to embody the Rules within national legislation and regulations, thus quoting also some aspects of Procedure 1.*

Procedure 3

The Standard Minimum Rules shall be made available to all persons concerned, particularly to law enforcement officials and correctional personnel, for purposes of enabling their application and execution in the criminal justice system.

Commentary. *This procedure stresses that the Rules, as well as national statutes and regulations implementing the Rules, should be made available to all persons concerned with their implementation, in particular law enforcement officials and correctional personnel. The effective implementation of the Rules might also involve the organization of training courses by the central administration in charge of correctional matters. The dissemination of procedures is discussed in Procedures 7 to 9.*

Procedure 4

The Standard Minimum Rules, as embodied in national legislation and other regulations, shall also be made available and understandable to all prisoners and all persons under detention, on their admission and during their confinement.

Commentary. *To achieve the goal of the Standard Minimum Rules, it is necessary to make the Rules, as well as the implementing national statutes and regulations available to prisoners and all persons under detention (rule 95), in order to further the awareness that the Rules represent the minimum conditions that are accepted as suitable by the United Nations. Thus, this procedure supplements the provisions contained in Procedure 3.*

A similar requirement, that the Rules be made available to the persons for whose protection they have been elaborated, has been already established in the four Geneva Conventions of 12 August 1949, of which articles 47 of the first Convention, 48 of the second, 127 of the third and 144 of the fourth state in common :

"The High Contracting Parties undertake, in time of peace as in time of war, to disseminate the text of the present Convention as widely as possible in their respective countries, and, in particular, to include the study thereof in their programmes of military and, if possible, civil instruction, so that the principle thereof may become known to the armed fighting forces, the medical personnel and the chaplains."

Procedure 5

States shall inform the Secretary-General of the United Nations every five years of the extent of the implementation and the progress made with regard to the application of the Standard Minimum Rules, and of the factors and difficulties, if any, affecting their implementation, by responding to the Secretary-General's questionnaire. This questionnaire should, following a specified schedule, be selective and limited to specific questions in order to secure an in-depth review and study of the problems selected. Taking into account the reports of Governments as well as other relevant information available within the United Nations system, the Secretary-General shall prepare an independent periodic report on progress made with respect to the implementation of the Standard Minimum Rules. In the preparation of those reports the Secretary-General may also enlist the co-operation of specialized agencies and of the relevant intergovernmental organizations and non-governmental organizations in consultative nexus with the Economic and Social Council. The Secretary-General shall further refer to the Committee on Crime Prevention and Control for consideration and further action, as appropriate.

Commentary. *It will be recalled that the Economic and Social Council in its resolution 663 C (XXIV) of 31 July 1957, recommended that the Secretary-General be informed every five years of the progress made with regard to the application of the Standard Minimum Rules and authorized the Secretary-General to make arrangements for the publication, as appropriate, of such information if necessary. Seeking the co-operation of specialized agencies and relevant organizations* *is a well-established United Nations practice. In the preparation of his independent report on progress made with respect to the implementation of the Standard Minimum Rules, the Secretary-General will take into account, inter alia, information available in the human rights organs of the United Nations, including the Commission on Human Rights, The Sub-Commission on Prevention of Discrimination and Protection of Minorities, the Human Rights Committee functioning under the International Covenant on Civil and Political Right, and the Committee on the Elimination of Racial Discrimination. The implementation work under the future convention against torture could also be taken into account, as well as any information which might be gathered under the body of principles for the protection of prisoners and detainees currently under preparation in the General Assembly.*

Procedure 6

As part of the information mentioned in Procedure 5 above, States should provide the Secretary-General with :

(a) Copies or abstracts of all laws, regulations and administrative measures concerning the application of the standard Minimum Rules to persons under detention and to places and programmes of detention;

(b) Any data and descriptive material on treatment programmes, personnel and the number of persons under any form of detention, and statistics, if available;

(c) Any other relevant information on the implementation of the Rules, as well as information on the possible difficulties in their application.

Commentary. *This requirement derives from both resolution 663 C (XXIV) of the Economic and Social Council and the recommendations of the United Nations Congresses on the prevention of crime and the treatment of offenders. Although the items of information suggested here are not specifically provided for, it seems feasible is collect such information in order to assist Member states in overcoming difficulties through an exchange of experience. Furthermore, the request for such information is analogous to the existing periodic reporting system on human rights originally established by the Economic and Social Council in its resolution 624 B (XXII) of 1 August 1956.*

Procedure 7

The Secretary-General shall disseminate the Standard Minimum Rules and the present implementing procedures, in as many languages as possible, and make them available to all States and intergovernmental and non-governmental organizations concerned, in order to ensure the widest circulation of the Rules and the present implementing procedures.

Commentary. *The need for the widest possible dissemination of the Standard Minimum Rules is self-evident. Close co-operation with all appropriate intergovernmental and non-governmental organizations is important to secure more effective dissemination and implementation of the Rules. Therefore, the Secretariat should maintain close contacts with such organizations and should make relevant information and data available to them. It should also encourage those organizations to disseminate information about the Standard Minimum Rules and the implementing procedures.*

Procedure 8

The Secretary-General shall disseminate his reports on the implementation of the Rules, including analytical summaries of the periodic surveys, reports of the Committee on Crime Prevention and Control, reports prepared for the United Nations congresses on the prevention of crime and the treatment of offenders as well as the reports of the congresses, scientific publications and other relevant documentation as from time to time may be deemed necessary to further the implementation of the Standard Minimum Rules.

Commentary. *This procedure reflects the present practice of disseminating such reports as part of the documentation for the United Nations bodies concerned, as United Nations publications or as articles in the Yearbook on Human Right and the International Review of Criminal Policy, the Crime Prevention and Criminal Justice Newsletter and any other relevant publications.*

Procedure 9

The Secretary-General shall ensure the widest possible reference to and use of the text of the Standard Minimum rules by the United Nations in all its relevant programmes, including technical co-operation activities.

Commentary. *It should be ensured that all relevant United Nations bodies include or make reference to the Rules and the implementing procedures, thus contributing to under dissemination and increasing the awareness of specialized agencies, governmental, intergovernmental and nongovernmental bodies and the general public of the Rules and of the commitment of the Economic and Social Council and the*

General Assembly to their implementation.

The extent to which the Rules have any practical effect on correctional administrations depends to a great extent on the measures through which they permeate local legislative and administrative practices. They should be known and understood by a wide range of professionals and non-professionals throughout the world. Therefore, there is a great need for more publicity in any form, which should also be attained by frequent references to the Rules, accompanied by public information campaigns.

Procedure 10

As part of its technical co-operation and development programmes the United Nations shall :

(a) Aid Governments, at their request, in setting up and strengthening comprehensive and humane correctional systems.

(b) Make available to Governments requesting them the services of experts and regional and interregional advisers on crime prevention and criminal justice;

(c) Promote national and regional seminars and other meetings at the professional and non-processional levels to further the dissemination of the Standard Minimum Rules and the present implementing procedures;

(d) Strengthen substantive support to regional research and training institutes in crime prevention and criminal justice that are associated with the United Nations.

The United Nations regional research and training institutes in crime prevention and criminal justice, in co-operation with national institutions, shall develop curricula and training materials, based on the Standard Minimum Rules and the present implementing procedures, suitable for use in criminal justice educational programmes at all levels, as well as in specialized courses on human rights and other related subjects.

Commentary. *The purpose of this procedure is to ensure that the United Nations technical assistance programmes and the training activities of the United Nations regional institutes are used as indirect instruments for the application of the Standard Minimum Rules, and the present implementing procedures. Apart from regular training courses for correctional personnel, training manuals and the like, particularly at the policy and decision-making level, provision should be made for expert advice on the questions submitted by Member States,* *including an expert referral system to interested States. This expert referral system seems particularly necessary in order to implement the Rules according to their spirit and with a view to the socio-economic structure of the countries requesting such assistance.*

Procedure 11

The United Nations Committee on Crime Preventions and Control shall :

(a) Keep under review, from time to time, the Standard Minimum Rules, with a view to the elaboration of new rules, standards and procedures applicable to the treatment of persons deprived of liberty;

(b) Follow up the present implementing procedures, including periodic reporting under Procedure 5 above.

Commentary. *As most of the information collected in the course of periodic enquires as well as during technical assistance missions would be brought to the attention of the Committee on Crime Prevention and Control, ensuring the effectiveness of the Rules in improving correctional practices rests with the Committee, whose recommendations would determine the future course in the application of the Rules, together with the implementing procedures. The Committee should therefore clearly define existing shortcomings in or the reasons for the lack of implementation of the Rules, inter alia, through contacts with the judiciary and ministries of justice of the countries concerned, with the view to suggesting appropriate remedies.*

Procedure 12

The Committee on Crime Prevention and Control shall assist the General Assembly, the Economic and Social Council and any other United Nations human rights bodies, as appropriate, with recommendations relating to reports of *adhoc* inquiry commissions, with respect to matters pertaining to the application and implementation of the Standard Minimum Rules.

Commentary. *As the Committee on Crime Prevention and Control is the relevant body to review the implementation of the Standard Minimum Rules, it should also assist the above-mentioned bodies.*

Procedure 13

Nothing in the present implementing procedures should be construed as precluding resort to any other means or remedies available under international law or set forth by other United Nations bodies and agencies for the redress of violations of human rights, including the procedure on consistent patterns of gross violations of human rights under Economic and Social Council resolution 1503 (XLVIII) of 27 May 1970, the communication procedure under the Optional Protocol to the International Covenant on Civil and Political Right and the communication procedure under the International Convention on the Elimination of All Forms of Racial Discrimination.

Commentary. *Since the Standard Minimum Rules are only partly concerned with specific human rights issues, the present procedures should not exclude any avenue for redress of any violation of such rights, in accordance with existing international or regional standards and norms.*

17

Custodial Justice : UN Principles for Protection of Prisoners

No State may permit or tolerate torture or other cruel, inhuman or degrading treatment or punishment. Exceptional circumstances such as a state of war or a threat of war, internal political instability or any other public emergency may not be invoked as a justification of torture or other cruel, inhuman or degrading treatment or punishment. - Declaration on the Protection of All Persons from Being Subjected to Torture and Other Cruel, Inhuman or Degrading Treatment or Punishment Adopted by General Assembly resolution of 9 December 1975

(Adopted by the General Assembly of the United Nations on 9 December 1988 by Resolution 43/173)

The General Assembly Recalling its resolution 35/177 of 15 December 1980, in which it referred the task of elaborating the draft Body of Principles for the Protection of All Persons under Any Form of Detention or Imprisonment to the Sixth Committee and decided to establish an open-ended working group for that purpose.

Taking note of the report of the Working Group, which met during the forty-third session of the General Assembly and completed the elaboration of the draft Body of Principles for the Protection of All Persons under any Form of Detention or Imprisonment.

Considering that the Working Group decided to submit the text of the draft Body of Principles to the Sixth Committee for its consideration and adoption.

Convinced that the adoption of the draft Body of Principles would make an important contribution to the protection of human rights.

---

* From U.N. Documents.

Considering the need of ensuring the wide dissemination of the text of the Body of Principles.

1. *Approves* the Body of Principles for the Protection of All Persons under Any Form of Detention or Imprisonment, the text of which is annexed to the present resolution;

2. *Expresses its appreciation* to the Working Group on the Draft Body of Principles for the Protection of All Persons under any Form of Detention or Imprisonment for its important contribution to the elaboration of the Body of Principles;

3. *Requests* the Secretary-General to inform the Members of the United Nations or members of specialised agencies of the adoption of the Body of Principles.

4. *Urges* that all efforts be made so that the Body of Principles becomes generally known and respected.

Body of Principles for the Protection of All Persons under Any Form of Detention or Imprisonment

Scope of the Body of Principles

These Principles apply for the protection of all persons under any form of detention or imprisonment.

Use of Terms

For the purpose of Body of Principles:

(a) "Arrest" means the act of apprehending a person for the alleged commission of an offence or by the action of an authority;

(b) "Detained person" means any person deprived of personal liberty except as a result of conviction for an offence;

(c) "Imprisoned person" means any person deprived of personal liberty as a result of conviction for an offence;

(d) "Detention" means the condition of detained persons as defined above;

(e) "Imprisonment" means the condition of imprisoned persons as defined above;

(f) The words "a judicial or other authority" mean a judicial or other authority under the law whose status and tenure should afford the strongest possible guarantees of competence, impartiality and independence.

Principle 1

All persons under any form of detention or imprisonment shall be treated in a humane manner and with respect for the inherent dignity of the human person.

Principle 2

Arrest, detention or imprisonment shall only be carried out strictly in accordance with the provisions of the law and by competent officials or persons authorised for that purpose.

Principle 3

There shall be no 'restriction upon or derogation from any of the human rights of persons under any form of detention or imprisonment recognized or existing in any State pursuant to law, conventions, regulations or custom on the pretext that this Body of Principles does not recognize such rights or that it recognizes them to a lesser extent.

Principle 4

Any form of detenton or imprisonment and all measures affecting the human rights of a person under any form of detention or imprisonment shall be ordered by, or be subject to the effective control of, a judicial or other authority.

Principle 5

1. These Principles shall be applied to all persons within the territory of any given State, without distinction of any kind, such as race, colour, sex, language, religion or religious belief, political or other opinion, national, ethnic or social origin, property, birth or other status.

2. Measures, applied under the law and designed solely to protect the rights and special status of women, especially pregnant women and nursing mothers, children and juveniles, aged, sick or handicapped persons shall not be deemed to be discriminatory. The need for, and the application of, such measures shall always be subject to review by a judicial or other authority.

Principle 6

No person under any form of detention or imprisonment shall be subjected to torture or to cruel, inhuman or degrading treatment or punishment.* No circumstance whatever may be invoked as a justification for torture or other cruel, inhuman or degrading treatment or punishment.

---

* The term "cruel, inhuman or degrading treatment or punishment " should be interpreted so as to extend the widest possible protection against abuses, whether physical or mental, including the holding of a detained or imprisoned person in conditions which deprive him, temporarily or permanently, of the use of any of his natural senses, such as sight of hearing, or of his awareness of place and the passing of time.

Principle 7

1. States should prohibit by law any act contrary to the rights and duties contained in these Principles, make any such act subject to appropriate sanctions and conduct impartial investigations upon complaints.

2. Officials who have reason to believe that a violation of this Body of Principles has occurred or is about to occur shall report the matter to their superior authorities and, where necessary, to other appropriate authorities or organs vested with reviewing or remedial powers.

3. Any other person who has ground to believe that a violation of the Body of Principles has occurred or is about to occur shall have the right to report the matter to the superiors of the officials involved as well as to other appropriate authorities or organs vested with reviewing or remedial power.

Principle 8

Persons in detention shall be subject to treatment to their unconvicted status. Accordingly, they shall, whenever possible, be kept separate from imprisoned persons.

Principle 9

The authorities which arrest a person, keep him under detention or investigate the case shall exercise only the powers granted to them under the law and the exercise of these powers shall be subject to recourse to a judicial or other authority.

Principle 10

Anyone who is arrested shall be informed at the time of his arrest of the reason for his arrest and shall be promptly informed of the charges against him.

Principle 11

1. A person shall not be kept in detention without being given an effective opportunity to be heard promptly by a judicial or other authority. A detained person shall have the right to defend himself or to be assisted by counsel as prescribed by law.

2. A detained person and his counsel, if any, shall receive prompt and full communication of any order of detention, together with the reasons thereof.

3. A judicial or other authority shall be empowered to review as appropriate the continuance of detention.

Principle 12

1. There shall be duly recorded:

(a) The reasons for the arrest;
(b) The time of the arrest and the taking of the arrested person to a place of custody as well as that of his first appearance before a judicial or other authority;
(c) The identity of the law enforcement officials concerned;
(d) Precise information concerning the place of custody.

2. Such records shall be communicated to the detained person, or his counsel, if any, in the form prescribed by law.

Principle 13

Any person shall, at the moment of arrest and at the commencement of detention or imprisonment, or promptly thereafter, be provided by the authority responsible for his arrest, detention or imprisonment, respectively, with information on and an explanation of his rights and how to avail himself on such rights.

Principle 14

A person who does not adequately understand or speak the language used by the authorities responsible for his arrest, detention or imprisonment is entitled to receive promptly in a language which he understands the information referred to in principle 10, principle 11, paragraph 2, principle 12, paragraph 1, and principle 13 and to have the assistance, free of charge, if necessary, of an interpreter in connection with legal proceedings subsequent to his arrest.

Principle 15

Notwithstanding the exceptions contained in principle 16, paragraph 4, and principle 18, paragraph 3, communication of the detained or imprisoned person with the outside world, and in particular his family or counsel, shall not be denied for more than a matter of days.

Principle 16

1. Promptly after arrest and after each transfer from one place of detention or imprisonment to another, a detained or imprisoned person shall be entitled to notify or to require the competent authority to notify members of his family or other appropriate persons of his choice of his arrest, detention or imprisonment or of the transfer and of the place where he is kept in custody.

2. If a detained or imprisoned person is a foreigner, he shall also be promptly informed of his right to communicate by appropriate means witha consular post or the diplomatic mission of the State of which he is a national or which is otherwise entitled to receive such communication in accordance with international law or with the

representative of the competent international organisation, if he is a refugee or is otherwise under the protection of an intergovernmental organisation.

3. If a detained or imprisoned person is a juvenile or is incapable of understanding his entitlement, the competent authority shall on its own initiative undertake the notification referred to in this principle. Special attention shall be given to notifying parents or guardians.

4. Any notification referred to in this principle shall be made or permitted to be made without delay. The competent authority may however delay a notification for a reasonable period where exceptional needs of the investigation so require.

Principle 17

1. A detained person shall be entitled to have the assistance of a legal counsel. He shall be informed of his right by the competent authority promptly after arrest and shall be provided with reasonable facilities for exercising it.

2. If a detained person does not have a legal counsel of his own choice, he shall be entitled to have a legal counsel assigned to him by a judicial or other authority in all cases where the interests of justice so require and without payment by him if he does not have sufficient means to pay.

Principle 18

1. A detained or imprisoned person shall be entitled to communicate and consult with his legal counsel.

2. A detained or imprisoned person shall be allowed adequate time and facilities for consultations with his legal counsel.

3. The right of a detained or imprisoned person to be visited by and to consult and communicate, without delay or censorship and in full confidentiality, with his legal counsel may not be suspended or restricted save in exceptional circumstances, to be specified by law or lawful regulations, when it is considered indispensable by a judicial or other authority in order to maintain security and good order.

4. Interviews between a detained or imprisoned person and his legal counsel may be within sight, but not within the hearing, of a law enforcement official.

5. Communications between a detained or imprisoned

person and his legal counsel mentioned in this principle shall be inadmissible as evidence against the detained or imprisoned person unless they are connected with a continuing or contemplated crime.

Principle 19

A detained or imprisoned person shall have the right to be visited by and to correspond with, in particular, members of his family and shall be given adequate opportunity to communicate with the outside world, subject to reasonable conditions and restrictions as specified by law or lawful regulations.

Principle 20

If a detained or imprisoned person so requests, he shall if possible be kept in a place of detention or imprisonment reasonably near his usual place of residence.

Principle 21

1. It shall be prohibited to take undue advantage of the situation of a detained or imprisoned person for the purpose of compelling him to confess, to incriminate himself otherwise or to testify against any other person.

2. No detained person while being interrogated shall be subject to violence, threats or methods of interrogation which impair his capacity of decision or his judgement.

Principle 22

No detained or imprisoned person shall, even with his consent, be subjected to any medical or scientific experimentation which may be detrimental to his health.

Principle 23

1. The duration of any interrogation of a detained or imprisoned person and of the intervals between interrogations as well as the identity of the officials who conducted the interrogations and other persons present shall be recorded and certified in such form as may be prescribed by law.

2. A detained or imprisoned person, or his counsel when provided by law, shall have access to the information prescribed above.

Principle 24

A proper medical examination shall be offered to a detained or imprisoned person as promptly as possible after his admission to the place of detention or imprisonment, and thereafter medical care and treatment shall be provided whenever necessary. This care and treatment shall be provided free of charge.

Principle 25

A detained or imprisoned person or his counsel shall, subject only to reasonable conditions to ensure security and good order in the place of detention or imprisonment, have the right to request or petition a judicial or other authority for a second medical examination or opinion.

Principle 26

The fact that a detained or imprisoned person underwent a medical examination, the name of the physician and the results of such an examination shall be duly recorded. Access to such records shall be ensured. Modalities therefore shall be in accordance with relevant rules of domestic law.

Principle 27

Non-compliance with these Principles in obtaining evidence shall be taken into account in determining the admissibility of such evidence against a detained or imprisoned person.

Principle 28

A detained or imprisoned person shall have the right to obtain within the limits of available resources, if from public sources, reasonable quantities of educational, cultural and informational material, subject to reasonable conditions to ensure security and good order in the place of detention or imprisonment.

Principle 29

1. In order to supervise the strict observance of relevant laws and regulations, places of detention shall be visited regularly by qualified and experienced persons appointed by, and responsible to, a competent authority distinct from the authority directly in charge of the administration of the place of detention or imprisonment.

2. A detained or imprisoned person shall have the right to communicate freely and in full confidentiality with the persons who

visit the places of detention or imprisonment in accordance with paragraph 1, subject to reasonable conditions to ensure security and good order in such places.

Principle 30

1. The types of conduct of the detained or imprisoned person that constitute disciplinary offences during detention or imprisonment, the description and duration of disciplinary punishment that may be inflicted and the authorities competent to impose such punishment shall be specified by law or lawful regulations and duly published.

2. A detained or imprisoned person shall have the right to be heard before disciplinary action is taken. He shall have the right to bring such action to higher authorities for review.

Principle 31

The appropriate authorities shall endeavour to ensure, according to domestic law, assistance when needed to dependent and, in particular, minor members of the families of detained or imprisoned persons and shall devote a particular measure of care to the appropriate custody of children left without supervision.

Principle 32

1. A detained person or his counsel shall be entitled at any time to take proceedings according to domestic law before a judicial or other authority to challenge the lawfulness of his detention in order to obtain his release without delay, if it is unlawful.

2. The proceedings referred to in paragraph 1 shall be simple and expeditious and at no cost for detained persons without adequate means. The detaining authority shall produce without unreasonable delay the detained person before the reviewing authority.

Principle 33

1. A detained or imprisoned person or his counsel shall have the right to make a request or complaint regarding his treatment, in particular in case of torture or other cruel, inhuman or degrading treatment, to the authorities responsible for the administration of the place of detention and to higher authorities and, when necessary, to appropriate authorities vested with reviewing or remedial powers.

2. In those cases where neither the detained or imprisoned person nor his counsel has the possibility to exercise his rights under paragraph 1, a member of the family of the detained or imprisoned person or any other person who has knowledge of the case may exercise such rights.

3. Confidentiality concerning the request or complaint shall be maintained if so requested by the complainant.

4. Every request or complaint shall be promptly dealt with and replied to without undue delay. If the request or complaint is rejected or, in case of inordinate delay, the complainant shall be entitled to bring it before a judicial or other authority. Neither the detained or imprisoned person nor any complainant under paragraph 1 shall suffer prejudice for making a request or complaint.

Principle 34

Whenever the death or disappearance of a detained or imprisoned person occurs during his detention or imprisonment, an inquiry into the cause of death or disappearance shall be held by a judicial or other authority, either on its own motion or at the instance of a member of the family of such a person or any person who has knowledge of the case. When circumstances so warrant, such an inquiry shall be held on the same procedural basis whenever the death or disappearance occurs shortly after the termination of the detention or imprisonment. The findings of such inquiry or a report thereon shall made available upon request, unless doing so would jeopardize an ongoing criminal investigation.

Principle 35

1. Damage incurred because of acts or omissions by a public official contrary to the rights contained in these Principles shall be compensated according to the applicable rules on liability provided by domestic law.

2. Information required to be recorded under these Principles shall be available in accordance with procedures provided by domestic law for use in claiming compensation under this principle.

Principle 36

1. A detained person suspected of or charged with a criminal offence shall be presumed innocent and shall be treated as such until proved guilty according to law in a public trial at which he has had all the guarantees necessary for his defence.

2. The arrest or detention of such a person pending investigation and trial shall be carried out only for the purposes of the administration of justice on grounds and under conditions and procedures specified by law. The imposition of restrictions upon such a person which are not strictly required for the purpose of the detention or to prevent hindrance to the process of investigation or the administration of justice, or for the maintenance of security and good order in the place of detention shall be forbidden.

Principle 37

A person detained on a criminal charge shall be brought before a judicial or other authority provided by law promptly after his arrest. Such authority shall decide without delay upon the lawfulness and necessity of detention. No person may be kept under detention pending investigation or trial except upon the written order of such an authority. A detained person shall, when brought before such an authority, have the right to make a statement on the treatment received by him while in custody.

Principle 38

A person detained on a criminal charge shall be entitled to trial within a reasonable time or to release pending trial.

Principle 39

Except in special cases provided for by law, a person detained on a criminal charge shall be entitled, unless a judicial or other authority decides otherwise in the interest of the administration of justice, to release pending trial subject to the conditions that may be imposed in accordance with the law. Such authority shall keep the necessity of detention under review.

General Clause

Nothing in the present Body of Principles shall be construed as restricting or derogating from any right defined in the International Covenant on Civil and Political Rights.

Index

J

K

L

O

P

S

T

U